Religious Identity in an Early
Reformation Community

Studies in Central European Histories

VOLUME XLV

Religious Identity in an Early Reformation Community

Augsburg, 1517 to 1555

By

Michele Zelinsky Hanson

BRILL

LEIDEN · BOSTON
2009

Cover illustration: *Admonition to the People of Augsburg*. Author: Johann Eberlin von Günzburg (1522). Artist unknown. Courtesy of the Rare Book and Manuscript Library, University of Pennsylvania.

This book is printed on acid-free paper.

Library of Congress Cataloging-in-Publication Data

Hanson, Michele Zelinsky.
  Religious identity in an early Reformation community : Augsburg, 1517
to 1555 / by Michele Zelinsky Hanson.
      p. cm. — (Studies in Central European histories ; v. 45)
  Includes bibliographical references (p.   ) and index.
  ISBN 978-90-04-16673-8 (hardback : alk. paper) 1. Reformation—Germany—
Augsburg. 2. Augsburg (Germany)—Church history—16th century. 3. Identification
(Religion) I. Title. II.
Series.

  BR359.A9H36 2008
  274.3'37506—dc22

                                                                    2008031289

ISSN 1547-1217
ISBN 978 90 04 16673 8

For Nora and Finn

CONTENTS

ACKNOWLEDGMENTS

On a hot afternoon in Philadelphia in the summer of 1993 I struggled to define my interest in history for a routine assignment in a dissertation workshop, and the conviction on which this book is based, that ordinary people living through the religious upheavals of the sixteenth century Reformation must have found some way to go on living with one another despite their differences, was born. I am very grateful to Thomas Max Safley, who directed that workshop and my dissertation, for having faith in me and my project at a crucial turning point in my career. I also wish to thank him for his ongoing support and interest in my work.

This project would have been inconceivable without the opportunity to conduct extensive research in the Stadtarchiv and the Staats- und Stadtbibliothek Augsburg. Grants from the German Academic Exchange Service (DAAD) and the Mellon Foundation provided much needed support for the years I spent in Augsburg. The German Historical Institute also allowed for travel in Germany and a valuable opportunity to present the project in the early stages of writing.

Many people in Augsburg contributed to the success of my research and the development of my ideas. The warmth of their welcome and the interest they showed in my work made my time in Augsburg a true joy. By so readily admitting a newly minted PhD candidate from the States to their circle of early modern European and Swabian specialists they deeply enriched my research experience with both formal discussions in colloquia and informal chats over dinner. Many thanks go to the Faculty of the University of Augsburg, especially Prof. Drs. Johannes Burkhardt and Rolf Kiessling and their students, including Thomas Nieding, Matthias Brei, Sabine Ullmann, and Anke Sczesny; to Wolfgang Weber and Stephanie Haberer at the Institut für Europäische Kulturgeschichte; and to the Historisches Verein für Schwaben. They offered me a warm welcome into Augsburg's scholarly community and helped me not only to navigate the campus and the city, but provided direction for my research when I wasn't sure where to begin. In addition, the members of Rolf Kiessling's Colloquium für Schwäbische Landesgeschichte served as the earliest audience for the writing on which this book is based. I am especially grateful to

Christine Werkstätter, Carl Hoffmann, and Gabi von Trauchburg who took me under their wings and shared their time with such kindness and generosity. Wolfgang Wüst and the staff at the Stadtarchiv provided essential research assistance, a great place to work, and often a good laugh. Particular thanks to Alois Senser for bringing me box after box of interrogation records, often several times in the same day. At the Staats- und Stadtbibliothek Augsburg, Wolfgang Mayer and Hans-Jörg Künast also provided valuable research support.

With great fondness I thank the members of our Archivstammtisch for many happy memories of Thursday nights. Among others, they have included at one time or another Allison Creasman, Georg Feuerer, Helmut Graser, Mitch Hammond, Christine Johnson, Hans-Jörg Künast, Erik Midelfort, Benedikt Mauer, Wolfgang Mayer, Beth Plummer, Kathy Stuart, Ann Tlusty, and Helmut Zäh. They offered support, advice, encouragement, friendship and good humor. Special thanks to Ann Tlusty, Beth Plummer, and Christine Johnson whose advice and suggestions at weekly "power lunches" were so helpful in the early stages of writing.

For providing collegial support and some much needed time for writing I thank the History Department at La Salle University. Many thanks also to the staff of the University of Pennsylvania's Rarebook and Manuscript Collection, especially John Pollack, Lynne Farrington, and Brooke Palmieri. Others, including Thomas A. Brady Jr., Thomas Max Safley, Edward Peters, Thomas Childers, Lee Palmer Wandel, Emily Fisher Gray, Jerry Drew, and Erica Gelser have read patiently, attentively, and critically—in the best sense of the term—many versions of this project over the years. They and others have helped to make this a much better book. I am grateful to the editors at Brill, Hendrik van Leusen, Boris van Gool and Birgitta Poelmans, for seeing its potential.

My family deserves a special thank you for their unfailing support and faith in me. My parents have been with me on this journey from the beginning even though they did not always understand why I wanted to go back to Germany...again. Christopher Hanson has helped me to see this project through to the end. His encouragement, understanding, and patience are often unacknowledged but never taken for granted. Chris has my heartfelt thanks for his willingness to make my dream his own.

My children have played a special role in the creation of this book. The notion of writing as a way of giving birth—in the sometimes painful and protracted process of labor, the deeply personal and emotional investment in its success, and the sense of creating one's legacy—took on a double meaning for me in the fall of 2006. I was in the early stages of labor with my son as I completed revisions on my last day of work, and he was born early the following morning. The printed book appeared a bit later. Nora and Finn have sacrificed time with Mommy to allow me to work, but they are the reason why I do it, and this book is for them.

A NOTE ON NAMES, TRANSLATIONS AND QUOTATIONS

Women's last names retain the Early New High German feminine "-in" ending. First names have been modified to modern German spelling, and last names that appear in varying forms in the sources have been standardized in the text but kept in their original form in the footnote references. English translations of quotations from the sources are my own. Quotations appear in the footnotes in their original Early New High German with the following variations: abbreviated word endings are expanded and punctuation is modified as necessary for clarity.

INTRODUCTION

The preachers here moved her to this baptism, because she attended their sermons for a good four years, one preached this, another preached something else, one held the Sacrament for a sign, the other held [it] for flesh and blood, So they preached against one another and confused her so much that she didn't know what she should believe, and therefore she wanted to listen to the others too...[1]

With these words Agnes Vogel explained how she had observed the religious debates of the 1520s, had been drawn to consider Anabaptism, and eventually had chosen to be baptized. She witnessed the bewilderingly controversial sermons of preachers who were active in the city of Augsburg, priests of the old religion and a whole array of reformers of a new Christianity based on the Gospel alone.[2] Vogel's testimony gives us an insight into how ordinary people in the early years of the Reformation understood the controversies swirling around them and tried to find a way of settling the issues in their own minds. She listened not to one preacher but to many, tried to make sense of their disagreements on the Eucharist, and in the end was driven by their confusing messages to keep an open mind, open enough to include radical Anabaptist preachers. While not everyone who witnessed the religious debates of the early Reformation found their answers in a new baptism, Vogel's experience seems to reflect what must have been a common reaction to the times: a desire to understand, to find one's own place in the crowd of Christians, to take a stand with which one could live. Like many people in the early sixteenth century, Vogel believed her soul was at stake in her search to find the true preaching of the Gospel, and the route passed through uncharted territory for most lay people.

Agnes Vogel lived in one of the Reformation's most notable cities. Martin Luther's famous first encounter with Papal Legate Cardinal Cajetan (1518); the first statement of Protestant faith, which became

---

[1] *"Zu solhem tauff haben sy bewegt die prediger alhie, dann sy sey wol vier jar an ir predig ganngen, hab ainer das, an ander an annders gepredigt, ainer im Sacrament ain zaichen, der ander flaisch und plut wellen haben, Also wider ain annder gepredigt, unnd sy ganntz irr gemacht, da sy nit gewißt, was sy glauben solle, und deßhalben begert die anndern auch zuhoren,"* StadtAA, Reichsstadt, Urg. 14 May 1528, Agnes Vogel.

[2] The term evangelical reform comes from the reformer's insistence on the preeminence of the Gospel or *evangelium*, from the Greek.

known as the Augsburg Confession (1530); the peace treaty that settled the Schmalkaldic War between Protestant princes and the Holy Roman Emperor, known as the Augsburg Interim (1548); and the Peace of Augsburg (1555), which ended religious warfare in the Empire for the next six decades, all took place there. The free imperial city on the Lech and Wertach Rivers in southern Germany was home to thousands of residents, whose lives shaped and were shaped by the extraordinary events of their day. For Augsburgers not only witnessed great events, they, like Christians throughout Europe, participated in history when they made their own choices about how to respond to the challenges presented by the religious Reformation of the sixteenth century. Between 1517 and 1555 the citizens of Augsburg witnessed tremendous changes, reacted with passion and restraint, and ultimately adapted to a new way of life.

Studying the experiences of ordinary people in the early years of the Reformation era provides a valuable perspective for understanding the impact that theological divisions had on the way people identified their religious beliefs and interacted with each other. In the first few decades of the sixteenth century the scale of internal religious conflict was new to Christians in Europe. Neither spiritual nor secular authorities could bring much order, and people, such as Agnes Vogel, had to cope with the mixed signals they received from their superiors. Before the Peace of Augsburg in 1555 established structures for preserving religious diversity (though not freedom) in Germany, a different set of circumstances more ambiguous, tenuous, and unfamiliar prevailed. Those circumstances can also make the search for material evidence of religious feelings and commitments more difficult to find, recognize, and understand. Looking at this earlier period in Augsburg, however, allows us to see how people responded to religious innovations and upheavals in the absence of institutions designed to enforce conformity.

Agnes Vogel and hundreds of others: women, men, adults, youths, the wealthy, the poor, the educated, the simple, the pious, the blasphemous, and the indifferent provide insights into what it was like to live through this time of great change. They are historically unimportant people; their words have been immortalized only because a scribe wrote down their responses during questioning by the city council of Augsburg in the course of judicial investigations. Some were defendants, detained by the council on various sorts of criminal charges, but many were merely witnesses, some friendly and some hostile. Some defendants cooperated willingly, and some only reluctantly, some put up a brave fight then collapsed under the threat of force, some withstood even the physical and psychological assault of torture. All of them left behind a paper trail that otherwise would not exist, a faint echo of their experiences of life in the first half of the sixteenth century. With the exception of tax records, there are very few sources that record even the existence of individual persons in this period, let alone their experiences, and almost none that capture their words. For the historian legal testimonies are a challenging but tremendously vital means for learning how ordinary people attempted to articulate their experiences of the rapidly changing world in which they lived.

Many insightful studies have examined the development of different confessions of faith that grew out of the Reformation and the impact of confessional differences on interactions between people or communities.[3] These works inevitably focus on the period after 1555, which is often referred to as the confessional age, a time when confessional lines were more clearly drawn and institutions were developed to enforce them, and when ordinary people, therefore, left clearer markers of religious affiliations, boundaries, and conflicts in written records. During the so-called confessional age, both secular and spiritual authorities apparently strived to create religiously obedient populations, and confessional differences defined relations between mutually hostile religious groups and, presumably, between individuals who belonged to different confessions. The resulting confessionalization thesis argues that authorities instilled distinct confessional identities in their subjects, more or less successfully, for the sake of modernizing their states.[4] This thesis has fomented much debate and discussion and has inspired valuable research into the second half of the sixteenth, as well as the seventeenth and even eighteenth centuries.[5] The theory of confessionalization presupposes that

---

[3] From this point on, the term confession will be used refer to a confession of faith, such as the Catholic, Lutheran, or Zwinglian.

[4] Classic texts on the confessionalization thesis include Heinz Schilling, *Konfessionskonflikt und Staatsbildung: eine Fallstudie über das Verhältnis von religiösem und sozialem Wandel in der Frühneuzeit am Beispiel der Grafschaft Lippe* (Gütersloh: Gütersloher Verlagshaus Mohn, 1981); Wolfgang Reinhard, "Zwang zur Konfessionalisierung? Prolegomena zu einer Theorie des konfessionellen Zeitalters," *Zeitschrift für Historische Forschung* 10 (1983), 257–277; and Ernst Walter Zeeden, *Konfessionsbildung. Studien zur Reformation, Gegenreformation, und Katholischen Reformation*, (Stuttgart: Klett-Cotta, 1985).

[5] For newer assessments: Wolfgang Reinhard and Heinz Schilling, eds., *Die Katholische Konfessionalisierung: Wissenschaftliches Symposion derGesellschaft zur Herausgabe des Corpus Catholicorum und des Vereins für Reformationsgeschichte*, (Gütersloh: Gütersloher Verlagshaus, 1995); and Thomas A. Brady, Jr., "Confessionalization—The Career of a Concept,"

confessionalism, the growth of distinct and exclusive religious groups, had already occurred, therefore, most studies begin with the second half of the sixteenth century or later. Once confessional boundaries are visible enough for the crossing of them to be observed, those studies can test the ideal of clearly defined confessional beliefs imposed by authorities against the reality of its reception and interpretation by subjects in the area under scrutiny. For example, Marc Forster's work on Catholicism in Southwest Germany finds that a genuine Catholic identity did not emerge among lay people until after the middle of the seventeenth century (and the Thirty Years' War) and that lay people played a vital role in fashioning that identity, which could vary by region as a result.[6]

More and more scholars have begun to explore the experiences of people during the confessional age by studying various regions of Europe. Many of those historians have emphasized the exceptions to and limits of confessionalization to the point that one begins to wonder if the notorious confessional antagonism of the latter sixteenth and seventeenth centuries has not been greatly exaggerated. Olivier Christin and Benjamin Kaplan, for example, argue persuasively that tolerance occurred far more often than has usually been recognized.[7] Christin identifies a number of significant territories in Europe that responded to religious disunity in the second half of the sixteenth century by devising some sort of official peace settlement that allowed different religious confessions to coexist. He includes the Holy Roman Empire, France, Transylvania, the hereditary Habsburg states, Poland, and the Netherlands, much of western and most of central Europe in that group, which is not to say that those settlements were not hard-fought. Kaplan argues that while toleration lacked the intellectual support to give it legitimacy as a principle, peaceful coexistence whether *de facto* or *de jure* (as in Augsburg) has been overshadowed by tales of conflict and intellectual histories that trace the origins of religious liberty to a later time.

Other regional studies of the Dutch Republic, Hungary, and Switzerland, for example, support their findings. Judith Pollmann argues,

---

in *Confessionalization in Europe, 1555–1700: Essays in Honor and Memory of Bodo Nischan*, ed. John M. Headley, et al. (Burlington, VT: Ashgate, 2004), 1–35.

[6] Marc Forster, *Catholic Revival in the Age of the Baroque: Religious Identity in Southwest Germany, 1550–1750*, (Cambridge: Cambridge University Press, 2001).

[7] Olivier Christin, "Making Peace," in *A Companion to the Reformation World*, ed. R. Po-chia Hsia (Malden, MA: Blackwell, 2004), 426–439; and Benjamin J. Kaplan, "Coexistence, Conflict, and the Practice of Tolerance," ibid., 486–505.

"the more we stress that in everyday life religious differences could
be overcome, the harder it becomes to explain this intolerance and
insistence on confessional difference."[8] Pollmann has examined religious culture in the Dutch Republic in the seventeenth century and
suggests that a person might be both tolerant and intolerant. A person
might prefer to obtain religious uniformity in his community, but he
also recognized that individuals could share a Christian piety held in
common by members of different groups. Pollmann asserts that the
recognition of this shared piety enabled people of different confessions
to get along on a daily basis in confessionally mixed areas. Studies
conducted in the Kingdom of Hungary (Croatia and Transylvania) by
Katalin Peter and Istvan Toth provide fascinating examples of relig-
ous tolerance from rulers and common people. Peter uses the example of
Isabella of Hungary (1519–1559), who believed it was her responsibility to protect the freedom of worship of all her people.[9] Toth has
argued that Hungary in the sixteenth century experienced a variety of
conditions that encouraged rulers to tolerate religious diversity.[10] The
Catholic Church was too weak to suppress evangelical reformers, and
rulers loyal to Rome could not afford to alienate Protestant subjects
while at war with the Ottoman Empire, an endeavor in which the
popes supported them. Moreover, he illustrates the ambiguous nature of
religious identity in Hungary in the first half of the sixteenth century:
parish priests who considered themselves loyal to Rome gave out communion in both kinds and married, while villagers continued to think
of and refer to Protestant ministers as priests. As he says, "the new
churches did not organize themselves into exclusive congregations...in
one area could be found a Lutheran, Calvinist, and Catholic bishop
simultaneously, because these denominations and churches were not
regionally separated."[11] Examples from the sixteenth century in Hungary
demonstrate how circumstances could encourage peaceful coexistence

---

[8] Judith Pollmann, "The bond of Christian piety: the individual practice of toler-
ance and intolerance in the Dutch Republic," in *Calvinism and Religious Toleration in the
Dutch Golden Age*, eds. R. Po-chia Hsia and Henk van Nierop (Cambridge: Cambridge
University Press, 2002), 53–71.

[9] Katalin Peter, "Tolerance and Intolerance in sixteenth-century Hungary," in
Tolerance and Intolerance in the European Reformation, eds. Ole Peter Grell and Robert
W. Scribner, (New York: Cambridge University Press), 249–261.

[10] Istvan György Toth, "Old and New Faith in Hungary, Turkish Hungary, and
Transylvania," in *A Companion to the Reformation World*, 203–220.

[11] Toth, 209.

even as new confessions emerged. Further examples from the work of
Frauke Volkland indicate that even when and where confessions were
clearly articulated, as in Bischofszell, Switzerland, people weighed the
merits of confessional loyalty against material goals and often found
the practical gains of conversion more persuasive.[12] Evidence of people
intrepidly crossing supposedly impervious confessional lines leads many
scholars to assert that confessionalization was a far more limited phenomenon than formerly believed.[13] One wonders then about the limits
to the usefulness of the confessionalization thesis. While it becomes
increasingly common for historians to cite the porousness or fluidity
of confessional boundaries in all parts of Europe and Britain, however,
none deny the existence of boundaries entirely. All of these studies
argue for the importance of understanding local circumstances, yet
despite the uniqueness of each situation, a pattern emerges. Humans
were capable of making eminently rational and pragmatic decisions,
long before the modern era of secularism and rationalism, and decisions apparently motivated by faith, such as conversion to a different
confession or hostility toward a member of a different confession, often
involved other factors besides religion alone. These observations suggest
looking earlier for signs of behaviors that were supposedly lost with
the growth of confessional distinctions, such as toleration of others,
or that are not supposed to occur until after confessionalization, such
as the privatization of religious beliefs. Hans Guggisberg, for example,
contends that arguments for religious freedom did not find intellectual
foundations until the secularism of the Enlightenment in the eighteenth
century.[14] People in Augsburg could not wait that long.

This book proposes to explore issues typically reserved for the post-
1555 confessional age, such as the formation of religious identities and
the impact of religious identity on relations with others, at the very
beginning of the reformation. From the moment that theologians and
preachers disagreed publicly, in writing and in sermons, lay people had
to begin making choices about whom to support or whether to support
anyone at all and how to feel about other people's choices. In Augsburg,

---

[12] Frauke Volkland in *Interkonfessionalität—Transkonfessionalität—binnenkonfessionelle
Pluralität: neue Forschungen zur Konfessionalisierungsthese*, ed., Kaspar von Greyerz, et al.,
(Gütersloh: Gütersloher Verlag, 2003), 91–104.

[13] Nicole Grochowina in *Interkonfessionalität*, 48–72; and Ralf Pröve, ibid., 73–90.

[14] Hans R. Guggisberg, "Wandel der Argumente für religiöse Toleranz und Glaubensfreiheit im 16. und 17. Jahrhundert," in *Reformation und Gegenreformation*, ed. Heinrich
Lutz (Munich: Oldenbourg, 1979), 455.

in the first half of sixteenth century, the development of religious identities and their impact on relations within a community took place in an
environment without confessionalization. Boundaries between confessions were not just less visible; they did not exist. The only religious
group in Augsburg that was treated by contemporary authorities as
remotely close to a distinct confession was the Anabaptists,[15] and the
Anabaptists' relations with other residents were so common and intimate
that one cannot really speak of a boundary between them. Although
it is difficult to find contemporary sources that speak directly to such
issues, they do exist, and the silences, as much as the statements, say a
great deal about how people tried to navigate a religiously divided and
diverse world when it was new and when—at least in Augsburg—civic
institutions had little interest in coercing belief or worship. Augsburg's
magistrates were divided on matters of religion and, thus, could not
agree on rejecting or endorsing one form of reform. This gives us an
opportunity to see how people adapted and what kinds of choices they
made about what religious faith(s) to pursue and how to interact with
relatives, friends, or neighbors who made different choices. It may also
suggest a way to view the subsequent period outside the framework of
confessionalization.

Therefore, this study examines how and to what extent people formed
religious identities in the first four decades of the Reformation and
how those identities had an impact on their relationships with other
people, particularly their families, friends, and neighbors. Distinctive
confessional entities, such as Lutheran or Catholic, that would emerge
later in the century, much later according to some studies, were barely
recognizable in the 1520s and 1530s and could not be identified with
the names used later. Before the Reformation began, if Europeans
identified themselves religiously at all, it would have been simply as

---

[15] In fact, Anabaptist theologians varied greatly in their beliefs and interpretations of
the Bible and are usually not thought of as comprising a single confession. What mainly
united them was their rejection of infant baptism, and contemporaries identified them
by their participation in adult baptism. To contemporary authorities that baptism served
as a clear sign of belonging to a particular religious faith, and in that sense alone could
Anabaptism be seen as a confession. On Anabaptist theology in southern Germany see
Hans Guderian, *Die Täufer in Augsburg: Ihre Geschichte und ihr Erbe*, (Pfaffenhofen: Ludwig
Verlag, 1984); Werner O. Packull Packull, *Mysticism and the Early South German-Austrian
Anabaptist Movement 1525–31*, (Scottdale, PA: Herald Press, 1977).

Christians.[16] In the early years of reform, most people seem not to have felt the need to articulate any particular religious identity. Confessional names, as an indication of one's religious affiliation, do not appear in either the questions asked or the responses of defendants or witnesses in the interrogation records. The absence of confessional labels testifies to the unimportance of such terms in the daily life of contemporaries. The sheer novelty of reform and religious disagreements alone is not a satisfying explanation for this omission. The embryonic state of definitive articulations of religious faiths (or confessions) would delay the use of confessional names, but that does not sufficiently explain the striking absence of terms used to define religious affiliation. Rather, it seems to have something to do with the way individuals pursued their spiritual life. People related to their religious beliefs and practices in a variety of ways ranging anywhere from idle curiosity to identification. A person might attend a sermon, listen to a preacher, or visit a clandestine gathering for any number of reasons not just belief. As a result, the modern notion of identity obscures the variety of ways or reasons that people affiliated themselves with a religious group or confession. In France, for example, Keith Luria observed that the importance of religious identity was dependent on various factors and conditions.[17] Thus, identity is not a simple category, and the term misleads us not only because confessional names were not used, or were used incorrectly and indiscriminately as also happened, but because participation did not always indicate belief and vice versa.

During this period many people seem to have had a considerable capacity for tolerating the religious differences of their peers, when they were able to recognize them. There are few incidents of hostility between residents as a result of religious differences and even those are about much more than religion. Whenever citizens appeared to clash over religious differences, the dispute always involved some other grievance as well. When religious discontent erupted, it was usually directed at clerical or civil authority figures or their property, not at fellow citizens. The point here is not to say that people did not have passionate feelings about religion, many did, but rather that they did not automatically destroy communal relations. No matter what the

---

[16] Lee Palmer Wandel, *The Eucharist in the Reformation* (Cambridge: Cambridge University Press, 2006), 46.

[17] Keith P. Luria, *Sacred Boundaries: Religious Coexistence and Conflict in Early-Modern France* (Washington, D.C.: The Catholic University of America Press, 2005).

imperial estates decided or theologians preached, the common people had to live with each other on a daily basis. As Robert Scribner so aptly points out, given that spiritual authorities, priests, ministers and scholars could not agree on the meaning of Scripture, most people considered it beyond themselves to condemn their fellow Christians for errors of faith. He argues that the "tolerance of practical rationality" explains the ability of ordinary people to coexist during this period.[18] Circumstances guided the outcome of encounters between people, rather than a philosophy of tolerance—or of persecution, I would add. It appears that when Augsburg's city council asked citizens to get along with each other and not to argue about religion, it was motivated by the desire for peace and order not by the appeal of religious diversity. Yet that ultimately turned out to be in the city's best interests, and they realized it without the benefits of eighteenth century Enlightenment secularism. Augsburgers, both magistrates and commoners, seemed to find guidance from traditional values, such as honor, friendship, peace, and modesty.[19] Those terms frequently appear in official decrees and ordinary speech. Likewise, Emily Fisher Gray finds that Augsburgers in the mid-sixteenth century used the principle of "good neighborliness" to explain why they shared space and facilities with people who belonged to a different faith.[20] Katarina Sieh-Bürens argues that Augsburg's confessionally mixed oligarchy recognized the benefits of coexistence even before the Imperial Diet of 1555.[21] Towards the end of this period, in the late 1540s and early 1550s, Augsburgers began to show signs of confessional rivalries that would grow in the following centuries as political platforms became linked with religious ones. The potential for conflict was a fact of life from the beginning of the reformation and one that contemporaries tended to deal with more pragmatically than is often acknowledged. What we are interested in

---

[18] Robert W. Scribner, "Preconditions of tolerance and intolerance in sixteenth-century Germany," in *Tolerance and Intolerance in the European Reformation*, eds. Ole Peter Grell and Robert W. Scribner, (Cambridge: Cambridge University Press, 1996), 32–47, especially 38.

[19] "*mit und gegen ain annder erbarklich, freündtlich, fridlich, und beschaidenlich halten, dann wer das überfaren, der wurde auch darumb ernstlich und hertigklich gestrafft werden*," StadtAA, Reichsstadt, Literaliensammlung, Zuchtordnung, 5 December 1529, (emphasis mine).

[20] Emily Fisher Gray, *Good Neighbors: Architecture and Confession in Augsburg's Lutheran Church of Holy Cross, 1525–1661* (Diss. University of Pennsylvania, 2004).

[21] Katarina Sieh-Bürens, *Oligarchie, Konfession und Politik im 16. Jahrhundert: Zur sozialen Verflechtung der Augsburger Bürgermeister und Stadtpfleger 1518–1618*, (Munich: Verlag Ernst Vögel, 1986), 183.

here is why differences seldom led to conflict and what people fought about when they did.

The city of Augsburg provides an excellent venue for examining the experiences of ordinary people in the early Reformation, because of its religiously diverse population and its rich archival sources. The Free Imperial City of Augsburg lay in southern Germany just south of the confluence of the Lech and Wertach Rivers as they flow northwards from the Alps. Nestled between these two rivers, about 35,000 inhabitants made Augsburg one of the largest cities in Germany in the early sixteenth century, and its founding by two of Caesar Augustus' nephews in 15 B.C. made it (as *Augusta Vindelicorum*) one of the oldest. The rivers served as a valuable means for transporting goods, while its canals, diverted into and around the city, aided the population with a water supply, sanitation, and defense. High walls and watch towers enclosed the city and guards at the gates monitored the entry and exit of residents and visitors. The city oriented itself along the main thoroughfare, with the cathedral toward the northern end, the city hall and its square in the center, and St. Ulrich and Afra near the southern end. The city's wealthiest families tended to locate themselves around one of these neighborhoods, though numerous artisans and shop-keepers made their homes throughout the city. Many weavers lived in the comparatively poor area known as the Jakob's Quarter, or the *Jakobervorstadt*, which joined the city on the eastern side near the Franciscan church.

The city's location along the major north-south trade route between Antwerp and Venice placed it in an enviable position for economic growth. In addition to printing, gold- and silversmithing, Augsburg represented one of the leading centers of textile production in southern Germany, and weavers formed one of the largest craft guilds in the city. Prominent merchant families, such as the Fugger, Welser, Baumgartner, Bimmel, Herwart, Höchstetter, Imhof, and Rehlinger, prospered in long-distance trade, banking, and mining ventures.[22] Their lucrative business enterprises in Italy, Spain, the Netherlands, Hungary, Switzerland, and Austria, not to mention closer to home in neighboring Bavaria, made at least a small portion of Augsburg's population some of the wealthiest people in the Holy Roman Empire. Although

---

[22] Katarina Sieh-Bürens, *Oligarchie, Konfession und Politik im 16. Jahrhundert: Zur sozialen Verflechtung der Augsburger Bürgermeister und Stadtpfleger 1518–1618*, (Munich: Verlag Ernst Vogel, 1986), 20–21.

Augsburg's elites prospered, in the early sixteenth century an increasingly large portion of the population ranked as "have nothings" in the tax records.[23] Also, fewer artisans seemed able to manage even the lowest level of property assessment. Tensions resulting from the widening gulf between wealthy and poor contributed to the unrest that erupted in the early Reformation.

Since the guild revolution in 1368, Augsburg's patricians had been forced to share the urban government with the guilds, a change that recognized the importance of the growing number of wealthy merchants who did not come from one of the patrician families. Artisans who belonged to guilds elected representatives to the city's large council (*Großer Rat*), but most council members came from the guild aristocracy of merchants, suppliers and traders rather than practicing craftsmen.[24] These men then chose the forty-two members of the small council (*Kleiner Rat*) of whom thirty-four were guild masters and eight patricians, the council of thirteen (*Dreizehner*), later known as the secret council (*Geheime Rat*), and the two mayors of the city (one patrician and one guild master). The council of thirteen, which included the mayors, formed the true center of power in the city government.[25] Thus, the cherished guild government in Augsburg came closer, in practice, to an oligarchy.

Of Augsburg's elites, the Fugger family had an especially close relationship with the ruling Habsburg dynasty and played a valuable role in securing the imperial throne for Charles V in 1519, by providing him with the financial means to persuade his electors. His grandfather, Emperor Maximilian I had had an especially close relationship with the city. He benefited from the generosity of Augsburg's bankers and they from his patronage.[26] Maximilian favored the city with as many as fifty-five visits both for business and pleasure; he held several imperial diets in the city and engaged many humanists, artists, and printers in his cultural pursuits. He visited the city so often that he eventually purchased his own house near Holy Cross church and won permission

---

[23] Philip Broadhead, "Guildsmen, Religious Reform and the Search for the Common Good: The Role of the Guilds in the Early Reformation in Augsburg," *The Historical Journal* 39, No. 3 (Sep., 1996): 582.

[24] Broadhead, "Guildsmen," 583.

[25] Sieh-Bürens, 30.

[26] Christoph Böhm, *Die Reichsstadt Augsburg und Kaiser Maximilian I: Untersuchungen zum Beziehungsgeflect zwischen Reichsstadt und Herrscher an der Wende zur Neuzeit*, (Sigmaringen: Jan Thorbecke, 1998).

from the city council to open a gate in the city walls to allow him entrance at night. Although Charles' relationship with Augsburg was not quite so intimate or pleasant for either party, Augsburg hosted a number of imperial diets that marked significant turning points in the history of the city, the empire, and the Reformation.

On the eve of the Reformation, Augsburg housed at least twenty-five churches, chapels, and cloisters including various orders for men and women.[27] In addition, a number of churches also had adjoining preaching houses (*Predigthäuser*) that served the lay population with special sermons on Sundays and feast days. The preaching houses were some of the earliest sites of evangelical preaching in the city, and the city appropriated them to hire preachers of their own choosing. The medieval bishops of Augsburg had exercised important functions in the city, especially in the area around the cathedral, the *Bischofsstadt*. The bishop, however, had lost most of his political power when Augsburg became a free imperial city in the thirteenth century and by the 1500s had no official role in governing the city. Bishop Christoph von Stadion had initially encouraged humanist-trained preachers in the cathedral parish church of St. John, such as Johann Oecolampadius in 1518,[28] but he later attempted to hinder evangelical reform in the city by censoring preachers who supported Luther, such as Urbanus Rhegius.[29] Until 1537, the bishop retained control over the cathedral and seven other churches in the city, until he and the other remaining Catholic clergy were forced by the city's Protestant church ordinance (*Kirchenordnung*) to settle in Dillingen.

The Reformation found early supporters in Augsburg, as it did in many imperial cities.[30] The Carmelite monks of St. Anna welcomed

---

[27] See Rolf Kießling, *Bürgerliche Gesellschaft und Kirche in Augsburg im Spätmittelalter* (Augsburg: Verlag H. Mühlberger, 1971).

[28] Wandel, *Eucharist*, 58.

[29] Horst Jesse, *Die Geschichte der Evangelischen Kirche in Augsburg*, (Pfaffenhofen: Ludwig Verlag, 1983), 65.

[30] For general histories of the Reformation in Augsburg, especially in the first half of the 16th century: Friedrich Roth, *Augsburgs Reformationsgeschichte*. 4 vols. (Munich: T. Ackermann, 1901–11), Wolfgang Zorn, *Geschichte einer europäischen Stadt*, (Augsburg: Wißner, 1994); Horst Jesse, *Die Geschichte der Evangelischen Kirche in Augsburg*, (Pfaffenhofen: Ludwig Verlag, 1983) and Philip Broadhead, "Guildsmen, Religious Reform and the Search for the Common Good: The Role of the Guilds in the Early Reformation in Augsburg," *The Historical Journal* 39, No. 3 (1996): 577–597; and "One Heart and One Soul: The Changing Nature of Public Worship in Augsburg, 1521–1548," *Ecclesiastical History Society Papers* (1997–1998): 116–127.

Martin Luther in 1518, though the Augustinians at Holy Cross hosted him, during his aborted meetings with the papal legate, Cardinal Thomas Cajetan. Despite Luther's precipitous flight from the city, his message of reform continued to find listeners in Augsburg. In addition to Carmelites, members of the Franciscans and even some of the preachers at the cathedral parish, such as Urbanus Rhegius in 1520, began preaching from the Gospel and against indulgences, monasticism, and clerical celibacy. Although Rhegius left the cathedral, the city later hired him to preach at St. Anna and St. Moritz. In 1523 the first marriage of a priest, Jakob Grießbeutel, took place in Augsburg and was attended by a number of clergy and several prominent citizens who paid for the wedding feast. By this time signs indicated increasing support for evangelical reform among residents of Augsburg, and some of them began organizing their efforts to pressure the council to reform the city's religious worship.[31] The city council itself, much like the city's population as a whole, remained divided or undecided. Some councilors remained loyal to the old faith, while many favored reform, but those in favor of reform could not agree on which reformer to follow: Luther, Ulrich Zwingli, Martin Bucer, or someone else. Despite much popular support for some kind of reform, ties to the Catholic emperor and business contacts nearby and abroad also made it difficult for the city to abandon the Catholic Church.

In 1524 the controversial monk Johann Schilling began preaching at the Franciscan Church, or *Barfüßer Kirche*. His sermons against the papacy, city council, and Jakob Fugger "the Rich" captured and vocalized the resentment many Augsburgers felt about their dwindling economic and political status. When his sermons became too dangerous for the council to ignore, Schilling was pressured to leave the city. Although he agreed to leave peacefully and slipped out of the city quietly, many of Schilling's supporters learned of his disappearance and a large crowd soon descended on the councilors in the city hall to demand his return. After several tense days, the council and the rioters managed to end the Schilling Uprising with little violence because of their willingness to compromise. Rioters finally dispersed with the promise that the council would hire a new evangelical preacher to

---

[31] StadtAA, Reichsstadt, Urgichten, 12 August 1523, Wilhelm Gemelich and Hans Bogenschutz.

replace Schilling. His first replacement at the Franciscan church was Rhegius, soon followed by the more popular Michael Keller in 1525, who was a supporter of Ulrich Zwingli. By 1527 Luther and Zwingli's literary war over issues like the Eucharist naturally drew in the city's evangelical preachers. Luther maintained that Christ was physically present in the host, while Zwingli contended that Christ's presence was spiritual and found in the gathering of the community rather than the wafer.[32] Augsburg's ministers participated actively in this debate in their writings, sermons, and petitions to the city council for endorsement. Johann Frosch and Stefan Agricola supported Luther, while Keller, who was later joined by Bonifacius Wolfart and Wolfgang Musculus in 1531, formed a core of Zwinglian preachers in Augsburg in frequent and vociferous opposition to them. While the ministers tended to support Luther or Zwingli, most, like Rhegius, are best described as championing their own ideas. In the 1520s every priest or minister in Augsburg preached according to his own best understanding of the Eucharist and the Mass, with the rather vague directive from the council to preach from the true Gospel.

Throughout the 1520s Augsburg's city council refused to take a firm stand on the issue of church reform. It intervened, as with Schilling, to keep the peace and stifle outbursts of violent or public protest, such as vandalism of church property,[33] but otherwise made no attempts to stop evangelical or Catholic worship by policy. On 9 November 1525, for example, the council directed the evangelical preacher Johann Speiser "if he wanted to continue to preach, he should preach God's word in such a way that no one would be angered,"[34] the most important point being to avoid stirring up conflict. Likewise, the Catholic humanist theologian, Ottmar Nachtigall, had retained his position at St. Moritz under Fugger sponsorship because he had promised the council that he would "avoid in his preaching anything that might cause a riot, ill-will, or rebellion."[35] When Nachtigall called the evangelical preachers in Augsburg heretics, the council reminded him of his promise to avoid

---

[32] For a detailed discussed of the Eucharistic debate in Augsburg see Wandel, *Eucharist*, 55–93.

[33] StadtAA, Reichsstadt, Urg. 8 May 1524, Georg Näßlin. Also *Die Chroniken der deutschen Städte vom 14. bis ins 16. Jahrhundert*, Clemens Sender (1524) p. 155.

[34] *"So er mer werde predigen, soll er das gotz wort dergestellt predigen damit niemandt darab geergert wurde,"* StAA Reichsstadt, Ratsbuch 15 (1520–1529) 9 Nov. 1525.

[35] *"das yhen, so zu aufrur, widerwillen, und emporung raichen mochte, abzusteen,"* StAA Reichsstadt, Ratsbuch 15 (1520–1529) 12 Sept. 1528.

inflammatory remarks in his sermons and ordered him to stay off the imperial streets (more for his protection than as a punishment, they said), but it did not order him to stop preaching. Preferring scholarship over preaching anyway, Nachtigall gained permission from the Fuggers to resign his post and leave the city.[36] Interestingly, in his negotiations with the council Nachtigall pointed out that he found it odd that he, who obeyed the emperor's edicts (against Luther and evangelical reform), should be accused of causing rebellion and forbidden the imperial streets, while the evangelical ministers who disobeyed the emperor should walk about freely.

While the council dealt rather carefully with the well-connected Nachtigall, it was clear that the council was not ready to take sides on the religious debates of the day. In light of the council's and the city's internal divisions and conflicting foreign interests, the magistrates saw their primary task as keeping the peace.[37] Thus, the city council's hesitancy to act for or against the religious innovations appearing in the 1520s enabled people in Augsburg to hear a variety of messages, each one as unique as the priest or minister in the church—or in the case of Anabaptists the house or the garden—where he met his audience. When Agnes Vogel was baptized, before the Feast of St. Michael (29 September) 1527, Anabaptism had not yet been outlawed in Augsburg, which may be why it became the site of a major gathering of Anabaptists in the summer of 1527. Anabaptism was not forbidden in the city until October 1527, and the council's prosecution of Anabaptists was noticeably milder than in other parts of the empire, such as Bavaria, where they were usually executed. Even after Anabaptism became illegal in Augsburg, residents still had access to a diverse assortment of preaching in both reforming and anti-reforming sermons. With the exception of the occasional dismissal of a preacher who riled up the people too much, such as Johann Schilling or Ottmar Nachtigall, the city council tolerated the tumult of conflicting messages. They tried to smooth over differences and encouraged people to discuss religious issues peacefully and not heckle ministers in the middle of sermons.

In the midst of these efforts to pacify the city's domestic squabbles, Augsburg became the center stage for imperial diplomacy as well.

---

[36] Friedrich Roth, *Augsburgs Reformationsgeschichte*, vol. 1, 306–308.
[37] For a list of Augsburg's mayors by confession, see Sieh-Bürens, *Oligarchie*, 347–350.

In 1530 Emperor Charles V returned to the city to hold an imperial diet in the hopes, once more, of settling the matter of religion in the empire. One year earlier, reformers, including Luther and Zwingli, had met in Marburg at Philip of Hesse's behest to reconcile their differences, so that the cities and princes, who had recently "protested" the Diet of Speyer in 1529,[38] could present a unified and, therefore, stronger opposition to the emperor and Catholic princes. In Augsburg in 1530, Luther's colleague Philip Melancthon modified the Marburg Colloquy's articles so as to offend the emperor's Catholic sensibilities as little as possible, yet the emperor, newly reconciled with the pope, rejected them. Melancthon's articles became known as the Augsburg Confession. A number of princes and cities signed it before leaving the diet, some created their own,[39] and others, such as Augsburg, refused put anything in writing. Like the Colloquy of Marburg, the Augsburg Confession failed to unify Protestants, many of whom rejected its meek terms. Rather than accomplishing a reunion and reconciliation, the imperial diet in 1530 led to a deeper rift with Catholics, when Protestant rulers decided later that year to create the League of Schmalkalden for their mutual defense.

While the emperor's grand entrance into the city surely impressed Augsburgers, Charles' request that all evangelical preaching be forbidden during his residence probably had a deeper impact on the average citizen. Augsburg's evangelical ministers were forced to leave the city for the duration. Rhegius and others never returned, while Keller, joined by Musculus and Wolfart, pushed for an official reformation of religion in Augsburg after their return. In the early 1530s, with the elections of a series of evangelical mayors, such as Mang Seitz, Ulrich Rehlinger, Georg Herwart, and Jakob Herbrot, who enthusiastically supported reform, the city council finally took a decisive stand to support religious reform and end the controversies in Augsburg. Beginning in 1533 the council sought a common statement of faith and form of worship from evangelical preachers in the city. In 1534 the council asserted control over preaching in the city's churches and preaching houses. They employed only preachers who conformed to the preaching of the Gospel as understood in Augsburg, something not quite Lutheran

---

[38] Cities and princes who protested the 1529 Diet of Speyer, which required them to enforce an imperial ban against Martin Luther, thus became known as Protestants.

[39] Strasbourg, Constance, Lindau, and Memmingen created a variation, the Tetrapolitan Confession.

or Zwinglian, though rather closer to the latter, and released any who would not conform.[40] While decisive, this move was hardly conclusive, as eight churches under the bishop of Augsburg's control continued preaching the old faith. For another three years Augsburg remained a place where ordinary citizens could easily and legally pursue multiple religious options.

The year 1537 was a real turning point in Augsburg's religious history, when the council prohibited the Catholic Mass and expelled the Catholic clergy. Bishop von Stadion retired to his seat in Dillingen, the remaining clerics fled, and citizens were forbidden to leave the city to attend Catholic services in the surrounding countryside. For the next ten years, Augsburg's council sought religious consensus in the city mainly by eliminating public debate and standardizing worship, rather than by policing private beliefs. The experiment with uniformity ended when Emperor Charles V defeated the Schmalkaldic League in 1547 and paraded his enemies—Philip of Hesse and Johann Friedrich of Saxony—as his prisoners at the "armored" diet held in Augsburg. Having sided with the league of Protestant princes and cities in the war, Augsburg faced the emperor's wrath when he settled affairs with his opponents. More importantly for residents of the city, Charles's arrival restored Catholic services and clergy to Augsburg and undermined evangelical preaching by requiring Augsburg's ministers (quite a few of whom chose exile instead) to conform to a very conservative statement of faith that allowed for communion in both kinds and marriage of ministers but otherwise differed little from Catholicism. This very compromised statement of faith, known as the Interim, was intended to resolve religious differences in the empire until the council held in Trent could reform the church. Catholic princes refused to accept the Interim as a confession of faith, while Protestants, having just lost the war had little recourse but to agree to it, at least officially. Since the terms of the Interim were enforced on evangelical ministers only and not on Catholic clergy or citizens, it did little to unify religious worship or belief in Augsburg. In addition, Charles imposed considerable indemnities on the cities that supported his enemies and made significant constitutional changes in Augsburg and twenty-six other cities. The emperor's dissolution of the guild-run government in Augsburg, replacing it with

---

[40] Wandel, *Eucharist*, 46–93.

patricians, antagonized large portions of the population and increased resentment against the emperor and the faith he represented.

For the next seven years, from the end of the diet in 1548 through 1555, Augsburg's citizens once again faced life in a religiously diverse community. After a decade in which only evangelical preaching had been permitted, Catholics could worship openly again and priests and their processions could be seen on the street. Protestants remained divided, especially on the issue of whether to accommodate themselves to the Interim, and many felt betrayed by the council that had accepted the emperor's terms and the ministers who cooperated with them. Added to these tensions was the growing threat, as war returned again, that military fortunes might establish a new religious settlement that would favor one side. Having allied himself with the emperor in 1546, Lutheran prince Moritz of Saxony shifted the balance of power in the empire once more in 1552, with the help of Henry II of France, Charles' enemy. A victory for Moritz' forces could mean the expulsion of the old religion from the city, while a victory for the emperor could mean a return to a world before the reformation ever started. Both of these dreaded scenarios briefly became real, when the city was occupied first by Duke Moritz in April and then imperial troops in August of 1552. Neither situation proved tenable or desirable, and once again the city's fortunes would be decided, at least in part, by imperial politics.

When the city hosted the diet in 1555, the estates signed a treaty that kept the peace within the empire until 1618, by allowing princes to choose the religion of their state and to exile dissenters. The Peace of Augsburg also established Augsburg's status as a bi-confessional community. The treaty's well-known principle of *cuius regio, eius religio*[41] was suspended in Augsburg and a few other cities in which it was determined that two legal religions should coexist.[42] Since the return of Catholicism to Augsburg in 1547, the city had *de facto* become bi-confessional, though one might more accurately say multi-confessional, if one considers the variations in Protestantism practiced and the lingering,

---

[41] *Cuius regio, eius religio,* or whose rule, his religion, asserted that every ruler could choose the religion of his state and exile dissenters.

[42] Along with seven other imperial cities, including Biberach, Dinkelsbühl, Donauwörth, Kaufbeuren, Leutkirch, Ravensburg, and Ulm, Augsburg identified itself as bi-confessional. Of the eight, the first four had Lutheran governments, and only the latter four, including Augsburg, shared the government between the confessions. For more on Augsburg, Biberach, Ravensburg, Dinkelsbühl see Paul Warmbrunn, *Zwei Konfessionen in einer Stadt*, (Wiesbaden: F. Steiner, 1983), 11–14.

though relatively obscure, presence of Anabaptism. Article Twenty-Seven of the Peace of Augsburg proposed to uphold the status quo by preserving a safe haven for Catholics in free imperial cities that were otherwise Protestant.[43] In Augsburg, the population of Catholics was sizeable and influential enough to warrant the sharing of government between the two faiths. While the evangelical churches in Augsburg had tended toward Zwinglianism, the Peace permitted only the Augsburg Confession, a very moderately Lutheran understanding of Protestantism, which insisted on Christ's real presence in the Eucharist and only hinted at justification by faith. Thus, Protestants in Augsburg were forced to endure more than just adjusting to Catholics in the city. The peace settlement might have aimed to preserve the status quo—no longer would Catholics or Protestants have to fear expulsion (until another crisis during the Thirty Years' War)[44]—but, in fact, it led to many changes. Already in 1548 signs of the stress caused by religious divisions became apparent, and citizens and magistrates tried to navigate the changing landscape.

With the exception of the decade between 1537 and 1547, Augsburgers lived in a community whose authorities encouraged toleration of differences, even if it was only seen as a temporary expedient. Despite the wishes of many for religious unity, legal religious coexistence ultimately became a way of life for them, far earlier than in most parts of the empire. By the seventeenth century this expedient settlement contributed to the entrenching of confessional divides and accompanying antagonism.[45] While clearly unique, in some sense, Augsburg serves as a sort of microcosm for the Empire as a whole, which also became officially bi-confessional in 1555. People of different religious leanings were not isolated from one other but, in fact, lived in neighboring states and communities, just as Protestant and Catholic Augsburgers lived in neighboring houses or floors of houses, and interacted on a daily basis. Their experiences indicate that people found the means for accommodation despite religious disagreements.

---

[43] C. Scott Dixon, "Urban Order and Religious Coexistence in the German Imperial City: Augsburg and Donauwörth, 1548–1608," *Central European History*, 40 (2007): 9.

[44] During the Thirty Years' War, first Catholic and then Protestant worship was temporarily banned in the city during the occupations of Swedish and imperial troops respectively.

[45] Etienne François, *Die unsichtbare Grenze: Protestanten und Katholiken in Augsburg, 1648–1806* (Sigmaringen: J. Thorbecke, 1991).

Augsburg possesses an incomparable collection of sources for examining how ordinary people expressed their religious experiences in the first half of the sixteenth century. The records of judicial hearings (*Urgichten* or *Verhörprotokolle*) form the foundation of this study, and they are supplemented by the city council's record books (*Ratsbücher*), correspondence and decrees, punishment books (*Strafbücher*), tax records (*Steuerbücher*), and account books (*Baumeisterbücher*). The hand-written transcripts of hearings conducted by members of Augsburg's city council have survived, with rare exceptions, intact from the period 1517 to 1555. These were criminal cases (adultery, prostitution, spousal abuse, libel, blasphemy, public disorderliness, trespassing, vandalism, or theft) not investigations into religious belief or practice, with the exception of Anabaptists. In the early sixteenth century, Augburg's Small Council stood at the center of Augsburg's criminal justice system.[46] When a person was arrested, the prisoner would be held (*"in eysen gelegt"*) in one of the cells beneath the city hall. This convenient location facilitated questioning by members of the Small Council, who took turns in pairs each month to hear the interrogations of prisoners. The two hearers (*Verhörer* or *Auditores*) of criminal cases would report to the council at its thrice-weekly sessions for further decisions and instructions on how to proceed. All decisions regarding whether to arrest someone, to pursue or continue the interrogation of a prisoner or witness, to use torture and under what conditions, how to sentence and whether to pardon were all made by members of the Small Council, with sometimes as few as a dozen of the forty-two members present. The list of questions (*Fragstück*), which formed the basis of the interrogation, would also be created in the council chamber, based on the initial complaint against the prisoner and often refined for subsequent interrogations after hearing testimony from witnesses. The council's appointed hearers interrogated the prisoner or witnesses, sometimes with the assistance of the city executioner, whose office included administering torture, and always in the presence of the city scribe who wrote down the entire proceedings as they occurred.[47] Prisoners were not represented or assisted by lawyers, but their families or friends could petition the city council or

---

[46] Reinhold Schorer, *Die Strafgerichtsbarkeit der Reichsstadt Augsburg 1156–1548*, (Cologne: Böhlau Verlag, 2001), 166.

[47] Schorer, 168; and Carl A. Hoffmann, "Strukturen und Quellen des Augsburger reichsstädtischen Strafgerichtswesens in der ersten Hälfte des 16. Jahrhunderts." *Zeitschrift des Historischen Vereins für Schwaben* 88 (1995), 91.

request petitions from influential persons to seek a pardon or leniency by explaining mitigating circumstances or making assurances of the accused person's good behavior in the future.

With the development of the inquisitorial process in Europe in the Middle Ages,[48] the criminal justice system began to rely on evidence or, in the absence of material evidence, a confession to establish a person's guilt. Thus, torture and the executioner became instrumental in the investigation of criminal cases, in order to extract the truth from an accused person. Strict rules regulated the application of torture, which Augsburg's council followed, under the guidance of legal experts, such as the humanist Conrad Peutinger in the first half of the sixteenth century. For example, torture could be applied if witness testimony indicated that a prisoner was lying or withholding information in a serious matter, if the gravity of offense warranted corporal or capital punishment, and only if the accused person's health could sustain torture without causing a life-threatening injury. In Augsburg, women who were pregnant, men who had hernias, and youths and children were routinely excused from torture in circumstances that would otherwise have indicated its use for an adult. If a prisoner did not respond to "friendly questioning," (*guter frag*) the council could choose various degrees of force, all of which—from the decision to use or threaten torture to its actual application and the response—would be noted by the scribe as it took place. At the mildest level, councilors might make verbal threats or warnings to give truthful questions. Next in severity was having the executioner show the prisoner the instruments of torture that could be used. For women this almost always meant the thumbscrews, and for men the *strappado*,[49] which, at this stage, would involve tying the hands together behind the person's back but not pulling him up. In some cases, a note at the end of the list of questions indicated that a prisoner was to have her fingers placed in the thumbscrews but without tightening, even if she did not answer the questions any differently, and the questioning stopped there. Thus, the council did not always use

---

[48] Schorer, 162–163. For a general history of this development in Europe, see Edward M. Peters, *Torture* (Philadelphia: University of Pennsylvania Press, 1996).

[49] The *strappado* involved tying a person's hands together behind his back and then lifting the hands to the point that the person's legs were lifted off the floor. If this did not have the desired effect, weights could be added to the feet to make the hoisting up more painful. This procedure often resulted in dislocating the shoulders, which would become increasingly painful after they had time to swell. Prisoners who withstood the first round of torture often succumbed when threatened with it a second time.

the fullest expression of power to which it was empowered in criminal investigations, though their reasons for restraint are not always clear. In serious cases the questioning might skip over these intermediate forms of pressure and proceed directly from the first round of questioning to the application of torture, tightening the thumbscrews or pulling up by the hands. It should be observed, however, that torture was not used in all cases and never for witnesses.

A variety of factors, including the accused person's age, gender, demeanor, mental capacity, petitions, degree of guilt or involvement, and the gravity of the offense, would influence the council's decision to release or sentence a prisoner. A person found innocent or only guilty of a minor infraction might be released or turned over to the punishment lords (*Strafherren*), who dealt with minor discipline issues.[50] The most common punishments ranged from reprimands (in front of the assembled council or in public), fines, time spent in a tower (from one day to three months),[51] or exile (from one year to lifetime). Corporal punishments usually meant whipping, occasionally branding, or, rarely, cutting out the tongue, such as for blasphemy. Of course, conditions in the prison were sometimes so miserable that simply being held in the cells during the course of interrogations constituted a corporal punishment in itself.[52] Execution was certainly the most severe punishment the council could impose but was used only rarely in the cases considered in this book.[53]

While records created during interrogation naturally pose some challenges in assessing the value and significance of testimony, their potential for revealing genuine emotions and sentiments is immense when used carefully. A number of methods serve to maximize the usefulness of these sources. First, comparing the interrogation records to the Punishment Books (*Strafbücher*) and Council Records (*Ratsbücher* or *Ratsprotokolle*) allows one better to understand the council's interpretation of the defendant's position and the gravity of the crime and to verify the outcomes of cases in which a defendant was sentenced. It also confirms

---

[50] Hoffmann, 77–78.

[51] The towers used for punishment were part of the city's fortifications. A prisoner would be kept under guard, and the council could worsen the punishment by limiting the food and drink allowed to him. Schorer, 178.

[52] Schorer, 177.

[53] This study does not entail a legal history of Augsburg, and, therefore, does not analyze statistics for the frequency or types of punishments used in the city's criminal justice system as a whole.

that there are very few missing cases. Also, this study considers all types of criminal cases not just cases of religious crimes, which ensures that one finds statements about religion that are presumably less calculated, since they were not relevant to the charge being investigated. Likewise, given that the council itself was divided on religious issues throughout most of the period studied, the hearers were not meant to represent a particular religious faith. Similarly, the use of witness testimony in many cases provides a body of information from people who were not being coerced to speak or at risk of punishment, and it can help to confirm (or challenge) the testimony of the accused person. None of the witnesses appearing in these cases were threatened with or subjected to torture or other forms of coercion; the use or threat to use torture would have been noted in these meticulously recorded hearings.

Most of the cases were written down by the same scribe, which makes differences in the speaker's tone, emotion, intelligence, cooperativeness or reticence more clearly observable. This is especially true when the interrogated persons were all subjected to the exact same list of questions, as a large group of Anabaptists was in 1528. The differences in their responses demonstrate that the hearing records are able to reflect the expressions and perspectives of unique individuals. It is also worth noting that even when a defendant or witness may have tried to mislead the council or obscure the truth, his or her testimony still has much to reveal about how people articulated their thoughts about religion and understood the religious issues of the day. An apparent weakness of the sources actually becomes a strength. At first it seems frustrating that the council did ask the questions that a historian might like to have asked, such as what religion a person followed or how a person felt about a certain faith or the followers of a particular reformer or priest. Yet the absence of those questions from the sources (even in cases investigating religious crimes, such as vandalism in a church or criticism of a preacher) tells us that those questions were not relevant to contemporaries. They conceived of the problems of their day very differently from what we would expect, and religious identity does not seem to have been one of them. The absence of such questions and the fact that these cases were not inquiries into religious belief or practice (with the exception of Anabaptists)[54] means that references to religion

---

[54] Even in the cases of Anabaptists, the council did not ask what they believed, why they were baptized, or how they felt about others, merely if, when, where, and by whom they were baptized.

or religious differences in the hearings tended to be voluntary or not in and of themselves vital to the investigation in the eyes of the contemporary speakers or listeners. Finally, people did not always feel fear or always face punishment when questioned. When used with caution, these sources certainly provide us with some of the best evidence available for the first half of the sixteenth century of the ways that ordinary people constructed and expressed their religious identities.

The chapters develop thematically and somewhat chronologically to show the emergence of different issues throughout the four decades under scrutiny. The first chapter opens with a brief look at a case that highlights the ambiguity of identifying religious affiliations in the early Reformation. There is a pervading atmosphere of uncertainty that characterized the experiences of many people negotiating social contacts in a new religious world. The second chapter explores the few cases that explicitly reflect religious conflicts in the 1520s and demonstrates the two points mentioned above, that people usually directed their hostility against authorities and that when they confronted neighbors other non-religious issues played a role—usually the dominant role—in inciting the conflict. The third chapter endeavors to reintegrate Anabaptists into the life of the city where they lived, by exploring their interactions with each other and non-Anabaptists. Thus, Anabaptists will appear in other chapters as well, just as non-Anabaptists appear in Chapter Three. The numerous hearings of Anabaptists, generated in part to discover how the group grew and organized itself, prove immensely useful for understanding how people might come to affiliate themselves with a particular religious group during a period of religious change like the early reformation. The fourth chapter examines Augsburg's decade-long experiment with religious uniformity when the city council banned the Catholic clergy and Mass. The cases during this time reflect surprisingly little resistance and the opposition that appears tends to be passive rather than aggressive, but then again, so was the council's policy. The last two chapters address the tumultuous period beginning in 1548 when Augsburg witnessed military occupation, political upheaval, the return of religious diversity and then its disappearance again, and finally a new religious settlement in favor of peaceful coexistence in 1555. Religious conflicts begin to emerge again in this period, similar to the ones in the 1520s (opposition to authorities and neighborly disputes with religious undertones) but now with higher stakes in a tense atmosphere in which imperial military conflicts rather than civil debate could determine the city's religious future.

From 1517 to 1555 Augsburg contained a community of families, neighbors, and foreigners who witnessed the appearance of religious innovation and diversity to a degree unparalleled in medieval Christian Europe. Circumstances in the city allowed an individual to experiment with religious innovations, by visiting different churches and meetings without committing to one kind. Even in the decade from 1537 to 1547, Augsburg's government was hardly a confessionalizing force. That period when Augsburg attempted to create religious uniformity actually witnesses fewer numbers of religiously-inspired hearings than the periods before and after, almost as if the council was content to have unified the preachers and preferred to let them see what they could do by persuasion alone. There is no concerted effort by the council to root out Catholics, who certainly existed in the city. Towards the end of this period, after 1548, the changing tone of religiously motivated conflicts seems to reflect a cultural phenomenon that bears similarities to the characteristics of the later confessional age. Between 1548 and 1555 religion and politics became intertwined to the point that people began to equate certain religious faiths with specific political agendas. Under those conditions, hostilities were more likely to flare than earlier, when one's religious affiliation seemed to have less impact on neighbors. From the beginning of the Reformation, people witnessed exciting and startling changes, namely the appearance of unprecedented diversity and controversy within western Christianity. They had to decide how to respond to innovations in and debates about religious beliefs and practices—even if they decided to withhold judgment—and how to react to other people's decisions. Surviving records indicate that Augsburgers had a considerable amount of freedom to determine their own opinions and, although tensions did sometimes erupt into conflict, they tended to respect the right of others to determine for themselves, even if they did not articulate their attitude in those terms. While religious freedom as a virtue might not yet have had widespread support, older principles, such as honor, friendship, and peace, or "good neighborliness," seemed to help people to negotiate new situations. Their behavior in such novel and unsettling circumstances reveals that the Reformation could inspire passionate and conflicting feelings about religion, as well as pragmatic and rational ways to handle them.

CHAPTER ONE

AMBIGUOUS IDENTITIES

The Kretzwescher's two daughters are Lutheran and Anabaptist… the Kretzwescher is neither Anabaptist nor Lutheran, but then he's not the master of his house.[1]

The Kretzwescher's neighbor offered the above description of the family's religious affiliations in apparently clear-cut terms. Upon closer scrutiny, we learn that he not only misinterpreted his neighbors' religious behavior but also had only a vague notion of what those terms meant. While one might expect that by the 1530s most urban residents would have a pretty good grasp of the different spiritual constellations emerging in the Reformation, this witness, a man named Aberlin Hasen, reminds us that not everyone cared passionately about reforming the church. He also indicates that it was not always easy to recognize other people's religious beliefs in this period. Hasen's testimony contributed to an investigation into the activities of a circle of Anabaptists conducted by the city council in March of 1533. The cases discussed below illustrate the indistinct nature of religious identities in the early Reformation and problems they presented.

Augsburg's interrogation records give us an insight into the ambiguous nature of the early Reformation and its implications for ordinary people. Due to its economic and political importance, the imperial city of Augsburg was the site of several significant Reformation events, including the signing of Confession of Augsburg in 1530, which constituted a declaration of Protestant beliefs. Despite its role in these important developments Augsburg remained neutral for quite awhile. Despite wide popular support for reform, the influence of powerful Catholic families, such as the Fugger, and the city's close ties to the emperor and Catholic trading partners, led the city council to pursue a cautious path.[2] When the city finally declared itself in favor of the Reformation in 1534,

---

[1] "*Des Kretzweschers zwo dochter seien luterisch unnd gartisch… der Kretzwescher auch weder gartisch noch luterisch doch seie er nit maister im hauß,*" StadtAA, Reichsstadt, Urg. 1 May 1533, Aberlin Hasen.

[2] Philip Broadhead, "Guildsmen, Religious Reform and the Search for the Common Good," 577–597. See also Roth, *Reformationsgeschichte* and Wolfgang Zorn, *Augsburg*.

it employed evangelical preachers, such as Wolfgang Musculus and
Michael Keller, who often disagreed with Wittenberg reformer Martin
Luther. Catholic services and clergy survived in the city until 1537 and
people loyal to the old faith survived longer. Anabaptists, who were not
welcome at any time, were generally left alone, unless their activities
became too blatant, as they did in 1533. At the time when these interrogations were conducted, many different forces inspired spiritual life
in Augsburg. The hearings reveal how people, and not just those who
were Anabaptists, dealt with the ambiguities inherent in identifying
religious groups in the early reformation. As numerous examples from
this period show, the Reformation did not have an impact just on the
individual's conscience but on communities, because those individuals
had to go on living with families and neighbors who did not always see
eye to eye on religious matters.

   An ordinary house in the Jakob's Quarter makes a particularly good
example of this extraordinary situation. In the course of the 1533
Anabaptist investigations, a house inhabited by four different families
came under the scrutiny of the city council. The council began by
questioning the carter, Aberlin Hasen, who lived with his wife on the
lowest floor, half underground. He later cites this awkward location as
one reason why he could not see too much of went on in the rest of
the house; most of his information came from talking with the maids
of the other residents, rather than first-hand. Above him, on the
second floor, lived the potion-maker Martin Roth, his wife, and their
maid. On the third floor lived the landlord, who was a tailor named
Michael Germair, with his wife, a brother-in-law, and their maid. On
the fourth floor lived Narciß Hieber (the Kretzwescher), his wife Sabina
Hieberin, her daughters (apparently from a previous marriage since
Elisabeth is referred to as Dr. Schenk's daughter), and the landlord's
stepsister, Ursula Germairin. His testimony does not mention if any
children lived there.

   Hasen was asked to describe the activities of the other residents of
the house and to identify the ones who were affiliated with Anabaptism. The man apparently tried to exonerate certain members of the
house by describing them as neither Lutheran nor Anabaptist ("*weder
luterisch noch gartisch*"), while accusing others of being both. As Hasen
describes it, the tailor (Michael Germair) and his wife, the potion-maker
and his wife and maid were neither Lutheran nor Anabaptist. The
tailor's unmarried stepsister (Ursula Germairin), the Kretzwescher's
wife (Sabina Hieberin), and her children (including Elisabeth Schenk)

were all Anabaptist or *gärtisch*. The Kretzwescher's two daughters are actually described as being both Lutheran and Anabaptist. Hasen said that Narciß Hieber was neither Anabaptist nor Lutheran, and explained "but then he's not the master of his household."[3]

The testimony of Aberlin Hasen proved, through further interrogation of the other residents, to have been at least somewhat accurate. This house contained families, and individuals within families, who had diverse religious leanings. The religious interests of the house's residents were known to the others, without being the cause of any apparent strife amongst them. One explanation for this could perhaps be found in Hasen's testimony. His description of the Kretzwescher, Hieber, as not being the master in his household, was his way of explaining how it could be that the man's wife and daughters were Anabaptists while he was not. For the landlord, Michael Germair, no such explanation is given. Instead, his tolerance of his stepsister and tenants' religious life, in spite of his own differing conviction, indicates that it was indeed possible for people of different religious persuasions to live peacefully together.

Michael Germair was questioned on the same day as Hasen. He vehemently denied having anything at all to do with anything Lutheran or Anabaptist. To paraphrase, he did not socialize with any of them, did not know anything about their business, did not house or host any of them, and could not possibly say anything at all about their activities.[4] In the course of his testimony, however reluctantly given, he admitted knowing that one of his tenants, Sabina Hieberin (also referred to as Kretzwescherin) was reputed to be a follower. About his stepsister, Ursula Germairin, who lived upstairs with the Hieber family, he stated that she had told him that they read and discuss the Bible upstairs while they spin. When questioned about the women's visitors, he contended "they did nothing upstairs but speak of good things."[5]

Being in a position of authority in the house, Germair naturally could not admit to having knowingly sheltered Anabaptists or permitted their meetings in his house. Aiding and abetting Anabaptists had been illegal

---

[3] "*Glaub auch das der Kretzwescher auch weder gartisch noch luterisch doch seie er nit maister im hauß,*" StadtAA, Reichsstadt, Urg. 1 March 1533, Aberlin Hasen.

[4] "*er hab weder mit den Gartischen noch den lüterischenn, gar nichts gehandelt, hab kein gemeinschaft mit inen, wiß gar nichts umb ir sach, hab sie weder gehauset noch gehofet, wiß umb ir thun und lassen gar nichts zu sagenn,*" ibid., 1 March 1533, Michel Germair.

[5] "*man thu nichts dan das man guet ding da oben sage,*" ibid.

since October 1527. Yet, he conceded that he knew of one incident, in which visitors came to see Sabina Hieberin, apparently for a meeting, but he claimed that he had turned them away and told her not to continue such activities, to which she supposedly agreed. He also admitted that he had been told of a meeting that had occurred in his house one evening while he was away. The interrogators, satisfied with Germair, released him on the same day, with the stipulation that he reappear if they should call him again for questioning, which they never did. None of the other witnesses or defendants gave the interrogators any reason to investigate him further. His Anabaptist stepsister refused to incriminate him, even after being tortured. The Hiebers' daughter, Elisabeth Schenk, readily confirmed that Germair, his wife and brother-in-law were not involved in Anabaptism, but she claimed that Germair did know of the comings and goings of her mother's visitors and refused them only on one occasion at night.[6] Other Anabaptists arrested during this investigation also testified that they had met at Germair's house on multiple occasions.

While Germair was not involved in any Anabaptist activities personally, he certainly knew that his stepsister and at least one tenant were members and even held meetings in his house. While not actually encouraging their participation, he seems to have seen very little wrong with their behavior except for where it might cast disrepute on the household. In other words, his concern was not aroused by their wanting to read the Bible together but by their receiving male visitors after dark, because of the impropriety or perhaps because of the noise from people climbing up the stairs to the fourth floor at night. Germair's reaction to the situation demonstrates that a neighbor's religious identity does not have to cause a conflict unless it upsets social mores. Even so, in this case, there does not seem to have been any conflict in the house before the city council began its investigation. The investigation was part of an attempt to break up a circle of Anabaptists that had been holding meetings.

Ursula Germairin, the tailor's stepsister, was questioned on 3 March 1533, two days after her brother. Her first interrogation consisted of three simple points. She described herself as a single woman from the Bavarian village of Bergheim. She had lived in Augsburg for ten years

---

[6] "*Der schneider hab die leit bei tag sehen auß und ein geen, und nicht mer dann ein mal bei der nacht nit leiden wollenn*," ibid., 3 March 1533, Elizabeth Schenk.

and had worked for her brother and an unnamed weaver. Secondly, she admitted to having been re-baptized along with Sabina Hieberin a year earlier. On the third point, the interrogators apparently asked her about her brother, but she refused to give any answer that might implicate him in any way, even after being "questioned with the thumb-screw"[7] twice. The interrogators held her for four days and approached her again on 7 March. This time she gave more detailed information regarding her activities and the names of a few of the people with whom she attended meetings, but she still said nothing against her brother. Except for the Kretzwescher's apartment and the Näßlins' house, she claimed not to have attended meetings anywhere else or any meeting over six people, which satisfied the legal proscription of large private gatherings of Anabaptists.

The limited scope of her involvement would have mitigated Ursula Germairin's culpability to some extent, as she may have intended in her testimony. Her naming of other followers was relatively circumspect and was most likely confined to people who were already known to the authorities. By 5 March, another family, the Näßlins, had already been arrested and interrogated. Regarding their activities, Germairin claimed that they did nothing but speak about the word of God. She also added that "she did not go there for wine-drinking but for divine nourishment."[8] In spite of her reticent posture, she absolutely refused to be swayed from her beliefs. In fact, she declared boldly to her inter-rogators: "If my lords, the mayors and the honorable council, should release her from the prison and show her mercy, she would not leave off the business but would pursue it as far as her body and life would sustain her."[9]

Not surprisingly, given Ursula Germairin's obstinate attitude and her relatively marginal social position, she was led out of the city and banished for life. As a single woman and a non-citizen, she was rela-tively insignificant from the point-of-view of the city council. If she had backed down, shown repentance, or even recanted, she probably would have been remanded to her brother's custody and released without

---

[7] "*Zu zwaien malen mit dem daumstock gefragt, sagt sie wolle iren bruder nit verraten*," ibid., 3 March 1533, Ursula Germairin.

[8] "*Seie...nit von wein trinken sonder von der himelischen speis wegen zu in gangenn*," ibid., 7 March 1533, Ursula Germairin.

[9] "*Wann meine herrn, die Burgermeister und ein Erber Rat sie gleich wol der fancknus erlieβ unnd ir gnad mittailte, wollte sie dannocht von dem handl nit steenn sonder den verfolgen alls weit ir ir leib unnd leben raiche*," ibid., Ursula Germairin.

further penalty. Instead, her defiance of the authorities forced them to remove her from the city. Although the council would not tolerate a threat to its authority, it demonstrated its relatively mild treatment of Anabaptists by not having her whipped on the way out.

Sabina Hieberin, wife of Narciß Kretzwescher, began her interrogation just as adamantly as her housemate, Ursula Germairin. She confessed immediately to having been re-baptized, but she refused to incriminate anyone else, even after torture with the thumbscrews. Like Germairin, she was interrogated again on 7 March. On this occasion she divulged more precise information about her baptism, where it took place and who was there, and about other meetings that she had held or attended. Her testimony confirms Ursula Germairin's in so far as the names of other members and when and where they met, though she did comment about their activities at these meetings. Also like Ursula Germairin, she refused the interrogators' offer to recant. She told them, "she had no thought of abandoning the business and, if she should ever have to do so, it would do great violence to her soul."[10] Despite this brave declaration, Sabina Hieberin did indeed recant in the end. Perhaps, because of her ties and responsibilities as a wife and mother, she had more to lose by defying the authorities. Or, perhaps, she merely had no intention of getting caught again.

As for her husband, Narciß Kretzwescher, Sabina Hieberin denied his involvement in Anabaptism quite emphatically, even claiming, "her husband is not a follower, rather he tells her he would like to be her executioner. He might as well be her executioner as any other."[11] It possible that Hieberin characterized his attitude so vehemently in order to protect him from any suspicion of complicity, but Hasen's testimony (and the fact that the council chose not to question him) confirms that Kretzwescher almost certainly was not an Anabaptist. Yet despite any alleged disapproval on his part, Hieberin had obviously managed to attend meetings and even to hold meetings in their home on more than one occasion. Then again, as Hasen pointed out, "[Kretzwescher] is not the master of his house." Since the interrogators did not question Narciß Kretzwescher, the only evidence for his beliefs comes from statements made by his wife and neighbor. Regardless of his feelings, the

---

[10] "*Sie gedenk von den handl nit zu steen unnd so sie das y thunn mußt wurd irer selenn ein grosser zwanck bescheenn,*" ibid., 7 March 1533, Sabina Hieberin.

[11] "*Ir man gee nicht mit dem handl umb sonder sag zuo ir Er wolle selbs ir hencker sein, sei gleich so guet er sei ir hencker als ain ander,*" ibid., Sabina Hieberin.

records clearly indicate that he had not been able to influence either his wife's or his stepdaughter's religious choices.

We have no way of knowing why Sabina Hieberin chose to recant, after standing up to her husband's alleged hostility and withstanding the interrogators' torture, nor why Ursula Germairin, whose brother winked at her activities, refused to recant. Under carefully scrutinized circumstances a prisoner could be tortured to elicit information, but the object of judicial torture was not conversion. Certainly, many other factors might persuade one to recant. In the case of Anabaptists, the council usually released those who recanted and exiled those who refused or those who were not citizens of Augsburg. Corporal punishment was reserved for the most active members who violated multiple laws by baptizing, preaching, and encouraging new followers, thereby helping the movement to grow.

On one point, Aberlin Hasen made a curious error in his description of the religious affiliations of his housemates. He accused Sabina Hieberin's daughter, Elisabeth Schenk of being both Lutheran and Anabaptist. His reason for this conclusion was that, "she, the one daughter, served at Hertnit the tavernkeeper's. Hertnit had ordered the daughter to go to [the Cathedral of] Our Lady for services, but the daughter did not want to do it."[12] Hasen obviously interpreted Schenk's refusal to attend Catholic services as compelling proof of her involvement in non-Catholic sects. The language of Hasen's statements indicates that he did not have a clear idea of what any of the Protestant faiths involved. For one thing, he did not mention Zwingli at all, even though his reforms were the most popular with ministers and lay people in Augsburg. Not to mention, by 1533 one could certainly not be both a follower of Luther and an Anabaptist at the same time, despite sharing a few common ideas. As it turns out, Elisabeth Schenk was neither.

The young woman described her situation in a very different way from Hasen. Elisabeth Schenk testified that she had not been re-baptized and was not a follower of Anabaptism. She did not state whether or not she was Lutheran, but most likely the interrogators did not ask her that, since it was not a crime in Augsburg. As for why she left the service of the tavernkeeper, Hertnit, she explained that she left because

---

[12] "*Des Kretzweschers zwo dochter seien luterisch und gartisch ursach sie hab die ein dochter verdingt zum Hernit Bierschencken der hab der dochter bevolhen zu unser frauen an die predig zu geen aber die dochter hab es nit thunn wollenn*," ibid., 1 March 1533, Aberlin Hasen.

she did not want to go to the sermon at the Cathedral of Our Lady (which still held Mass in the old way). She had complained about it to her mother, Sabina Hieberin, who told her daughter "she would not force her to do anything. If she did not want to go to Our Lady, and someone did not want her in service because of it, then she should come back home."[13] We do not know if she was actually fired, but she did return home and continue to attend services at Holy Cross Church and the Franciscan Church instead. At the time, both Holy Cross and the Franciscan churches were employing evangelical preachers, Wolfgang Musculus and Michael Keller, respectively. Neither man could be defined by a particular confessional identity, based on later definitions; but as was common in southern Germany, both ministers had much more in common with Zwingli than Luther.[14] Although she never declared herself as belonging to a particular group by name, Schenk indicated her religious leaning by declaring her preference for services at those places.

Elisabeth Schenk's testimony along with the other interrogation records from Augsburg raises some interesting questions about the forming of religious identity early in the Reformation. For one, they indicate the very indistinct manner in which people identified the various religious faiths and their own participation in them. Rather than identifying a religious group by name, Elisabeth Schenk indicated her religious preferences by naming the churches where she did or did not want to attend services. Aberlin Hasen, the basement informer, recognized Elisabeth Schenk's refusal to go to the Cathedral as a sign of where her loyalties lay, though he misread the sign. Testimony from other cases also indicates that people did not feel compelled to attend services at only one church, but instead visited several places. It is also worth noting that the city council never used confessional names to identify or learn a defendant's religious preferences.

---

[13] "*Sie hab sich nit lassen tauffen, seie auch kein garten schwester und umb das sie von dem hertnit bierschencken komen seie die ursach das sie nit gen Unßer frauen an die predig gen wollen, des sie irer muter geclagt, die hab ir geantwort sie welle sie zu nichten noten, wann sie nit zu unßer frauen wolle geenn und man sie darumb am dienst nit haben welle mog sie wol wider haim geenn, des sie gethann also mit irer Anfrauen vor und nach gem Creutz zu den parfuessen und ander ort zu predig gangen,*" ibid., 3 March 1533, Elizabeth Schenck.

[14] Wandel argues that Augsburg's preachers actually devised their own evangelical reform that was unique to that city, though influenced by important leaders elsewhere, including Zwingli, Bucer, and Luther.

Furthermore, in the course of this series of interrogation records, the German term for Anabaptist, *Wiedertäufer* (literally re-baptizer), is never used. Throughout their testimonies, the suspects and witnesses referred to their religion as "the matter" (*Sache*) or "the business" (*Handel*). The council never asked a prisoner if he or she was an Anabaptist (*Wiedertäufer*), only if they had been baptized. Just like the magistrates, Ursula Germairin and Sabina Hieberin defined membership in the sect by whether or not one had been re-baptized as an adult. Aberlin Hasen, on the other hand, referred to them not with the noun *Wiedertäufer* but with the adjective, "*gärtisch*," or "*gartisch*," derived from the term *Gartenschwester* or *Gartenbruder* (Gardensister or Gardenbrother). This term alluded to the gardens in- or outside the city walls in which Anabaptists sometimes met, since they could not gather in public places or buildings. This manner of identifying one's religious inclinations with where one meets or attends services reflects the fluidity of pre-confessional religious boundaries in this period.

Elisabeth Schenk's interrogation demonstrates how family members with differing religious beliefs could tolerate and even facilitate each other's faith. In the course of her interrogation, Schenk was questioned about her mother's activities and some of the people with whom her mother met. She testified that she had overheard them talking about their existence and about God, but other than that she had not paid attention.[15] She was present but did not participate. She testified that she knew of no inappropriate behavior, but she added that when someone from the society was poor or in need, they would be introduced and taken care of by the others. The only other meeting place that she could name for the interrogators was the house of a shoemaker, Georg Näßlin, where she had once met her mother to escort her home from a meeting.[16] Elisabeth Schenk was released by the city council without further questioning or punishment. The mother and daughter's interrogation records suggest that the members of the Hieber household pursued their own religious interests rather independently of one another.

These interrogation records shed light on the interactions of persons who identified themselves with different, even contentious, religious

---

[15] "*So sie also zu samen komen hab sie gehort das sie von irem wesen unnd von got gesagt aber sie hab sich der sach nichts komert,*" ibid., Elizabeth Schenk.

[16] "*Wann eines auß der gesellschaft arm unnd mangelhaft gewesenn so habenn die andern der selben person fur gestellt und gaben,... Bruder und Schwester gangenn gen der Neßlerin auch ursach sie hab ir muter daselbs i mal da selbst geholet,*" ibid., Elizabeth Schenk.

groups. Within the Hieber family, we see at least three different religious leanings, one towards Zwinglianism (Elisabeth Schenk), one towards Anabaptism (Sabina Hieberin), and one for an indistinct "neither Lutheran nor Anabaptist," group (Narciß Hieber a.k.a. Kretzwescher) which most likely meant the traditional Catholic Church. The mother and daughter showed an apparent disinterest in each other's religious beliefs yet supported each other's right to choose for herself what she would believe. Sabina Hieberin supported her daughter's right to leave her place of work for religious reasons, and Elisabeth Schenk described her mother's re-baptism and related activities with sympathy rather than any hint of disapproval. Aberlin Hasen's unclear ideas about the various religious groups reflect not just ambiguity but an uninformed state of mind. Further, his denial of being "*lutherisch*" himself is striking and somewhat puzzling, given that the council was not hunting for Lutherans. Augsburg's population was mostly Protestant in 1533, so Hasen ran no risks by identifying himself as Lutheran, except perhaps from the Zwinglians. Instead, his statements seem to reflect either a complete rejection of religious reform or a distinct lack of interest in or even awareness of the religious developments in his community.

The very existence of this house, with four families of diverse spiritual inclinations and involvement living under one roof, captures the essence of common people's experiences in the early years of the Reformation. Under one roof we find some people who rejected reform, some who embraced it, and even a few who risked their safety for an illegal sect. Yet they lived peacefully with each other before they came to the attention of the Augsburg city council. Ernst Walter Zeeden has argued that the exclusive claims of each confession to Christian truth made intolerance of every other confession essential,[17] yet the testimonies of these residents reveal if not outright sympathy, then at least a distinct hesitancy to condemn people of other faiths, even Anabaptists who were denounced by every other confession. As Judith Pollmann has observed in the Dutch Republic in the seventeenth century,[18] it seems that some people, such as the tailor Germair, could recognize the shared Christian piety evident in the meetings of Anabaptists who came together to discuss the Bible. The unique circumstances of this pre-confessional period also permitted a form of pragmatic tolerance or what Robert

---

[17] Zeeden, *Konfessionsbildung*, 104–5.
[18] Pollmann, "The bond of Christian piety," 69.

Scribner has named the "tolerance of practical rationality."[19] The
religious situation in Augsburg in 1533 lacked two important elements
that would later threaten the potential for tolerance. First, there were
no clearly defined or uniform principles to establish distinct confessions
and, secondly, there was no active participation of secular authorities
to support one confession exclusively and eliminate all others. These
elements, which, like Zeeden, Wolfgang Reinhard and Heinz Schilling
also find necessary to the process of confessionalization, had not yet
been realized in Augsburg.[20] In 1533, eight churches still held Catholic
Masses, and Protestants debated the relative merits of Luther versus
Zwingli. Augsburg's government still tolerated a religiously diverse community. The various groups had much in common and still attempted
reconciliation. Preachers argued over petty details until parishioners
were no longer sure whom to believe. In this atmosphere, the behavior
of the Germair household begins to look like a natural reaction to the
conditions of the time.

The related case of the Näßlins presents another sample of intra-
family relations tested in the pursuit of religious identity. In the Näßlin
family, we find both accommodation and conflict within the family over
religious issues. On 5 March 1533, between the initial and final interrogations of the three women mentioned above, two more suspects,
Georg and Barbara Näßlin, were arrested. Georg Näßlin, a shoemaker,
steadfastly denied being a follower of Anabaptism, but he acknowledged
that he had permitted meetings to take place in his home at his wife's
insistence. He explained his complicity in her behavior as follows:

> Though he did not want the brethren in his home and told his wife so,
> she threatened to leave him because of it. He considered his situation
> as a poor artisan and decided that if he opposed her, he might lose her.
> So, he figured it would be better to let them meet in his house than not
> or for her to go elsewhere.[21]

---

[19] Scribner, *Tolerance and Intolerance*, 38.

[20] See Heinz Schilling, "Die Konfessionalisierung von Kirche, Staat und Gesell-
schaft—Profil, Leistung, Defizite, und Perspektiven eines geschichtswissenschaftlichen
Paradigmas," in *Die Katholische Konfessionalisierung: Wissenschaftliches Symposion der Gesellschaft
zur Herausgabe des Corpus Catholicorum und des Vereins für Reformationsgeschichte*, eds. Wolfgang
Reinhard and Heinz Schilling, (Gütersloh: Gütersloher Verlagshaus, 1995), 1–49; and
Wolfgang Reinhard, "Zwang zur Konfessionalisierung?" 257–277.

[21] *"Er seie der sachen durch schlechts nichts verwannt, dann sovil das er die bruder nit leden
wollenn inn seiner hauß, hab sein fraw gesagt sie kond mog und wolle sie nit lassen, wann es aber
ye sein muß, unnd werd sie sich sein alls ires Eemans verzeichenn, Uff das er gedacht er seie ain
handtwerckman hab ain wenige armut so er dem weib wider wertig wer, mocht ime entzogen werden*

In her testimony, Barbara Näßlin confirmed that "she had no intention of giving up the matter, she would rather leave her husband; he was not a follower." She further stated that when her husband confronted her about it and did not want to allow her visitors, she told him "she would leave the house and follow them."[22]

In March of 1533 Georg Näßlin's attempts to keep his wife by tolerating her Anabaptist activities went further than just permitting meetings at home. Barbara told the interrogators that her husband accompanied her to at least one assembly near the outskirts of the city, where they spoke about the word of God.[23] In addition, Georg confirmed her testimony that their servant Leonhart was also a follower. So, although he disapproved of his wife's re-baptism, he knowingly facilitated her faith and also tolerated that of his servant. As a sign of his combined disapproval and concern for his wife, Georg took quite an unusual action, by adding a request to the council at the end of his testimony. He asked the honorable council to see if his wife could be dissuaded from the business, either through preachers or in some other way.[24] As it turned out, she did indeed recant, though by what method or with what argument they convinced her, we do not know. Like her friend, Sabina Hieberin, there is a simple note on the back of her hearing record: Recanted.

The Näßlins present a rather poignant example of two people struggling to overcome conflicting religious beliefs. Barbara's display of conviction despite her husband's objection to her re-baptism, forced him into a difficult situation. In order to keep his wife happy he was able to overcome the disapproval he felt for a faith which he claims he saw as wrong or, at the very least, illegal. Apparently, he decided that any compromise of conscience on his part was justified by his economic and emotional needs. His own beliefs never became an issue in the

---

unnd dabei es were besser das er den zugang in seinem hauß dan das er nit oder gestatet das sein fraw an andere ort gienge also zu gesehenn, den zu und abgang der bruder in seiner hauß," StadtAA, Reichsstadt, Urg. 5 March 1533, Georg Näßlin.

[22] *"Sie konnd und wiß den handl nit zu lassenn, Ee wolt sie irem man lassenn, er seie der sach nit anhengig…Wann ir man sie umb den handl ankomen sei unnd ir kein zuogang wollen lassen hab sie zu ime gesagt, So woll sie auß dem hauß und inen nach geenn,"* ibid., 5 March 1533, Barbara Näßlin.

[23] *"Vergangen Somers seien sie und ir man bei den Siben Pronnen gewesenn, derend die obgmelte personen auch under ein ander vom wort gots geredt,"* ibid., Barbara Näßlin.

[24] *"Bit auch ein erber rat wolle verordnen ob sein weib von den handl gewisenn wordenn mocht es seie durch predicanten oder inn ander weg,"* ibid., Georg Näßlin.

course of the trial; for the interrogators, it was enough that he denied being an Anabaptist.

It seems unlikely that the tolerance which Georg Näßlin showed toward his wife would have stemmed from any philosophical views about the freedom of conscience. He may, however, have been familiar with the teaching of St. Paul who advised people to remain with unbelieving spouses.[25] He admits (or boasts?) in his testimony that, when he first found out that Barbara had been re-baptized, he had struck her so hard that her head was cut open.[26] According to him, it was this action which first prompted her threat to leave him, because she would not leave her faith. Therefore, his acceptance of her activities was probably forced on him by circumstances rather than by principle. He decided to value her social and economic role in his life over her religious affiliation. As it turns out, Barbara's threats and Georg's fears came to fruition. Within the year Barbara Näßlin left her husband to run away with another Anabaptist. His efforts at appeasement clearly fell short, and so did Barbara's recantation. Georg received a certificate of divorce from Augsburg's evangelical preachers and later ran into trouble with the law yet again, when he attempted to sell a copy of it to facilitate someone else's remarriage.

Georg Näßlin's behavior in 1533 points to another interesting trend which emerges from the interrogation records, that of people who speculated with religious movements without committing to them. In this case, Georg had not only permitted Anabaptists to meet in his house, he had also accompanied his wife to meetings at other places. The testimonies of several other Anabaptists arrested at this time list Georg Näßlin among those who attended meetings with them. This degree of facilitating seems to extend beyond the call of duty of a tolerant spouse, so one wonders where he really stood on religious issues.

Another case, from nine years earlier, further complicates what we know about Georg Näßlin's position on religious matters. In 1524 Näßlin was arrested on charges of iconoclasm. He had been accused of collaborating with his servant, Leonhart, who had vandalized and

---

[25] 1 Corinthians 4:12–15.

[26] "*des seie sein Neßlins weib gewar worden Und die sach auch angenomenn des er ir ye nit erwören noch laiden konden noch mogenn, hab sie mer dan ain mal geschlagen, Unnd das ain mal in loch in kopff, hab sie ime hin unnd weck lauffenns getraet daruf er besorgt wie vor,*" StadtAA, Reichsstadt, Urg., 5 March 1533, Georg Näßlin.

desecrated holy images in the Cathedral of Our Lady. Unfortunately, we do not know if the Näßlin's Anabaptist servant Leonhart in 1533 is the same man who had worked for them in 1524, although it seems likely. According to the chronicler, Clemens Sender, Georg Näßlin and his servant had smeared cow's blood on the sacred paintings and statues and memorial tablets in the cathedral.[27] After initially fleeing the city, Näßlin turned himself in and faced the council's questioning. In his testimony from 1524, Georg admitted that he had known of his servant's intentions beforehand but claimed that he had immediately reprimanded him and forbidden him to carry them out. He even knew how the young man had acquired the blood from a butcher by sending Georg's young son to fetch it for him, while Georg was away from home. Georg credited the inspiration for the crime to a priest who had stayed with him for some time. This priest, Herr Veit, had read to Georg from the Bible and spoken to him about the evils of idolatry, while Leonhart also listened.[28] Näßlin's suspected complicity in the iconoclastic plot of 1524 and his activities in 1533 suggest that Georg Näßlin was not nearly as innocent of radical religious interests as he wished to appear. One cannot help wondering if perhaps this brush with the law in 1524—four days in prison and once tortured—served to dampen Georg's enthusiasm for religious innovation. He may have been more comfortable with observing and learning from others than committing himself personally. Although official records do not indicate that Näßlin was punished by the council in 1524, Sender claims that Näßlin was initially banished for a year but was then soon readmitted "and became much more Luther-ish than he was beforehand."[29] Again, we are left wondering what it meant to be called "*luterisch*" at this time.

---

[27] "*Am 13. tag aprilis in der nacht hat Jerg Neslin, ain Schüster, mit seinem knecht alle tafflen, den todten zu degechtnus gemacht und gemalt, mit den figuren, crucifix, ölberg, unser liebe frauen und der heiligen bildnus geziert, mit kieplut auff dem kirchoff und creuzgang zu unser liebe Frauen vermeilgt, geplindt und verwiest. diser schuster hat sich 3 tag verborgen, darnach hat er solichen seinen mutwillen selbs anzeigt. da hat man im die stat 1 jar verbotten; aber über kurtz hernach ist im die stat wider erlaupt worden, und ist noch vil grösser lutherisch worden, dan er vor gewest ist.*" Clemens Sender, *Die Chroniken der deutschen Städte vom 14. bis ins 16. Jahrhundert*, (1524) p. 155.

[28] "*Er hab ain priester lannge zeit bey im gehabt, genant Her Veit, . . . der hab im vil inn der Bibell von der Abtgotterey gelesen, und anzaigt wie die bilder und gotzen nichts sollen, sey allain abtgotterey, in dem were ain knecht genant Leonhart, der hette solhs auch vom obegemelten priester horen lesen, darauff derselb knecht, ain hertz gefangen die bilder in den kirchen hin und wider gesetzt,*" StadtAA, Reichsstadt, Urg. 8 May 1524, Georg Näßlin.

[29] Clemens Sender, 155.

Later that year, in June of 1533, a case of spousal abuse came before
the court in which the issue of religious belief makes an unexpected
appearance. Hans Karrer, who happened to be a former Anabaptist,
was arrested for hitting his wife. He explained that their fight started
with an argument over some domestic issue. According to Karrer, his
wife's harsh verbal abuse drove him to strike her, a common defense
from men accused of spousal abuse in this period. He claimed that it
was something he had not done in five years. He added that he did
not mind when she refused his advances or even kicked and pushed
him away. "He would gladly put up with that, if she would just treat
him properly…but she can't control her tongue."[30]

In the midst of this investigation into marital strife, the interrogators apparently considered the possibility of a religious motive for the
altercation. The list of questions (*Fragstück*) no longer exists for us to
see exactly what the councilors asked Hans Karrer, but his answer
indicates their intentions. He responded to their last question with the
following explanation.

> It was six years ago that he was baptized, [he is] no longer a follower,
> [he] takes care of his work. There also is no other reason that he hit his
> wife than her abusive speech and nothing at all to do with religion. She
> may, as far as he's concerned, believe what she wants; he doesn't want
> to force her to anything.[31]

The council must have been familiar with Karrer's past religious activities, in order to have posed a question about religion playing a role in
his abuse of his wife. What is interesting is that the interrogators saw
his faith, or rather they saw a discrepancy in faith between husband
and wife as a potential cause of marital strife. It may be that the interrogators had additional information, unavailable to us, that led them to
explore this possibility. Perhaps they feared that an Anabaptist would
coerce his wife to adhere to his heretical principles, and they wished
to protect her soul. In any case, the interrogators did not pursue the

---

[30] "*Sein weib hab ine auch offter malen mit fauschten geschlagenn wann er leipliche werck mit ir
ye zu zeiten zepflegen begert mit fuessen von ir gestossen das alles hab er guetlich geliten wolt es noch
gern leydenn, wan sie das nun zimlich gegen im hiellt. Wann sie ine hielt wie ein knecht unnd gebe im
guetenn grueß wolt er es geren leiden Aber sie sey ires munds nit maister.*" StadtAA, Reichsstadt,
Urg. 12 June 1533, Hans Karrer.
[31] "*Es seie bei sechs jar lang das er getauft worden, hanng der sachenn nicht mer an, wart seiner
arbeit, Seie auch kein ander ursach das er sein weib geschlagen dann ir heftig mund unnd der glaub
gar nichts, sie mog sein halb glauben was sie wolle, er woll sie zu nichts notenn,*" ibid., Hans
Karrer.

questioning beyond this point. They not only accepted Karrer's explanation, they released him on the same day, sending him to appear before the council to receive a reprimand for his abusive behavior.

The cases discussed in this chapter illustrate the challenges that people faced when pursuing religious faith in a time of great ambiguity and the impact their behavior could have on family relations. In particular, the last two cases explore the tensions that might arise when spouses differed in their convictions. In all of the cases discussed, the disparity between the spouses either led to conflict, in the case of the Näßlins, or was expected to lead to conflict, in the case of the Karrers. That is to say, the husbands, like Kretzwescher mentioned above, were expected to take an interest in their wives' faith.[32] It is worth noting that some Anabaptist men also said that their wives tried to dissuade them from baptism or attending meetings. Yet despite this anticipated strife, which sometimes became violent or threatened to become violent, Näßlin and Hieberin did not allow their husbands to influence their spiritual choices. Both women went ahead to be baptized and meet with other followers. Näßlin's husband reconciled himself to his wife's conviction to a remarkable degree by attending meetings with her and permitting meetings in their home. Likewise, Hieberin practiced her faith in spite of her husband's alleged opposition, but then again, as we learned, he was not the master of his household. One wonders how vehement the opposition was. Hans Karrer, on the other hand, plainly stated that he would not interfere in his wife's faith. In spite of the potential for friction, these couples found ways to live with their differences. We saw Michael Germair showing a great deal of tolerance and even sympathy for his sister's Anabaptist activities, and a mother who supported her daughter's right to choose her religious faith, even though it differed from her own. In this period of religious innovation, individuals as well as communities struggled to make these new sources of conflict fit into their picture of harmonious life.

These cases demonstrate the possibility for accommodation in a period usually characterized by its conflicts. In addition, these cases show the difficulty of using terms like confession, Lutheran, Zwinglian, or even Anabaptist. The use of such terms is anachronistic and only vaguely

---

[32] It could also happen the other way. Hans Aspach (a.k.a. Aurbach) stated that his wife did not want to let him attend Anabaptist meetings. StadtAA, Reichsstadt, Urg. 4 May 1528, Hans Aspach.

representative of the fledgling religious groupings that were emerging in the early sixteenth century and of the way that people participated in them. Those names mean something different today than they did then, and, as seen in many of these cases, the Augsburgers did not use those terms to describe their religious affiliations. As a result, the term tolerance is also not necessarily appropriate to describe the often peaceful relations between people in this period, because without clear differentiations there was not necessarily anything to tolerate. Instead, there seems to have been a kind of openness to disagreement or variety among people, just as some people were open to discrepancies within their own beliefs.

CHAPTER TWO

RELIGIOUS TENSIONS IN THE 1520S

> *It amazes me that the poor Christians are persecuted in every way to such a degree. For a small 'misbelief,' a poor Christian must suffer… in the whole world, only the poor people are persecuted.*[1]

In this way an Augsburg resident lamented the harassment religious dissidents faced in the 1520s. Georg Zeindelweber was an experienced soldier, guardian of the city's arsenal, and he had seen the suffering of peasants and Anabaptists firsthand. Ironically, with all the weapons and skill at his disposal, even he was vulnerable to the contemporary fear of religious deviance. While individuals often coexisted peacefully despite differences, tensions fueled by the religious disputes of the early Reformation could also lead to conflicts with one's neighbors or authorities. Like most places in the Empire, Augsburg experienced a rise in tensions in the 1520s due in part to the intensifying of religious disagreements. Combined with economic and social grievances, the reforming spirit led to a number of incidents that threatened to shake up both the spiritual and secular institutions of Augsburg. Several cases from the mid to late 1520s illustrate the presence of tension and conflict between the citizens and their spiritual and secular authorities. For the most part, these incidents involved people protesting against authority figures, such as priests or the bishop's officers and even occasionally the city council. As we see in a number of cases, the city council strived to keep the peace by suppressing the rebellious elements and mitigating religious tensions without committing themselves to any particular type of reform. Regarding the impact of religious disunity on the city's inhabitants, however, the most interesting incidents concern conflicts between Augsburg's citizens. Both the government and populace attempted to go about business as usual, in spite of the potential for religious friction.

---

[1] "*in dem hette Zeugwart gesagt, es nem in wunder, das man sich allenthalben dermassen an die armen Christenn Richtet, Ettwan von ains klainen mißglaubens wegen mußt ain armes Christ herheben, in nome nur wunder an eine hern, und in der ganzen welt, so richt sich nur an die armen leut,*" StadtAA, Reichsstadt, Urg. 12 June 1529, Peter Sölber.

Several of incidents in the mid 1520s illustrate the nature of religious rebellion directed against the spiritual and secular authorities in Augsburg. The year 1524 saw a series of spectacular events in Augsburg. One of the earliest events took place in April, when Georg Näßlin's servant splashed blood onto paintings and statues in the Cathedral of Our Lady.[2] Näßlin anticipated being blamed and initially fled justice. When he eventually turned himself in he was interrogated three times over the course of four days, from 8 to 11 May. Despite undergoing torture Näßlin confessed only that he had known of his servant's plans ahead of time but refused to admit that he had countenanced or participated in the iconoclastic plot in any way.

The same day that Georg Näßlin turned himself in, a number of his friends were arrested for an incident at the Franciscan church. On 8 May 1524, a group of men and women, who had gathered in the church for Mass, confronted one of the friars who had arrived to bless the holy water in the font. When the friar refused to perform the blessing in the vernacular instead of the traditional Latin, a man grabbed the prayer book out of the friar's hand and threw it into the basin of water. Another man retrieved the book, tried to tear it in two and, when the parchment would not tear, threw it back into the water. Other testimony confirms this basic narrative with only negligible differences in the details. An interesting variation appears in one witness's account, which claims that the women who were present had suggested throwing the friar himself into the water.[3] Arriving shortly after the incident, one man asked the friars why they were not holding Mass, and they told him that they were afraid to go back into the church for fear of being injured.[4] Going into the cloister the same witness, Sixtus Saur, asked the church's lector,[5] to convince the friars to say Mass, but that only led to another bitter argument between the lector, Johann Schilling, and the verger.[6] The Franciscans' verger, Herr Laurenz, declared that "the devil had brought [Schilling] into the cloister," while the lector responded that "[Herr Laurenz] should thank God that many abuses

---

[2] Georg Näßlin's case is discussed in more detail in Chapter One.
[3] StadtAA, Reichsstadt, Urg. 8–11 May 1524, Hans Beringer, Franz Lamenit, Bartholome Nußfelder, Ulrich Richsner, Sixt Saur, and Peter Scheppach.
[4] Ibid., Sixt Saur.
[5] The lector or reader is one who reads lessons in a church service.
[6] The verger is the caretaker or attendant of a church.

were being done away with."[7] In fact, a number of the suspects testified that they had discussed the issue of the holy water with the lector ahead of time, which suggested that he had conspired with them in a plot to put his sermons against superstitious abuses, such as blessing holy water, into action.

The incident of throwing the prayer book into the holy water, together with the subsequent argument back in the cloister, served as a prelude to the most dramatic demonstration of resistance against the city council in Augsburg during the reformation, the Schilling Uprising.[8] Schilling, the Franciscans' lector, had been stirring up his listeners at the Franciscan church by criticizing both the Catholic Church's spiritual abuses and the city council's economic policies, both of which took advantage of the poor, according to Schilling. In attempting to defuse the situation, the council critically miscalculated by making a pact with Schilling to leave the city voluntarily and in secrecy. From 6 to 9 August 1524, an angry mob of people gathered in front of the city hall to protest the council's decision to force Johann Schilling into exile. The demands of the uprising's leaders included a variety of issues ranging from the religious to the mundane. Protesters wanted to return Schilling to his office obviously, but also to exile two unpopular preachers at the cathedral, to begin taxation of the clergy, to end the paying of ground-rents (*Grundzins*) to the clergy, to use the old (larger) measure for beer, and to brew beer in the old way and without fees.[9] These demands offer an excellent example of how spiritual and secular interests intermingled. The council's main worry was the people's willingness to use force to have their demands met. These incidents in the spring and summer of 1524 (iconoclasm, drowning of holy books, and the riot at the city hall) show that people began to express dissent against the Church in increasingly aggressive ways. Council members responded by suppressing threats to the peace, especially when it involved violence against themselves. The resolution to the conflict about Schilling replaced him with another reforming preacher, whom the council considered less radical, while ignoring the other grievances. A number of participants

---

[7] "*Herr Laurenz gesagt, . . . in hette der teuffel in das Closter bracht, . . . Darumb er Herr Laurenz mit ettlichen worten gestraft auff maynung er solte got danncken, das ettlich mißbrauch abkemen,*" ibid.

[8] For a more in-depth study of the Schilling Uprising, see Jorg Rogge, *Für den gemeinen Nutzen*, Tübingen, 1996.

[9] StadtAA, Reichsstadt, Urg. 6 August 1524 (anonymous report about participants in the uprising).

were publicly whipped, branded and then exiled from the city, and two
men, who were only marginally connected to the incident but were
suspected of planning another revolt were beheaded.[10]

The Schilling Uprising appears as both a precursor to the Peasants' War in 1525 and a landmark in the progress of reform in Augsburg. The Peasants' War was an uprising that spread across southern
Germany (and much of central Europe) from approximately 1524
to 1526. Thousands of peasants, often supported by urban workers,
banded together in leagues to demand the address of grievances, most
memorably articulated in the Twelve Articles.[11] Their demands ranged
from wanting to install clergy who would preach the Gospel purely, to
returning the use of natural resources (such as waterways or woods)
to the community, to ending serfdom. These demands were at least
partly inspired by reforming preachers who taught that the Gospel
could serve as a standard for all worldly institutions, not just the church.
Many supporters of the early reform movement in the 1520s believed
religious reform would be accompanied by a socio-economic revolution, because true Christian practice would lead to greater compassion
and equity among Christians. Although the war had some shocking
successes, it was suppressed fairly quickly and brutally by the nobility
with the support of clergy, like Martin Luther, who were appalled by
what they considered to be an abuse of the Gospel for personal gain.
Many radical reformers, such as Thomas Müntzer, and their followers
were prosecuted as a result of the war, and some who had supported
reform feared the direction it could take without the intervention of
authorities to guide it. Augsburg remained essentially untouched by the
Peasants' War,[12] but this moment in May of 1524 demonstrated to the
city council it would have to consider popular interests in the future.

----

[10] StadtAA, Reichsstadt, Urg. 11–15 September 1524, Hans Kag and Hans Speiser.
Philip Broadhead, ("Guildsmen," 589), asserts that they were executed secretly and
not as an example to others, but this seems to contradict the judgment that was read
at their execution, "so that everyone knows to avoid this (*davor sich menigclich wiß zu
verhueten*)," which took place on the square in front of the city hall, as noted on the
back cover of Kag's *Urgicht*.

[11] Peter Blickle, *The Revolution of 1525* (Baltimore: The Johns Hopkins University
Press, 1981), 195–201.

[12] Johann Schilling reappeared in Augsburg during the Peasants' War dressed as a
soldier. The council ordered him to be escorted out of town and required him to swear
to earn his money elsewhere and not come near the city again. StadtAA, Reichsstadt,
Ratsbuch 15, 25 March 1525.

It also shows us that supporters of reform were increasing in the city and becoming more insistent.

In the course of the 1520s, council members represented a variety of religious sympathies. Most favored some form of reform, with most of those preferring Zwingli to Luther, while quite a few still supported the old church. Given this mixture inside the council chambers, it is no surprise that in its dealings with the populace the council attempted to restrain expressions of dissent from both supporters of the old religion and reformers. For this reason the council would prosecute people who published anti-reforming polemics. The council arrested the physician Sigmund Grimm in 1526 for printing a pro-Catholic *pasquille* written by the theologian Johann Eck, one of Luther's most vehement opponents.[13] At the same time, the council also punished verbal abuse of the Catholic clergy. Two days after Grimm's arrest a group of young men were arrested for singing an allegedly anti-clerical song in the street one evening, although they and their witnesses insisted that the song was not about a priest but a knight.[14] Two years later in 1528, the council forced a Catholic priest, Ottmar Nachtigall, out of his position at St. Moritz Church. Nachtigall, who had been sponsored the by the Catholic Fugger family, was known for his aggressive anti-reform preaching and support for the Mass. Trained as a humanist, Nachtigall initially took an interest in studying the Gospels, especially in more accurate translations from the Greek, but he ultimately remained committed to the old church. The council silenced him, because his invectives angered many of his listeners, and the council feared that an outburst of violence might result.[15] Thus the council tried to keep all forces that might inspire religious conflicts to a minimum, whether for or against reform.

The council chose to avoid confrontation over religious matters and thereby recognized and even encouraged the continuation of diverse opinions and practices in the city. For example, on 16 April 1527, the council ruled that patients in the city's Holy Ghost Hospital would not be forced to receive the Eucharist whether in one or both forms, either bread alone or bread and wine together.[16] The council refused to endorse

---

[13] Ibid., 30 May 1526, Sigmund Grimm.
[14] Ibid., 1 June 1526, Clement Obrecht, etc. (witnesses).
[15] Ibid., Ratsbuch (1520–29), 7–19 September 1528.
[16] "*Hat ain Erber rhat erkandt, das man Niemandt nöten soll, under ainer oder bederlay gestalt, das Sacrament zu entpfahen,*" ibid., 16 April 1527.

one particular form of the Eucharist, and it would not require anyone
to receive it in a form that went against his or her wishes.

Thus, in the 1520s Augsburg's populace pursued a diverse array of
religious movements. Some townspeople remained loyal to the Catholic
Church, others became interested in Anabaptism, while most seemed
to prefer the teachings of one of the reformers, Luther, Zwingli, or
one of Augsburg's own evangelical preachers, to name just the most
prominent of the emerging religious groups. Although many people
wanted the Church to reform, they differed widely on the type of
reform they wanted and how to accomplish it. During this time the
city council, whose members were also divided on religious issues,
attempted to steer a neutral path, avoiding a commitment to a specific
religious establishment until the 1530s. Augsburg's townspeople seemed
to respond positively to the council's efforts to keep the peace. Though
clashes did occur between townspeople, the struggles were not nearly as
vicious or as numerous as one might expect. More importantly, cases
that initially seem to reflect antagonism against another religious group
are better described as anti-clerical or anti-institutional in nature. In
other words, hostility usually was directed not at the individual followers of another religious group but at their authority figures, such as
the clergy, or their property. The interrogation records reflect the city
council's efforts to keep hostility to a minimum, always on the watch
for potentially disruptive elements. These cases also reveal the sensitivity of lay people to religious tensions in their daily interactions. This
chapter examines two cases in closer detail in order to investigate the
nature of conflicts among citizens.

TRESPASSING

The first case comes from 1526; it involves a group of young men,
apprentice cabinet-makers (*Kistler*), who were accused of illegally
entering a garden to steal wood from the bishop of Augsburg.[17] The
wife of the bishop's custodian, the *Rentmeisterin*[18] wrote a letter to the

---

[17] The three men charged in this case, as well as most of their witnesses, lived in the
tax district known as "Von Sant Antonino," which included the area surrounding the
bishop's palace and estate in Augsburg. StadtAA, Reichsstadt, Steuerbuch 1526.

[18] The *Rentmeister* was an official of the bishop of Augsburg, who supervised the
bishopric's holdings, including the bishop's property in the city. In 1526 the *Rentmeister*
was Wolfgang Schick. For information on Wolfgang Schick, see *Das Bistum Augsburg:*

city council to report the transgressions which Georg Othmar and his apprentices had allegedly committed against her and her daughter. The story, summarized from the testimony of the defendants and witnesses, follows. The Rentmeisterin's daughter had found Georg Othmar's apprentices in the garden acting suspiciously; they claimed that they were picking flowers. She immediately demanded to know what they were doing and how they got in. When they explained that the gate had been standing open, she accused them of lying and threatened to send for her master, if they did not leave. In response, one of the apprentices, Heinrich Kron, ran home to Georg Othmar's house to get his knife, while the other apprentice, Marcus Schickart, remained in the bishop's garden holding his ground against the Rentmeisterin's daughter. By the time Kron returned, armed and accompanied by his master, Othmar, the Rentmeisterin had also appeared. Othmar and the Rentmeisterin began to argue and eventually started hurling insults at each other, like "Lutheran dog" (*luterischen hundt*) and "priest's whore," (*pfaffen hur*). The religious aspect to the insults and the context of the argument reveal some of the tensions underlying the apparent dispute over trespassers in the garden.

The cabinet-maker and his apprentices contended that the Rentmeisterin and her daughter initiated the insults and name-calling, as well as the religious nature of them. In addition to the usual assortment of rogue, thief, and dog,[19] the two women allegedly also used the appellation Lutheran, as in Lutheran rogue, Lutheran thief, or Lutheran dog.[20] Although the records do not refer to the cabinet-makers as Lutheran, it seems certain that they sympathized with some kind of reform, and that the Rentmeisterin knew it. The apprentice, Marcus Schickart, stated that the Rentmeisterin's daughter called them "fools and Lutheran dogs" from the moment she found them, and, when his attempts to be courteous with her failed, he then responded, "may Saint Valentine's

---

historisch und statistisch beschrieben, vol. 8, Alfred Schröder (Augsburg 1912–32). The feminine form "*Rentmeisterin*" refers to his wife, who appeared in this case. Since the title *Rentmeisterin* also serves as her proper name in all the case documents, I will us it in that sense and not italicize it in the text after this reference.

[19] The terms "*schelm*," "*dieb*," and "*hund*" appear in several places throughout the defendants' testimonies. StadtAA, Reichsstadt, Urg. 5 April 1526, Georg Othmar.

[20] For example, in Schickart's testimony, appears "*luterischen hundt*," ibid., 5 April 1526, Marx Schickart. Hans Freitag's wife overheard the apprentices being called, "*luterisch schelmen*" and "*luterisch dieb*" in her testimony, ibid., 7 April 1526, Hans Freitag's Ehewirtin.

[disease] strike you, like all priests' whores."[21] Heinrich Kron also testified that the Rentmeisterin's daughter had slandered and threatened
them first and that his master, Othmar, called her a priest's whore only
when she would not stop insulting them.[22] Kron, however, did not say
that either woman had used the term Lutheran. Did he not remember
or not notice? Their master, Georg Othmar, also claimed that he had
only insulted the Rentmeisterin in response to her slanderous abuse. As
he stated, "the Rentmeisterin came to him and called him a Lutheran
rogue and dog, to which Othmar answered, if she called him a rogue
and a Lutheran dog, then she was a priest's whore."[23]

The witnesses, who were the cabinet-makers' neighbors, concurred
more or less with the cabinet-makers' version of the story and tended
to defend their behavior. The whole of the cabinet-makers' defense
lay in the explanation, which several witnesses corroborated, that the
door to the bishop's garden had been standing open all week long and
many neighbors, including children, had gone in to take wood and pick
flowers. Hans Freitag, a city soldier whose house stood near the garden
door, testified that, "the garden had been open on Saturday, Sunday
and Monday, and his wife and children were also in the garden about
an hour before the defendants."[24] Freitag's young son, also named Hans,
testified that he and his little brother had been in the garden with the
defendants (as they picked flowers) and ran out when the Rentmeisterin
began to yell "Lutheran rogues," at the young men, but he could not
hear what the defendants answered. He added, understandably, that
"he was glad to have gotten out of there."[25] Apollonia Satlerin testified

---

[21] "*ain weibspil…geredt, ir Narren und luterischen hundt get auß dem gartn er Marx ir guete
wort geboten aber nichts an ir helfenn wollenn, und daruf zu ir geredt das dich Sant Veltin ankomn
aller pfaffenn huerenn*," ibid., 5 April 1526, Marx Schickart. The term "*Sant Veltin*" is a
version of St. Valentine, in this case meaning St. Valentine's disease, which usually
referred to epilepsy.
[22] "*Unnd als das weib nit wolen aufhoren schelten hete Otmar gesagt vin ich dan ein schelm so
bistu ein pfaffen hur*," ibid., 5 April 1526, Heinrich Kron.
[23] "*sie Rentmeistrn an ine auch komen und ein lutherischen schelmen und hund gescholtn Othmar
daruf geantwort wan sie in ain schelmen und lutherisch hund schelt so wer sie ain pfafn huer*," ibid.,
5 April 1526, Jorg Othmar.
[24] "*Der garten were samßtag sontag unnd montag offenn gewesenn dann Sein weib und kind
weren ungefarlich ain stund vor den gefangn auch im gartn gewesenn*," ibid., 7 April 1526, Hans
Freitag.
[25] "*Hans des Freitags Sonn sagt er wer mit sein brudlin inn den gartn mit den gefangn gangn
hete veiel gebrechen, unnd ebenn weit von den gefang wer die Rentmeisterin komen und gesagt, ir
narren geen d. auß dem gartn was macht ir da, als er solhs gehort wer er her fur unnd hinauß auß
dem gartn gelaufenn inn dem gehort das sie die gefangn luterisch schelmenn gescholtenn, wißt aber nit*

that she had also gone in on Sunday to pick flowers and had seen the garden standing open for a long time before that and people going in and out.[26] Moreover, two locksmiths were questioned regarding the condition of the door, which, to all appearances, had indeed been standing open for several days, owing to a problem with the lock.

The interrogation of the witnesses, especially the locksmiths, focused on the status of the door itself, as if the condition of the door would determine the extent of defendants' guilt. In fact, before the introduction of the Charles V's new legal code, the *Lex Carolina*, in 1532, traditional German law determined the nature of a crime by whether or not there had been an actual break-in.[27] The council did not seem at all concerned with whether or not the apprentices had a right to pick flowers in the bishop's garden or with the name-calling. Although it may seem to us a poor excuse for an alleged thief to argue that the door was already open, or that other people had gone in to take things too, this seems to have satisfied the council. Perhaps they felt that they could not punish the two young men for doing something the entire neighborhood had been doing. The neighbors clearly considered the invitation of the open door to be a legitimate indication that visitors were welcome. Nonetheless, the Rentmeisterin did not feel that way at all, and she was not inclined to dismiss the incident. All that mattered to her was that they had trespassed on the bishop's grounds. As Sebastian Bermiller, the locksmith, stated, "the Rentmeisterin had said [to him] the next day, she did not know if they had broken in or found the door open, but they were in the garden."[28]

In her letter of grievance to the city council, the Rentmeisterin explained her version of the story, which contained several elements left out by the defendants. Her daughter had approached the apprentices in the garden, she related, but they refused to leave when asked and instead declared that it was their garden and announced that they wanted to

---

und het auch nit gehort was die gefangn geantwort dann er wer fro das er davon komen," ibid., 7 April 1526, Hans Freitag's Sohn.

[26] *"Wer selbs am sontag hinein gangen blumen gebrochenn und het auch lang, vor oftermal den garten offen leut auß und ein geen gesehenn,"* ibid., 7 April 1526, Apolonia Satlerin. Further, *"die gefangen hete den garten nit aufzustossen es weren auch teglichs darvor die kinder auß und ein, wan sie von schul gelafen, veyel darinn gebrochenn,"* ibid., 7 April 1526, Anna Copin.

[27] Heinrich Brunner, *Deutsche Rechtsgeschichte* (Leipzig: Duncker and Humblot, 1906–1928), 835–836.

[28] *"Sie wißte nit ob die gefangn die thur aufgestossen oder aufsprochen odr ob sie sonnst offenn funden hetenn, aber sie werenn im garten gewesenn,"* ibid., 7 April 1526, Sebastian Bermiller.

go in and make a preaching house (*Predigthaus*). A preaching house was a meeting house attached to a church, usually of a monastic order, which served as a public chapel for services and preaching to the laity. Augsburg's preaching houses were some of the first sites of evangelical preaching in city, because they belonged to the city government rather than to the bishop. When the daughter told the young men that they should leave because she wanted to close up, they drew their knives and grievously insulted her.[29] The Rentmeisterin's story places the blame firmly on the cabinet-makers and implies that she and her daughter were in danger. The Rentmeisterin stated that they had called her a priest's whore when she tried to lock them out, but she did not mention insulting the cabinet-makers' honor in any way, in religious terms or otherwise. Surprisingly, given the traditional law on the significance of open doors in trespassing incidents, the Rentmeisterin readily admitted that the door to the garden had been left open. Unlike the city council, the defendants and the witnesses, the Rentmeisterin did not feel that the status of the door made any difference in the cabinet-makers' offenses. She also charged them with treasonously insulting the bishop of Augsburg and the emperor. Her report initiated an investigation by the council, which gave special attention to the question of treason rather than trespassing or religious insults.

In her report, the Rentmeisterin emphasized Othmar's belligerence, in particular depicting his resentment towards the Church authorities. By her account, Othmar had said, "call your thieving priest in here, who betrayed us with the garden and took it from us with lies. We'd like to give him one on the tonsure, so that his brains would run out his nose."[30] In addition, she said, Othmar had "reproached her with the words of Saint Paul and wanted to dispute with her, which she did not want to permit, since she was not trained for that."[31] Furthermore, she stated that one of the apprentices had claimed that they had as

---

[29] "*Alhie ist unnser wurtz gart, unnd wollen herein, unnser predig hauß machen da hat mein dochter guetlich begert, sy sollen auß dem garten geen, so woll sy den zu schliessen, da hand sy gegen ir in die messer, griffen und mit frevenlichen schelt worten begegnet,*" from the Rentmeisterin's letter with ibid., 5 April 1526, Jorg Othmar.

[30] "*Hat Jorg Otmair kystler von newem angefangn und gesagt, haiß deinen diebischen pfaffen hereinkomen, der uns umb den garten betrogen, und den uns hat abgelogen, so wollen wir im ains auff die platten geben, das im das hiren zu der nasen hinaus trieffen muß, und der gleichen wort vill und oft geyebt,*" ibid., Rentmeisterin.

[31] "*[Hat Jorg Otmair] mir den Paulum fur geworffn mit mir wollen dispothiern, das ich im die weil ich nit dartzu geordnet bin, kain stat hab wollen geben,*" ibid., Rentmeisterin.

much right to be there as [she], because all things were free.[32] Calling the bishop a thieving priest, who had stolen the garden with lies, and claiming to have a prior right to the garden recalls similar grievances expressed in the Twelve Articles of the Peasants' War which had taken place just the previous year. Among other things, the rebellious peasants demanded the return of lands and natural resources which had been taken unfairly from the common people.[33]

The question of property ownership and entitlement were key elements in the argument between the Rentmeisterin and the cabinet-makers. Unfortunately, since the council did not pursue that aspect, we do not know whether or not this argument indicated a genuine legal grievance on the part of the bishop's neighbors who believed the garden really belonged to them, or a broader criticism of the church's ownership of property in general. Also, it may simply have been a defensive tactic designed to deflect guilt away from the cabinet-makers. Regardless of the intention, it reflects the possibility in the 1520s for grievances to be expressed through hostile religious epithets.

One could certainly question the veracity of the Rentmeisterin's account, but it seems highly unlikely that any of the participants involved were telling the entire truth in this case. Although the apprentices portrayed their actions as purely defensive, it is clear from the context of their testimony that there was more to the incident than merely their being yelled at by the Rentmeisterin and her daughter. They were not the innocent victims of the women's bullying. Not only did they not leave when asked by the bishop's custodians, but one of men even went to get a weapon and returned with his master as reinforcement. This suggests that they wanted a confrontation. Even more revealing, one of the witnesses, Anna Copin, a furrier's servant, corroborated the Rentmeisterin's version of the story. Copin testified that, "one of them...said, 'hey, if we take the garden and make a preaching house out of it, what are you going to do about it?'" Yet Copin showed no sympathy for the Rentmeisterin, claiming that "[the Rentmeisterin] had said lots of mean things, but she didn't hear anything bad from the

---

[32] "*Gesagt sy habend als frei alda als ich dann es sey alle ding frei,*" ibid., Rentmeisterin.

[33] See, in particular, the fourth, fifth, and tenth articles which all pertain to the returning of common lands and resources unless a bill of sale could be produced which documented the community's sale of the usage rights. The fifth article claims that, "the community should be able to allow...each man to gather firewood for his home and building timber free...," Peter Blickle, *The Revolution of 1525*, pp. 195–201.

men."[34] The fact that Anna Copin, who was otherwise unsympathetic to the Rentmeisterin, confirmed even part of her statement suggests that there may have been some truth to the Rentmeisterin's allegations.

In addition to accusing the young men of trespassing and challenging her authority, the Rentmeisterin raised a very sensitive issue for the city council. She accused the cabinet-makers of having insulted Emperor Charles V and his brother, Ferdinand. According to the Rentmeisterin, one of the apprentices, whose name the Rentmeisterin did not know, suggested that the emperor would come, even if the bishop did not, and his master, Othmar, allegedly responded, "I crap on the emperor and his brother, on the head and in the face."[35] The magistrates of an imperial city could hardly ignore threats against the emperor. After all, disrespect towards any authority could indicate subversive tendencies amongst the population, about which the council was very nervous in the years immediately surrounding the Peasants' War. At the end of each of the three defendants' interrogations they were asked about the seditious remarks. All three responded that they did not know of anything else being said. Marcus Schickart, for example, stated that "[he] had heard nothing at all further about either priests, the bishop, the emperor, or his brother."[36] The council apparently accepted this answer, because they did not pursue the matter with any of the three men or the witnesses. Moreover, there is no account of any punishment for the men in any of the related legal records. The treatment of the case gives the overall impression that the council pursued the investigation halfheartedly to appease the bishop's custodian. The council seems to have been inclined to exonerate the defendants in this case, perhaps to avoid drawing attention to it.

With all its complex and sometimes hidden layers, this case offers one of the clearest examples of tension during the early Reformation in Augsburg, as it shows how differences over secular and spiritual

---

[34] *"wer die Rentmeisterin komen und vil böser redn getribenn aber nichts boß von den gesellen gehort dan das ainer auß inen wißte nit wolher, geredt ey wann man den garten nem und machte ein predig haus darauß was woltest du darzu thunn,"* StadtAA, Reichsstadt, Urg. 7 April 1526, Anna Copin. The underlining appears in the original interrogation record, indicating that the council also took special interest in this particular statement.

[35] *"Darauff spricht ain ander des namen ich nit waiß, kompt der bischoff nit, so kompt aber der kayser, auff die red spricht Jorg Otmair, ich schiß dem kayser und seinem bruder, auff den kopff und in das angesicht,"* ibid., Rentmeisterin.

[36] *"Also ferr weder von pfaffenn, bischof, kaiser noch von sein bruder gar nichts horen reden,"* ibid., 5 April 1526 Marx Schickart.

issues could overlap. It also stands out as one of the few examples of religious name-calling to appear in the city's interrogation records in the first half of the sixteenth century.[37] It is worth noting, however, that the issue of name-calling was not of interest to the contemporary examiners, though it is intriguing to historians today. Once again, we do not know if the Rentmeisterin's use of the term "Lutheran" for the cabinet-makers was accurate. She may have used it, like Aberlin Hasen, to refer to anyone who supported church reform, which she observed from their demands to create a preaching house. Also, the cabinet-makers' use of the term "priest's whore" for her reflected the fact that the Rentmeisterin was indirectly employed by the bishop through her husband, which made use of a traditional slur on a woman's sexual honor as well as on the reputed immorality of the clergy. It may not actually have been intended as an attack on the Rentmeisterin's beliefs. None of this interested the council. The council pursued the incident for two reasons, the charge of trespassing and the charge of sedition. The religious insults were considered irrelevant, merely a means for both parties to illustrate the offensive behavior of the other.

In a period in which anti-clericalism flourished, the fact that the garden belonged to the bishop probably fueled the antagonism already produced by jealousy over use of the property. In addition, the Rentmeister, Wolfgang Schick, and his family were probably viewed as outsiders by the defendants and witnesses, due to their status as landlords and as representatives of the bishop. That they were not citizens of Augsburg, just like the apprentices, probably mattered less than the distinction of their episcopal connections and status as landed property owners. It was their association with the clergy that caused the women to be called "priest's whores" rather than just whore which would have been a more common insult to a woman at this time. Characteristic of the early decades of the sixteenth century, people tended to express religious dissent through attacks on spiritual authorities, in which doctrinal issues are difficult to recognize.

The cabinet-makers' counter charge, that the women had called them "Lutheran scoundrels" (rather than just plain scoundrels) presents a unique terminology that appeared for the first time in this case 1529 and not again until 1552 in Augsburg's documented legal cases. Only

---

[37] One other case surfaced in 1552. See the Sundau-Sonntag case in Chapter Six.

the defendants mentioned this name-calling, which suggests that they
expected it would somehow reflect badly on the Rentmeisterin to have
used "Lutheran" in a pejorative way. Since they obviously demonstrated
sympathy for reform, the cabinet-makers would not have raised the
issue if they thought it would get them into trouble. The witnesses
clearly sympathized with the defendants, and the defendants possibly
expected sympathy from the council as well. That the Rentmeisterin
did not mention the defendants' religious position explicitly in her
report shows that she did not expect the council to pursue the case
on the grounds of the cabinet-makers' religious beliefs. It seems that
the name-calling did reflect real religious differences between the parties, but was not the basis for the conflict. As the Rentmeisterin said,
she did not want to engage in a theological dispute with the master
cabinet-maker. Rather, it served to express a variety of issues regarding authority, property, and anti-clericalism. The incident did not arise
from a dispute over religion, but the cabinet-makers' resentment of the
bishop does seem to have inspired their resistance to the Rentmeisterin
and her daughter. Likewise, the two women seem to have viewed the
evangelical sympathies of the cabinet-makers as making them more
threatening than they might otherwise have been. The Rentmeisterin
wanted to punish a group of men who expressed radical religious ideas,
flouted her position, insulted her honor and her superiors' authority.
Also, the defendants and their neighbors, who constituted most of
the witnesses, seem to have been held together by a solidarity which
probably included sympathy for church reforms (including the church's
ownership of land), resentment for clerical authority figures, and other
bonds of association, such as neighborhood.

Neither the parties involved nor the council seems to have given these
religious issues any attention in the case. The council may have chosen
to ignore the religious aspects in order to soothe hostilities, may have
unconsciously neglected it because of its very ordinariness at that time,
or may have avoided it simply because the religiously-divided council
was not in a position to take sides. Another likely possibility is that the
council probably sympathized with the cabinet-makers' situation, in
entering the garden as so many others did, but they could not ignore
a grievance filed by a woman having such powerful connections. As a
result, they pursued the case on two issues on which all council members could agree—and not very aggressively at that—on the basis of
offenses to property and authority.

Blasphemy

The other example of conflict from the 1520s presents a different kind of neighborhood interaction, and gives us a rare opportunity to see neighbors discussing their convictions with each other. This case from 1529 revolves around two military men, whose participation in a casual conversation among neighbors led to a bitter argument and one man's trial for blasphemy. The resulting interrogation records reveals well-to-do artisans and soldiers taking an active interest in theological debates and, ironically, their opinions about the use of force in regulating religious belief. When the incident came to their attention, the city councilors treated the incident solely as a case of blasphemy. As seen in other examples, although the council pursued its own interests in its investigations, a careful examination of the documents reveals that a great deal more can be found beneath the surface. In the midst of mounting religious tensions, the council members tried to maintain order through standards which they still shared in common; above and beyond religious bickering, impiety was still wrong.

On a Friday evening in early June 1529, neighbors gathered to sit and talk in front of the house of Georg Zeindelweber, the *Zeugwart*, custodian of the city's arsenal and a master gunsmith.[38] A maid who sat with them did her spinning as she listened to the conversation. When the goldsmith's wife saw the neighbors gathering together, she asked her husband to go with her to join them. Eventually the gathering included about fifteen men and women who ended a day of toiling at various crafts and household chores to sit for a while and talk. They included Zeindelweber, Peter Sölber (the goldsmith), Sigmund Berger (another gunsmith), Heinrich Meckenloher (a city guard), a toothpuller, a weaver, and a clockmaker, along with their wives and their maids. What appears to have been an ordinary event for them—neighbors congregating to discuss the topics of the day—becomes an extraordinary opportunity for us to eavesdrop on their discussion. However the

---

[38] Georg Zeindlweber was a master gunsmith and *Zeugwart* employed by the city of Augsburg. As the *Zeugwart* he was in charge of Augsburg's entire arsenal of weapons. He entered the city's employ in 1519, along with Sigmund Berger, who was also a gunsmith. StadtAA, Reichsstadt, Baumeisteramt, Baumeisterbuch 1519. The witnesses also referred to Zeindelweber by the title "*Zeugwart*" as a proper name. His name also appears as Zeinwedelweber and Zeinlinweber.

conversation began, we know that they eventually came around to talk
about religion. Out there on their street the neighbors talked about the
Commandments, the carrying of prayer beads, the virginity of Mary,
and the punishment of religious dissent. The debate eventually led to
a quarrel, which then erupted in name-calling between Zeindelweber
and another neighbor, Heinrich Meckenhloher.[39] A fist-fight threatened
to break out between the two men until the goldsmith Peter Sölber
forcibly led Meckenloher home. Even then, Zeindelweber called out
a challenge bound to provoke and humiliate his retreating opponent,
"Sure, you're a fighter! What Peasants' War were you in? How many
have you killed? You cripple!"[40]

The next morning Meckenloher began to spread the news of the
previous evening's altercation; in particular, he accused Zeindelweber
of having blasphemed against the Mother of God. He went to the
City Hall where he reported the incident to two captains of the guard.
According to their testimony, Meckenloher claimed that he would have
strangled Zeindelweber, if he had not been held back. The captains of
the guard showed no special sympathy for his complaint in their statement. In fact, they did report the incident at all until by the council to
testify about it. They stated that according to Meckenloher, "Zeindelweber had said that the kings, princes, and lords tolerate the Jews, who
say that Mary was a whore and Christ a bastard."[41] In other words,
Zeindelweber had simply repeated what he had heard of Jews who
blasphemed. Captain Scheitlin actually claimed to have reprimanded
the accuser, Meckenloher, because, as he said, "he saw that Meckenloher was going around telling everyone about the incident, so he told
him, he was doing the mayors no favor by spreading the story, maybe

---

[39] Heinrich Meckenloher was employed by the city of Augsburg as a *Reisiger*. In
other words, he was hired to ride as a guard, escort, messenger or in any other capacity that served the military interests of the city. He had been a city servant since at
least 1493 and continued until his death in 1537. StadtAA, Reichsstadt, Ratsbuch
1492–1498 and Baumeisterbuch 1537. Given the dates of their service, it seems that
Meckenloher was probably at least in his mid-fifties by 1529, and Zeindelweber was
most likely a younger man.

[40] "*Syha wol biß ain fechter, in welhem pawren krieg bist gewesen, wie vil hast zu tod geschlagen
du krupel,*" ibid., Urg. 12 June 1529, Peter Sölber (witness).

[41] "*und under andern gesagt wie Zeugwart hette geredt die kunig fursten unnd herren liden die
Juden, die sagten das Maria ain hur und Christus ain banckhart were,*" ibid., 15 June 1529,
Hauptman Schludin (witness).

it wasn't that serious."[42] Despite the captains' dismissive attitude, the case was taken seriously by the city council, and proceedings began just two days after the fateful argument took place.

The minutes of the Small Council record Meckenloher's original complaint and Zeindelweber's response as follows:

> Meckenloher complained against Georg Zeugwart: on the previous Friday evening, as honorable people were gathered together, and the Ten Commandments were considered, Master Georg said, among other things, when Meckenloher referred to the Mother of God, that he heard a Jew say that Mary was a whore and had born a bastard or a whore's child. Furthermore, [Zeugwart] said himself that Mary was a whore and had born a whore's child, and that was Christ, and he yelled after [Meckenloher] that she wasn't God's mother but the devil's mother.[43]

Zeindelweber was then allowed to answer this accusation. The scribe recorded the following statement for Zeindelweber, "Zeugwart's God had no mother, because if God had a mother, then she would be older than God. She was Christ's mother."[44] The secretary further noted that Zeindelweber denied that he had called Mary a whore or Christ a bastard. Despite Zeindelweber's clarification, Meckenloher would not retract his accusation. Instead, he swore that he could prove his claim and that if he could not prove it he would wager his body on it and suffer interrogation under torture against one another.[45]

After this passionate display of resolve from Meckenloher, the council began an investigation by collecting reports from the witnesses, in order to establish the facts of the case. In total, fourteen witnesses, Zeindelweber and Meckenloher's neighbors, were questioned, many of them twice, on 9 and 12 June. The two captains of the guard were

---

[42] "*er hab den Meckenloher gestrafft, dann er hette gesehen das Meckenloher zu Jederman gangen were und die Hanndlung anzaigte deßhalben er zu im gesagt, er solte wol den herren Burgermaistern kain gefallen daran thun, das er den hanndel also umbtrieg, es were veleicht nicht als hefftig,*" ibid., 15 June 1529, Haubtman Scheitlin (witness).

[43] "*Meckenloer clagt, wider Jorgen Zeugwart freitag nechst vergangen abents als erber leut bei ain ander gewesen, und der X pot gedacht sei worden, hab Maister Jorg under andern, als Meckenloer die Muter Gots genant, gesagt Er hab von ainem Juden gehort, das Maria ain hur sei, und hat ain Banckhart oder ain hurn kind tragen, Weiter geredt auch sich selbs, Maria sei ain hur und hat auch ain hurn kind tragen, das sei Christi und ime nachgeschrien sie sei nit ain Muter Gots sonnder des teufels Muter,*" ibid., Protokolle der Dreizehn, 8 June 1529.

[44] "*Antwort, Zeugwarts Got hat keine Muter gehabt, dan wa Got ain Muter gehabt, so were sie elter dan Got, Christus' Muter sei sie gewesen, Bestat nit das er die Muter Gots ain hurn gehalten oder das sie ain hurn kind tragen hab,*" ibid.

[45] "*Meckenloer, Er well sein furpringen beweisen und wo er das nit kondt beweisen wolt er sein leib an ine wagen und peinlich fragen gegen ainander leiden,*" ibid.

also finally questioned on 15 June, the day Zeindelweber's interrogations began. Slight variations in wording appear, as the neighbors
attempted to recapture what the two men had said to one another,
but no meaningful contradictions emerge. The witnesses described a
variety of contentious issues which catch the eye of a historian, such
as evangelical devotion to the rosary or Christian-Jewish relations.
Augsburg's city council pursued one point with single-mindedness: the
accusation of blasphemy.

Zeindelweber's interrogation introduces the story. He explained to his
interrogators that the argument with Meckenloher evolved from a discussion of the Ten Commandments. Meckenloher had asserted—quite
pompously, as far as Zeindelweber was concerned—that he had only two
Commandments: to believe in one God and to love others as oneself.[46]
At hearing this Zeindelweber had exclaimed that Meckenloher must be
a saint. According to Peter Sölber, Zeindelweber had even reached out
to grab Meckenloher's feet in order to kiss them.[47] Meckenloher had
responded that he was no saint but a sinner like everyone else, and he
thanked Almighty God and his dear Mother. Zeindelweber had then
claimed that God had no mother, because if he did, then she would
be older than he was. Therefore, the mother whom people attributed
to God was really the devil's mother.[48] Zeindelweber believed that Jesus
Christ, on the other hand, did have a mother, and she was the Virgin
Mary. According to him, they had talked about how and why the Jews
were allowed to insult the Virgin Mary. Zeindelweber had heard them
call her a whore and Jesus a whore's child. He refused to admit, however, that he had ever said it himself. Instead, he adamantly affirmed his
respect for both Mary and Jesus. In his own words, "such a thing never
entered his heart or soul. He honored the Virgin Mary daily by saying

---

[46] "*inn dem Meckenloher auch hin zu komen, under andern worten geredt er hab nich mer dan
zwei gepot,... die seyen die 2 gepot, Namlich ains gelauben inn ainem got, das ander den nechsten
mentschen alle lieb zu haben als sie selbs,... dem Meckenloher angesagt, so seyt ir hailig dar gegenn,*"
ibid., Urg. 15 June 1529, Georg Zeindelweber.

[47] "*So seidt ih ain heilig, hebt, laßt euch die fueß kuessen unnd im also noch den fuessen griffen,*"
ibid., 12 June 1529, Peter Sölber (witness).

[48] "*Meckenlocher geredt und wider geantwort er sey nit hailig sonder er sey ein synnder und jeh/jeder
danck dem allmechtigen got und seiner lieben muter, daruf Zeugt weit gesagt der allmechtig gott hab
kein, muter dan wann er ein muter hete so mußt die muter elter sein wan der allmechtig got, unnd die
Mueter so man dem allmechtigen got wolle zu siezenn seie des teufels Mueter, und der allmechtig got
hab kein muter,* ibid., 15 June 1529, Georg Zeindelweber.

a Hail Mary and every year by fasting on the eve of her birthday."[49] Again he attempted to give further proof of his piety.

> He had never had such a thing in his heart, because he always and in every way placed his trust and hope in God the Almighty and in Christ and the same in Mary...when he had been shot the previous year he vowed to send a silver picture to Our Lady in Aachen...for which he paid six gulden.[50]

He continued to deny the accusation that he had blasphemed, and, when the interrogators threatened to use torture, he insisted on his innocence.

Two days later, when the interrogation resumed, Zeindelweber tried to explain once more that he had not blasphemed and that if he had, then it had happened without his knowledge, because he was not a blasphemer at heart. He even brashly declared that "if it could be proven that he had knowingly [insulted the Virgin Mary], he deserved to be burned without further hesitation."[51] He refused to admit any wrong-doing, and the council, supported by witness testimony, refused to believe his vigorous defense: they were at an impasse. At this point, the interrogators turned to torture in order to extract a confession.

When the city executioner, who also administered judicial torture, bound Zeindelweber's hands behind his back, the defendant reiterated his innocence and claimed that the witnesses had wronged him. Then he was hoisted up off the ground, by his bound hands, with a weight tied to his feet.[52] This means of torture, called the *strappado*, often caused the prisoner's shoulders to be dislocated. At the very least it caused muscle injury and severe pain; the greater the weight, the greater the pain. Each subsequent episode would cause an increasing amount of pain, as the muscles began to swell and stiffen, especially after an interval of a day to two. After being pulled up once, Zeindelweber pleaded

---

[49] "*Dann ime solhs sachenn in sein herz und gemuet nie komen ursach er Ere die junckfrauenn maria noch teglich mit ainer spruch Ave Sancitissima Maria, etc. unnd jarlich irer geburt aubent mit vasten darumb sein will und mayung weder Christen noch Mariam zu uneren nie gewesen und noch nit seie,*" ibid.

[50] "*hete er doch solh sachenn inn seinem herez nie gehabt, Dannn er ye unnd allweg sein hoffnung und trost zu got dem allmechtigenn und Christo gehabt, unnd noch deßgleichen zu Maria ursach er seie vergangner jar geschossen worden hab er ein silberin pild gen Ach zu unser frauen verhaissen das er auch herab bracht sechs gulden darumb bezalt,*" ibid.

[51] "*Ob sich erfinde das er die wort wissennhaft geredt hete so seie er wert on underlassen zuverbrenen,*" ibid.

[52] See Michael Kunze, *The Highroad to the Stake* (Chicago: University of Chicago Press, 1987), pp. 57–59 for a description of the *strappado*.

his innocence. They threatened to pull him up again, and this time he declared, in addition to denying the charges repeatedly, "that if he knew he had blasphemed, then he would give judgment over himself, that he be robbed of God's sight forever and be burned without mercy."[53] The fact that the interrogators used a weight the first time, instead of trying initially without it, is rather unusual for Augsburg's criminal interrogations. In most other cases, torture was applied gradually, beginning with hoisting up the prisoner without weights, then adding a weight or two, if the first application was ineffective. Using weights straightaway could indicate that Zeindelweber's physical condition required a weight in order to make the hoisting up effective. As an active soldier, he may have been in very good shape and toughened to pain. It could also indicate that the council was convinced of his guilt and the serious of his offense and had no intention of wasting any time. In response to further threats of being pulled up with additional weight, he maintained his innocence and repeated his self-declared judgment. At the end of that day's questioning Zeindelweber conceded only that if he had blasphemed then it must have happened in a fit of rage, of which he had no knowledge. "But actually, he wasn't drunk at the time," he concluded, honestly but rather unhelpfully.[54]

The interrogators left Zeindelweber to sit in his prison cell under the city hall for four more days, with time to think about his deed, worry about his family, and let his already aching body stiffen. On 21 June they questioned him again. Over and over again he told them that if he had blasphemed, he had done it in anger and had only repeated the Jews' opinion, not his own. He acknowledged that if the witnesses said he had blasphemed, then he must have done it indeed, but that it did not represent his true feelings, which were to honor Mary. The interrogators listened to this defense three times in a row and then bound his hands together and threatened him once more with further

---

[53] "*wann er wiß das er die wort geredt habe gebe er die urteil uber sich selb das er des angesicht gots ewig beraubt seie, und das er on alle gnad verprennt werden,*" StadtAA, Reichsstadt, Urg. 17 June 1529, Georg Zeindelweber.

[54] "*Aber aigentlich seie er dazumal nit mit wein beladen gewesenn,*" ibid. Although hundreds of defendants used this excuse, Zeindelweber voluntarily gave up this potential explanation both for committing blasphemy in the first place and for his apparent ignorance of it. The council's acceptance of drunkenness as an excuse for behavior was subjective. It could easily lead to an extra fine. In the case of blasphemy, anger was considered as legitimate an excuse as drunkenness. Regarding the use of drunkenness as an excuse for illegal behavior, see B. Ann Tlusty, *Bacchus and Civic Order: The Culture of Drink in Early Modern Germany* (Charlottesville: University Press of Virginia, 2001) 80–102.

torture. Consequently, Zeindelweber finally confessed that he had in fact blasphemed, but he insisted that "it had happened only in the provoked heat of anger and it was never in his heart to dishonor the mother of God."[55]

Unlike most interrogation records from this period, Georg Zeindelweber's dossier does not state the decision of his case on the back cover. He certainly was removed from his office as *Zeugwart*, as the city's financial records show. A later entry from the Small Council's records indicates that he most likely suffered mutilation, by having his tongue cut out, and then banishment from Augsburg.[56] Given Zeindelweber's passionate and unswerving defense, it seems amazing that the council pursued his confession so tenaciously. Throughout his week-long interrogation he maintained that he was not a blasphemer, and one wonders why the council was so anxious to prove him, a handpicked city official, to be a blasphemer. Perhaps they wanted to make an example of him. Yet if this was the case, why did the council attempt to limit publicity about his crime? On 16 June, just after Zeindelweber's interrogation began, his accuser, Meckenloher, was called to appear before the council. He was told to keep quiet about what Zeindelweber had said and "neither to reveal nor publicize *other things as well*," (my emphasis) as instructed by the mayors.[57] The answers to the council's enigmatic behavior may be found in the testimony of Zeindelweber's witnesses.

---

[55] "*Gebunden unnd uf betrauung der Marter gesagt er hab die wort geredt, seienn aber auß bewegter Hitz des zorns beschechenn unnd sein gemuet Nie gestanden die muter gots zu schmechenn,*" StadtAA, Reichsstadt, Urg. 21 June 1529, Georg Zeindelweber.

[56] On September 1, Georg Zeindlweber was questioned regarding the whereabouts of various items which belonged to the Zeughaus. It seems that they were preparing to remove him from his office and wanted to make sure anything he had removed was returned and anything in the Zeughaus belonging to him was identified as well. We do not know if he was still being held in prison or if he was called back in. In late August the council decided to punish a man with a very similar name for the same crime with which Zeindelweber was charged, blasphemy. "*Dem Jorg Leinweber ist erkandt von der gotzlesterung wegen etc. das ym die zungen abgeschniten werden und soll davor uber die vier welde schweren, etc.,*" StadtAA, Reichsstadt, Geheimeratsprotokolle 26 August 1529. English: "Jorg Leinweber is informed that his tongue will be cut out for blasphemy, and he shall swear an oath over the four forests beforehand." Jorg and Georg are interchangeable names, while Leinweber is very similar to Zeindlweber and Zeinlinweber, which were other forms of the *Zeugwart's* name. The council recorded no other blasphemy cases during this period. If it is the same person, the sentencing from August 26 was probably delayed until September 1 in order to question Zeindelweber about the Zeughaus before removing his tongue made it impossible to get answers from him.

[57] "*Dem Hainrich Meckenloer ist in ainem Erbern Rath gesagt, das er der reden halben, so zeugwart gethan haben, hinfuro schweigen unnd davon noch anndern sachen halben niemant nichtzit*

The witnesses' testimonies considerably illuminate the picture of the events on 7 June 1529. The witnesses were allowed more freedom to explain the chronology of events and the development of the conversation than Zeindelweber, who was questioned narrowly on the one theme of blasphemy. The most detailed descriptions come from three persons: Peter Sölber the goldsmith, who pulled Meckenloher away from the fight; Sölber's wife, who was the first person questioned; and Sigmund Berger the gunsmith, who worked with Zeindelweber but was related to Meckenloher's wife.[58] From them, as well as the other eleven witnesses, we get a rough outline of how the argument developed.

Taken together, the interrogations of the suspect and witnesses provide a relatively coherent sketch of what occurred on that evening. A casual religious discussion among neighbors quickly got out of hand and became a battle of wills between two men of very different temperaments. Zeindelweber's inflammatory and imprudent speech, which was meant to irritate the self-righteous Meckenloher, led instead to a trial for blasphemy. The charge of blasphemy, which alarmed the city council, is by no means the most interesting aspect of this case. From the text of the story emerges a scene from the daily life of ordinary citizens during the early sixteenth century. The many, often only fleeting, references to contemporary events and issues, which are scattered throughout the rather emotional dialogue, allow us to explore a variety of themes. The case also demonstrates once again that the hostility between the two men evolved from something other than just differences over religious belief or practices. Also, the council's goals in dealing with the case may have had very little to do with blasphemy. Blasphemy may simply have been an easy way to get rid of a potential troublemaker.

Early on in the neighbors' discussion, Zeindelweber had asked Meckenloher why he carried a rosary.[59] Meckenloher answered that he carried them so that the *Aichellin*,[60] a man known for persecuting peasants in

---

anzaigen noch offennbaren, sonder an ort unnd ennden da sich gepurt, als bei den Herren Burgermaister anzaigt," ibid., Geheime Ratsprotokolle 16 June 1529.

[58] In the *Baumeisterbuch*, under the heading for *Büchsenmaister*, the first name is Georg Zeindlweber's, with the additional title of Zeugwart, and the second is Sigmund Berger's, ibid., Baumeisteramt, Baumeisterbuch 1529. In 1538, Sigmund Berger petitioned the city council on behalf of Meckenloher's wife, "his female relative," for a pension after her husband's death, ibid., Ratsbuch 1529–1542.

[59] The term *Paternoster* refers to a rosary, as in *"lieber warum tregst du ain paternoster?"* ibid., Urg. 9 June 1529, Peter Sölber's wife (witness).

[60] The term Aichellin refers to a provost, by the name of Peter Aichellin or Aychelin, who served the Swabian League in the 1520s. He gained a notorious reputation as an

nearby Bavaria, would not hang him. Zeindelweber responded that the princes, currently meeting in Nuremberg, would create a new *Aichellin* so that the people would no longer be hanged.[61] He found it amazing that people were being hanged everywhere, while nothing was done to the Jews who were true blasphemers. Zeindelweber reported to his friends that, according to the Jews, the Mother of God had borne children before and after the birth of Jesus and that Christ was not God's son. He added that the Jews called Mary a whore and Christ a bastard. For this reason, he wondered why "poor Christians" were slaughtered for misbelief while the Jews were tolerated. According to Sigmund Berger, "the Zeugwart said…that the Jews say that the Mother of God bore children before and after and that Christ is not God's son, and we tolerate them among us and burn the Christians."[62] Zeindelweber's expression of concern for the fate of "poor Christians" who were persecuted for an error of faith was almost prophetic.

Hearing Zeindelweber's allegation against the Jews, Meckenloher rashly declared that if he came across a Jew who said such a thing, he

---

executioner of peasants (*Bauernhenker*) during the Peasants' War, 1525–26. In addition to executing 1,200 peasants, he also had the pastor and preacher of Ellwangen executed in Dillingen in 1525 and seven Lutherans in Schwäbisch Gmünd in 1529. From Peter Aychelin's reputation came the expression, "To the gallows, said the Eichel." See *Bosl's Bayerische Biographie: 8000 Persönlichkeiten aus 15 Jahrhunderten*, Karl Bosl (Regensburg, 1983) and *Fischer's Schwäbisches Wörterbuch*, ed. Hermann Fischer (Tübingen, 1908).

[61] "*Hette Zewgwart zum Meckenloher geredt, lieber warumb tregst du ain paternoster, darauff Meckenloher geantwurt, Ich trag in umb des willen das mich der Aichellin nit henck, hette Zeugwart gesagt, Ja lieber, Es wirt jetzo ain anderer Aichellin zu Nurmberg aufsteen,*" StadtAA, Reichsstadt, Urg. 9 June 1529, Peter Sölber's wife (witness) and "*Hette Zewgwart gesagt, die Fursten wern jetzo zu Nurnberg bei ain ander, die wurden ain andern aichellin machen, das man die leut nit mer allso hencket, dann Zeugwart hette zum Meckenloher gesagt, Er [HM] treig ain paternoster darumb, das in der der aichellin nit hennckt, Er trawet aber got, man wurde jetzo ain aichellin machenn das man die leut nit mer also hencket,*" ibid., 12 June 1529, Peter Sölber (witness).

[62] "*Hette Zeugwart gesagt, … mich nymbt wunder das man die armen leut allenthalben im lannd, mit hencken, verprennen unnd anderm also plagt, und man sich nit an die Juden Richt, die sagen doch unverholen, unnser fraw sei kain junckfraw sy sei ain hur, und Christus sei ain hurenkind,*" ibid., 9 June 1529, Peter Sölber's wife (witness); "*Der Zeugwart hette under andern worten geredt, die Juden sagen die mutter gots hab vor und darnach kinder tragen und Christus sei nit gottes Sone, und wir leiden sy unnder unns, unnd die Christen verprennt man,*" ibid., 9 June 1529, Sigmund Berger (witness); and "*Hette Zeugwart gesagt, warumb todt und verprent man jetzo allenthalben die armen leut, und die Juden leiden wir under unns, beschutzen, beschirmen, unnd behawsen, die sagen, wie die Mutter Gots kinder vor unnd nacht tragen hab unnd schenden die Juden Got und Jhesus,*" ibid., 12 June 1529. In comparison: "*in dem hette Zeugwart gesagt, es nem in wunder, das man sich allenthalben dermassen an die armen Christenn Richtet, Ettwan von ains klainen mißglaubens wegen mußt ain armes Christ herheben, in nome nur wunder an eine hern, und inder ganzen welt, so richt sich nur an die armen leut, Warumb richtet man sich nit an die Juden, die sagen durch aus Maria sei ain hur, und Christus sei ain bannckhart,*" ibid., 12 June 1529, Peter Sölber (witness).

would make sure that he never said it again.[63] This boastful statement
was like waving a red flag in front of Zeindelweber, who did not believe
that Meckenloher had the nerve to carry out his threat and refused
to let Meckenloher get away with such posturing. Zeindelweber dared
him, "if you're so tough, why don't you go to the Franciscans and kill
Master Michael,[64] he says that the Mass is a blasphemy." Meckenloher
answered, "I have nothing to do with him, I'll let someone else kill
him." He stood up and announced that he was leaving, because he
would not stay where the Mother of God was blasphemed. Zeindelweber responded, "God never had a mother," and then stood up angrily
and said, "she isn't God's mother, she's the devil's mother. God had no
mother, she is Christ's mother."[65] Meckenloher was led away by Peter
Sölber, while Zeindelweber continued to call after him and attack his
masculinity with a variety of colorful insults mentioned above. The
neighbors went their separate ways, with the quarrel apparently over,
but the contest continued the next day when Meckenloher brought
Zeindelweber up on charges.

Zeindelweber and Meckenloher raised a variety of interesting contemporary religious issues in the course of their discussion. First and
foremost there was, of course, the subject of Mary's virginity, which
had long been maintained by the Catholic Church. Protestants in
the 1520s did not challenge the validity of this item of the Christian
faith, but they did question the veneration of Mary.[66] Furthermore,

---

[63] "wan ich solchs von ainem Juden horet,... So wolt er in darumb straffen das er solhs nymer thett," ibid., 12 June 1529, Sigmund Berger (witness).

[64] Meister Michael was the preacher Michael Keller, a Zwinglian, who preached at the Franciscan church in Augsburg from 1524 to 1544 and then at St. Moritz.

[65] "dagegen Zeugwart geantwurt, bißt du dann also schlägerlich, warumb geest du nit hin ab zu den parfussen und schlechst Maister Michel, der sagt wie die meß ain gots lesterung sei, hete Meckenloher gesagt, ich hab nichts mit im zuschaffen, ich will in ain andern lassen schlahen, Were in dem auffgestannden, und gesagt da beleib ich nymer, dann wa man die Mutter gottes schmecht, da mag ich nit bei sein, hette Zeugwart geredt, got hette kain mutter nye gehabt, und also gleich im zorn auffgestannden und gesagt, sy ist nit gots mutter, sy ists teuffels mutter, dann got hat kain mutter gehabt, sy ist Christus mutter, in dem hette der Sölber denn Möckenloher weckgefuert," ibid.

[66] Although Protestant reformers revised the traditional veneration of Mary, they still upheld her "perpetual virginity," including at the time of Christ's birth. Martin Luther and Huldrych Zwingli agreed that her entire significance stemmed from God's grace, which raised her from nothingness, making her an example for Christian living but not an advocate. Neither considered the *Ave Maria* to be a prayer but rather a greeting or praise, and Luther referred to the rosary as an "abuse." Nonetheless, even in areas where Prototestantism was popular, many traditional devotional practices continued. "Mariology," *Oxford Encyclopedia of the Reformation*, ed. Hans J. Hillerbrand (Oxford: Oxford University Press, 1996).

Zeindelweber brought up the distinction of her being the mother of Christ as opposed to the mother of God, which he apparently took very literally. Zeindelweber was hitting on a sore point, as Meckenloher showed when he responded to Zeindelweber's barbs so viscerally. Meckenloher asserted, "I won't attend the sermon anymore, because the mother of God should only be respected."[67] Had he been attending Keller's sermons? The introduction of the Reformation had called many traditional beliefs into question, which was upsetting to people who cherished and trusted those customs. As this case shows, it led to disagreements not only among theologians but among ordinary lay people as well.

In response to Meckenloher's threat, that he would punish a Jew for blaspheming, Zeindelweber responded with a philosophical viewpoint that sheds some light on the perspective of a sixteenth century military professional. As one witness briefly stated, "Zeindelweber said, it's all the same if you or I die as if a fly dies, God is so great."[68] His neighbor, Peter Sölber, described Zeindelweber's theory in more detail.

> After this Zeugwart began and said, dear Heinz, it's all the same if you or I die...God is so mighty, that if you or I die, he can make another Meckenloher or another Zeugwart. He made the whole world, he can do away with it and make another one. It's not our business. If we die in faith, we'll be saved. If we die in unbelief, it means nothing, like fly dung.[69]

At first glance it seems incongruous that a man who showed such total humility in his conception of his role in the universe, respective to God, could also have blasphemed. Yet his assertion—that Mary was Christ's

---

[67] "*an der predig pleib ich nymer, dann die mutter gotts soll nur unveracht sein,*" StadtAA, Reichsstadt, Urg. 9 June 1529, Peter Sölber's wife (witness).

[68] "*Hette er vom Zeugwart gehort, das er, wiß aber nit gegen wem, geredt, es ist gleich wan ir oder ich sterben, als wan ain fleug stirbt, also groß ist got,*" ibid., 12 June 1529, Ulrich Urmacher (witness). A Sixteenth-Century miller, Domenico Scandella, reportedly said something similar: "When man dies he is like an animal, like a fly," which Carlo Ginzburg thinks may have come from a similar verse in Ecclesiastes. Carlo Ginzburg, *The Cheese and the Worms: The Cosmos of a Sixteenth-Century Miller,* trans. John and Anne Tedeschi (Baltimore: Johns Hopkins University Press, 1980) 69.

[69] "*Nach solhem hette Zeugwart, angefanngen, und gesagt, lieber Haintz Es ist gleich ain ding, wan ir oder ich sterben, als wan ain fleug an ain wandt scheißt, wan got ist so mechtig, wan ich und ir absterben, das er ain andern Meckenloher, oder Zeugwart machen kan, hat er die ganntzen welt gemacht, so kan ers widerumb abthun, und ain anndere machen, es ist nichts unnser ding, sterben wir im glauben ab, so werden wir selig, sterben wir im unglauben, so ists nichts, gleich wie ain fleugen dreck, mit beschaidenhait zu melden,*" ibid., 12 June 1529, Peter Sölber (witness).

mother but not God's—fits very well with his reverence for the creator
of the world. Moreover, his cosmological statement denied Meckenloher
the right to punish anyone for misbelief—"it's not our business"—and
reflected his previous expression of sympathy for those who had already
been killed.[70] Zeindelweber may have had in mind the peasants who
were executed in 1525, to which he alluded in their discussion of the
Aichellin, as well as the Anabaptists, who had been persecuted more
immediately in and around Augsburg just the previous year. Just one
year earlier, in February 1528, two of his fellow gunsmiths, Christof
Walch and Matheis Miller, had been removed from their posts with the
city artillery for being Anabaptists.[71] If Zeindelweber had taken their
dismissal to heart, he might have had personal reasons for challenging
the widely asserted principle of government, that rulers have the right
to punish religious unorthodoxy, a precept that haunted early modern
society in the wake of the Reformation. As testimony in this case shows,
he was not always one to keep his temper or opinions to himself. The
council may have pursued Zeindelweber's case aggressively in order to
silence him not only because of the alleged blasphemy but because of
his sympathy for religious dissidents—"the poor Christians"—and his
criticism of official policy. The fact that Zeindelweber was a foreigner
(a non-Augsburger) may have weakened his position also, even though
he was a city employee. Could the opinions he expressed that night
have made the council doubt his trustworthiness, if he was ordered
to take military action against dissidents in the city? Throughout the
1520s, the council was deeply concerned about threats to its authority
and to the security of the city. Of all the people to support dissent, the
last one the council would want in the city is someone with military
experience and access to weapons. Ultimately, the council's motives will
remain a mystery, but the attempts to silence both Meckenloher and
Zeindelweber suggest that there is more to this case than the official
charge of blasphemy.

Although the conversation circled around religious issues, it is not easy
to categorize either man as following a particular religious faith. Zein-

---

[70] "*in dem hette Zeugwart gesagt, es nem in wunder, das man sich allenthalben dermassen an die armen Christen Richtet, Ettwan von ains klainen mißglaubens wegen mußt ain armes Christ herheben*," ibid.

[71] "*Eodem die [11 February 1528] hat ain erber Rat Cristoffen Walchen und Matheis Millern, baid Büchsenmaistern, des widertaufens halben, irer baider dienst geurlaubt, und abkindt, incraft hievor eingeschriben erkantnus.*" StadtAA, Reichsstadt, Ratsbuch 1520–1529, 11 February 1528.

delweber challenged Meckenloher to kill Michael Keller, the reforming preacher at the Franciscans' church, for calling the Mass a useless
sacrilege.[72] While this suggestion might indicate Zeindelweber's own
animosity towards Keller, it was actually meant to goad Meckenloher,
whose sensitivity on the subject was obvious. Something Zeindelweber
said, as Sölber was leading Meckenloher away from the quarrel, makes
a more compelling observation about the men's respective religious
positions. Zeindelweber shouted after him, that "he would like to see if
[Meckenloher] could drive him from the street with the devil or if he
could drive [Meckenloher] from the street with the Gospel, because he
wanted to stay with the Gospel."[73] With this statement, Zeindelweber
placed himself on a different side of a religious struggle from Meckenloher. By invoking the reformers' battle cry—the supremacy of the
Gospel—Zeindelweber seems to sympathize with evangelical reformers. Likewise, by relegating Meckenloher to the devices of the devil,
he indicated that he did not consider Meckenloher to be a follower of
the Gospel, and so, perhaps not a supporter of reform. However, that
still does not necessarily make Meckenloher a Catholic. The theological
disputes which abounded between Lutherans, Zwinglians, and others in
the 1520s left plenty of room for reformers to have bickered amongst
themselves in this way. The fact that Meckenloher was carrying a rosary
in 1529 could mean that he had remained loyal to the Catholic Church,
but many supporters of reform also continued to carry them throughout
the sixteenth century. Keep in mind, his excuse for carrying the rosary
was to avoid being hanged by the Aichellin not religious devotion, or
so he said. To some contemporaries, however, the carrying of rosaries
was seen as evidence of old-fashioned superstition and was cause for
derision.[74] Taken together, Meckenloher's fervent defense of Mary, his
rosary, and his support for the Mass suggest that if he was not Catholic,
then his notion of reform was more conservative or less certain (even
to himself) than Zeindelweber's. Zeindelweber's position is somewhat
more ambiguous. He supported the Gospel, derided Meckenloher for
carrying a rosary, and expressed sympathy for religious radicals, such as

---

[72] Augsburg's ministers were in the midst of heated debates that involved theologians
from all over the empire and Switzerland about the Eucharist and Mass. Most agreed
on abolishing the Mass but could not agree on what should replace it.

[73] "*Hette im der Zeugwart nach geschrien, er wolte doch gern sehen, ob er in mit dem teuffel, oder
er in mit dem Evangelium ab der gassen konndte treiben, dann er wolt bei dem Evangelum pleiben,*"
ibid., 12 June 1529, Maria Weygandt (witness).

[74] Consider the case of Agnes Braun, 16 November 1529, discussed below.

the Anabaptists. At the very least it seems probable that Zeindelweber supported evangelical reform more enthusiastically than Meckenloher did, but he also showed himself to be capable of uttering statements he did not necessarily believe, just to start a fight.

In spite of the conspicuous religious aspects of this case, they do not seem to have been the only factor at play in engendering such bitter antagonism between the two neighbors. Personal issues, as well as temperaments, influenced the course of their interaction. The tone and progression of Zeindelweber's expressions suggests that he was trying to push Meckenloher to a confrontation. At every opportunity his remarks were designed to get at Meckenloher's sore points, whether it was the Jews' insults to Mary or Michael Keller's criticisms of the Mass. His mistake lay in going too far to get Meckenloher to react and, thereby, stepping over the line to commit blasphemy himself.

Peter Sölber suggested, at two different points, that Zeindelweber was speaking in anger rather than out of conviction. On the first occasion, Meckenloher had declared that if he ever heard a "knave of a Jew" insult the Virgin Mary, he would stake his life that he never did it again. Sölber stated, "at these words from Meckenloher, Zeugwart became angry, because he believed that Meckenloher had called him a knave."[75] Calling someone a knave (*Bösewicht*) was considered an open invitation to fight; it virtually required a physical defense of one's honor.[76] Meckenloher refused, however, to be goaded into a fight, saying, instead, that he would only deal with a Jew that way but not with a Christian. So he did not give Zeindelweber the opportunity to redeem his honor physically. He then refused Zeindelweber's challenge to attack Michael Keller instead, so Zeindelweber proceeded to taunt him, finally uttering the fateful words, "Yes, she is a whore, and Christ is a bastard." Sölber told the interrogators, "in his opinion, Zeugwart said these words to Meckenloher so angrily, because he forgot himself. [He intended that] Meckenloher should attack him, because [Meckenloher] had made it clear that he would do that, if he heard it from a Jew, but he wouldn't acknowledge it from Zeindelweber."[77]

---

[75] "*Wan ichs dann von ainem boßwicht aim Juden hort, so wolt ich mein leib daran henncken, das ers nymer solt thun, Er mueßts mich berichten, oder ich wolts in berichten ab solhen des Meckenlohers worten, were der Zewgwart zornig worden, dann er nit anderst vermerckt, wan der Meckenloher hete in ain boßwicht gescholten,*" ibid., 12 June 1529, Peter Sölber (witness).

[76] Tlusty, *Bacchus and Civic Order*, 129–130.

[77] "*Ja sy ist ain hur, unnd Christus ist ain banckhart, unnd wie er Sölber vermaint, So hette Zeugwart, dise wort darumb so hitzig gegen Meckenloher geredt, das er sich versehen, Meckenloher*

What started out as a religious discussion, though never truly just that, clearly involved a personal competition between the two men. Zeindelweber attacked Meckenloher's reputation, questioning his courage and ability and even doubting his piety, in response to a grievous insult to his honor and shameless boasting from Meckenloher. Leonhart Martinfein, a neighbor who was called to the window by his child, said he heard Zeindelweber calling after Meckenloher, "Come on, fighter! Come here, come here! What war were you in? Where are the ones you've slaughtered and killed?" In response to which, Meckenloher's wife said to Zeindelweber, "God be thanked and praised that he hasn't killed anyone...she has a pious husband."[78] When Meckenloher's wife defended her husband's piety, Zeindelweber responded, "the devil is in him, he's got him by the forelock, he speaks out of him!"

Zeindelweber's taunts about Meckenloher's prowess may have had special significance for him, given their profession; both served in the city's military forces. Zeindelweber was not only a master gunsmith, like his neighbor Sigmund Berger, but he was also the *Zeugwart*, the official in charge of all weapons in Augsburg's artillery, for which he earned seventy gulden a year.[79] He had also served in military engagements and been shot on at least one occasion. According to Jürgen Kraus, the *Zeugwart* became an increasingly important official in the early modern period, with the post often held for lifetime by people from socially privileged backgrounds. Unlike Berger and Meckenloher, however, Zeindelweber was not a native of Augsburg. In the course of his interrogation, Zeindelweber asked the council to take care of his wife and children who were strangers in Augsburg and, therefore, friendless.

---

solt an in komen sein, die weil er sich vorhin dermassen, wan er solhs von ainem Juden hort, das er ims nit nachgeben wolt hette lassen mercken," StadtAA, Reichsstadt, Urg. 12 June 1529, Peter Sölber (witness).

[78] "*Losa krieger, kum her, kum her, in welhen krieg bist du gewesen, und wa sind die die du erstochen und zu tod geschlagen hast, darauff des Meckenloher weib gesagt, Nun sei got gedanckt und gelobt, das er kain zu tod geschlagen hat,...sy hette ain frumen man,*" ibid., 12 June 1529, Leonhart Martinfein (witness).

[79] Gunsmiths in this period, especially those on the city's employ, were hired to use the weapons as well as make them. As the Zeugwart, Georg Zeindelweber would have been in charge of overseeing the maintenance and security of the city's munitions. He would also have taken part in the city's military engagements, including outside the city walls. In this role, Zeindelweber may have served with the Swabian League during the Peasants' War, 1524–1526. See Jürgen Kraus, *Das Militärwesen der Reichsstadt Augsburg 1548–1806* (1980) pp. 326–327. For Zeindelweber's and Meckenloher's respective incomes, see StadtAA, Reichsstadt, Baumeisteramt, Baumeisterbuch 1529.

Meckenloher, on the other hand, served as a *Reisiger*, a type of soldier who rode on the city's behalf, for example, as a messenger or armed escort for traveling dignitaries or merchants.[80] He came from a tradition of civil service in Augsburg. His brother Achacius had served with him as a *Reisiger* until his death, and his father had been *Burggraf* in the late fifteenth century. The *Burggraf* was a city provost who had once administered low justice and regulated crafts on behalf of the bishops of Augsburg in the Middle Ages.[81] As the bishop lost judicial and political authority in the city in the fourteenth century, the office of the *Burggraf* also declined but remained part of the administration of the diocese of Augsburg, just under the position of *Rentmeister*. In addition, the Meckenloher family had been members of St. Ulrich's Brotherhood, a fraternity named for Augsburg's patron saint, which had been expanded in 1468 to include the laity and clergy.[82] The Emperor Maximilian I, Charles V's grandfather, had also belonged to this brotherhood.[83] So, Heinrich Meckenloher came from a family with a tradition of service and intimacy with the ecclesiastical and secular government of Augsburg.

According to the city's account books, Meckenloher's employment with the city had begun by 1496 at the latest but probably even earlier. An entry in the council records in 1492 shows that Meckenloher was directed to leave the city with his wife and family until allowed to return. A subsequent entry in 1496 recorded that he was to be permitted to return to the city and reassume his former post as a soldier. Unfortunately we do not know what caused this temporary exile. Other entries from the council records indicate that Meckenloher had also had a run-in with a group of huntsmen in 1523, after which he was directed to leave them alone. In the same year, another entry directed Heinrich Meckenloher to apologize to a Franciscan conventual and "take back" something he had said to him.[84] Meckenloher was no stranger to conflict and no stranger to the city council, who had admonished him on two

---

[80] *"Raisigen:...gerichtet und verpflichtet zum Reisen, specifisch zum kriegerischen Ausmarsch, und zwar stets zum Pferd. Eine Gemeinde hat reisige Diener...ein Besoldeter Kriegsmann oder reisiger Amtmann, [etc.]," Fischer's Schwäbisches Wörterbuch.* See also Kraus, pp. 170–171.

[81] See "Burggrafenamt" in the *Augsburger Stadtlexikon* (Augsburg, 1998).

[82] A. Haemmerle, *St. Ulrichs-Bruderschaft Augsburg: Mitgliederverzeichnis 1466–1521* (Munich: (privately printed), 1949).

[83] "Maximilian I," *Augsburger Stadtlexikon.*

[84] StadtAA, Reichsstadt, Ratsbuch (1520–1529), f. 23.

previous occasions for harassing people. Perhaps this is why the captains of the guard initially dismissed Meckenloher's accusations.

Having been a family man for at least thirty-seven years by 1529, Meckenloher was probably much older than Zeindelweber. Despite his impressive background, Meckenloher earned fifty gulden a year, a third less than the younger foreigner, Zeindelweber. Furthermore, Zeindelweber's contempt and Meckenloher's wife's defense of her husband indicate that he may never have proved himself in battle. Despite Meckenloher's employment as a soldier for the city of Augsburg, his wife said that he had never killed anyone. The two men may have been rivals on several levels. Although Meckenloher retreated from the fight which Zeindelweber's sharp words had invited on Friday evening, he took his grievance to the city council for retribution on Saturday—by far the more effective revenge.

This case demonstrates more importantly the active interest of ordinary lay people in religious matters. The men involved in this altercation held their own opinions and drew their own conclusions about their faith. Whether it had to do with the proper respect for the Mass or the treatment of religious dissenters, they considered themselves entitled to choose for themselves and to express their own thoughts. In the course of their discussion, they each made certain religious preferences clear, which indicate that they inclined toward different religious positions. Yet this was not the focus of their debate. Meckenloher's claim that he would take it upon himself to punish blasphemy from Jews infuriated Zeindelweber, who sympathized with other victims of religious persecution, like his former colleagues. In turn, Zeindelweber's unrelenting and escalating insults to Mary, in order to force Meckenloher to fight him or give up his macho claims, drove Meckenloher to denounce Zeindelweber to the council for blasphemy.

Of all the fascinating issues which appear in the witnesses' testimonies, the only aspect which interested the city council was the charge of blasphemy. In a time of uncertainty, regarding the religious destiny of the city, the council members ignored the undertones of conflict, not wanting to bring more attention to an issue already plaguing them. Instead they latched onto the charge of blasphemy as one of the elements of religion which they could legitimately control and which the various developing religious groups united in denouncing. Afterall, the confusion surrounding the diversity of religious interests was troublesome enough already, it could not be allowed to lead to impiety and disrespect as well. In police ordinances throughout the

1520s, the council consistently condemned blasphemy. The council's prosecution of Zeindelweber's transgression, while keeping other aspects of the case quiet, as illustrated by the Small council's instructions to Meckenloher, reflects the council's characteristic approach to religious conflicts in the 1520s.

A few months after this case occurred, the city council issued a police ordinance (*Züchtordnung*) reiterating the typical admonishments against immorality, including swearing, blasphemy, adultery, drunkenness, and gluttony, among other things. The ordinance is completely commonplace except for the very last item which contained something new. For the first time, the council used the forum of a police ordinance to address the issue of religious conflicts by adding a clause at the end stating that the discussion of religious issues in public should be carried out in a friendly fashion, without bitterness or antagonism.

> No one should insult another concerning our holy Christian faith and godly evangelical teaching, nor dishonor them with offensive, heated, riotous, or shameful words. Also do not publicly argue with the preachers before the congregation while they are preaching. Rather, where a conversation takes place between people, these same should conduct themselves with and towards one another honorably, friendly, peacefully, and humbly. Whoever transgresses this, will be gravely and heartily punished.[85]

The interrogation and other civic records from this period reveal the tensions in the city and the city's efforts to contain them by encouraging harmony and downplaying conflict in the midst of religious disunity. The values of honor, friendship, peace and humility find great resonance throughout the testimonies gathered in the first half of the sixteenth century. During this period, those traditional ideals were reminders of the common values that could help the community to navigate and survive a crisis like the religious divisions of the early Reformation.

By looking at the experiences of ordinary people, through a detailed investigation of interrogation records, we see that the disagreements inspired by religious movements could be upsetting to communal as well

---

[85] "*Es solle auch menigklich unsers hailigen Christlichen gelaubens, und Götlicher Evangelischer leer halben, den andern, nit schmähen, noch mit frevenlichen, hitzigen, aufrürischen, noch schentzierlichen worten, an sein Eeren antasten, Auch den Predicanten dieweyl sy predigen, vorder versamlung offenlich nit einreden, Sonder wa sich derohalben zwischen yemandt, reden zütragen und begeben, sollen sich dieselben, insolhem, mit und gegen ain annder erbarklich, freündtlich, fridlich, und beschaidenlich halten, dann wer das überfaren, der wurde auch darumb ernstlich und hertigklich gestrafft werden,*" StadtAA, Reichsstadt, Lit., Zuchtordnung, 5 December 1529.

as personal relationships. However, it seems that religious differences alone were not usually enough to cause conflicts; other factors always came into play, such as property rights or injured pride. How many other disputes over religion could be traced to these personal levels, if the sources existed to reveal them? Zeindelweber and Meckenloher were not arguing about Mary or the Mass but whether Meckenloher would really engage in a fight with someone over blasphemy. Zeindelweber had to utter a blasphemy himself in order to test him.

A few weeks before the new police ordinance appeared, a woman named Agnes Braun was harassed by a group of people as she went into St. Moritz carrying a rosary.[86] They taunted her for carrying a rosary in her hand but the devil in her heart. Was she being attacked for superstitious behavior or did she have a dubious reputation that made rosary-carrying appear hypocritical? Although she appears to have been the victim in this situation, it was Agnes Braun and not her tormentors who was arrested. Her interrogation was brief and seems to have led to no punishment. Without a list of questions, it is difficult to ascertain the council's reason for arresting Braun, but her testimony indicates that it was her response to the hecklers that got her into trouble. When they scolded her for carrying a rosary, Braun retorted, "surely, the wolf preaches there."[87] Presumably she was referring to one of the preachers, but it is unclear which one, since no one is mentioned by name in the hearing record. Calling the preacher "the wolf," seems to have been meant as an insult rather than a reference to a person's name. She defended herself as having spoken in anger with no ulterior motives for going to the sermon at St. Moritz that day. The apparent harmlessness of the incident suggests that the council was quite sensitive to eruptions of religious strife.

The incidents in the bishop's garden, on the Zeugwart's front step, and at the doors of St. Moritz provide rare glimpses into the lives of Augsburg's citizens. These cases reveal ordinary citizens discussing ideas about religion outside of church and expressing religious opinions to empower themselves in interactions with their neighbors. The people

---

[86] "*Als sie hinein sei ganngen auf die Bred, hab sie ein pater noster inne ir hand getragenn, haben sie die leut angesprochenn, sie trag ein pater noster inn ir hand, und den teufel im hertzen,*" ibid., Urg. 16 November 1529, Agnes Braun.

[87] "*sicha, wol predigt der wolff da,*" ibid.

involved made their own choices about what to believe and how to articulate their faith. The study of official decrees and religious treatises clearly cannot capture fully the ways that ordinary people experienced this age of religious debate. Looking at people, such as the Rentmeisterin, Georg Zeindelweber, or Agnes Braun, adds a new facet to our picture of how people in the sixteenth century responded to religious reform and the controversies it introduced. Arguments over property could have religious overtones or elements to them. People confronted each other over religious differences and brought up religious differences in their confrontations with each other. Often the use of religious expressions seems to have served as a language for venting other grievances with authority figures or neighbors. The cases discussed in depth here also reflect the difficulty of assessing people's real religious beliefs even when they are provoked into arguments related to religion. In this period, the whole notion of confessional identity just does not seem relevant from the perspective of ordinary people.

CHAPTER THREE

ANABAPTISTS: A SPECIAL CASE?

[Magdalena Wisingerin] was not ashamed of doing what honored God. She had given herself to the Lord. She would die in prison as gladly as anywhere else.[1]

Sedelmairin told Magdalena Seizin, who had no more than one underskirt, that if she let herself be baptized, she would bring her a whole arm full of clothing.[2]

When speaking of their religious life, some Anabaptists revealed passionate commitments to their faith while others seem to have been inspired more by worldly concerns. Their statements hint at the wide variety of interests that might lead someone to follow a religious movement. As we will see, the numerous records collected on Anabaptists in Augsburg show that in this way, as in others, Anabaptists were not as different from other contemporary Christians as sometimes thought. They did not live in isolation from the rest of the city but intermingled with non-Anabaptists on a daily basis, and the record of their activities gives us a chance to see how religious communities form within a larger urban setting. The followers of the movement do not fall neatly into the categories of either theologians or martyrs, rather they were like Augsburgers, ordinary people living in extraordinary times.

Of the various religious movements that appeared in Augsburg in the first half of the sixteenth century, the Anabaptists present a special case in some respects. Only they were systematically prosecuted for their faith. While a supporter of reform might get arrested for criticizing the city council or insulting the Catholic Church in public, he would not be arrested simply for supporting Luther or Zwingli. For a brief time, between 1537–1547, people could get into trouble for leaving the city to attend Catholic services, but there was no concerted effort to uncover circles of secret Catholics. The Anabaptists, on the other

---

[1] "... *dann sy schem sich nit was got zu lob kom, sy hab sich dem herren ergeben, sy welle gleich als gern in der fengknus, als anderstwa sterben, es gelt ir alles gleich,*" StadtAA, Reichsstadt, Lit. 1528, March–April, Magdalena Wisingerin, 15 April 1528.

[2] "*Die Sedelmairin hab der Magdalena Seitzin ir der Butzin haußfrauenn so nicht mer dan ein under rock gehabt sie soll sich tauffen lassen so welle sie ir ein ganzen arm vol claider bringen, was sie ertragen möhe,*" ibid., Anna Butzin, 16 April 1528.

hand, could be arrested merely for meeting with friends to read and
discuss the Bible. In fact, an imperial mandate from February 1527
demanded that Anabaptism be banned and its followers punished;
Augsburg's council eventually followed up with its own prohibition on
11 October 1527.

Although each of the various Christian faiths growing in the early sixteenth century had its opponents, only the Anabaptists were universally
condemned by all other faiths. In fact, it could be said that denouncing the Anabaptists was one of the few things on which Catholics and
Protestants could agree. Up to 1537 Augsburg still tolerated Catholic
worship in eight churches while supporting evangelical preachers in the
churches' preaching houses. In that atmosphere, people were exposed
to a variety of religious messages which could lead people in many
directions. The Anabaptist Agnes Vogel gives us an idea of how the
confusion of religious messages in the early reformation could affect
people.

> She was moved to this baptism by the preachers [in Augsburg], because
> she attended their sermons here for a good four years. One preached
> this, the other that; one held the Sacrament for a symbol, the other for
> flesh and blood. So, they preached against one another and confused her
> so much that she didn't know what she should believe, and, therefore,
> wished to hear the others as well.[3]

Vogel sought spiritual guidance from the preachers in Augsburg but
wound up going elsewhere. Fortunately for us she speaks more directly
than most about her own feelings regarding her spiritual life. She was
disappointed by the officially accepted preachers and did not trust them.
How could she know who was right when all the preachers claiming to
know the true Gospel disagreed with each other so vehemently? When
an Anabaptist minister read to her from the Bible, he persuaded her
that the way to salvation lay in being baptized. Like others, Vogel sought
out answers in a variety of places. In her case, it led to Anabaptism.

In this twilight state before abolishing the Mass in 1537, the city
council expected citizens of different religious inclinations to live and
let live. By its own prohibition, however, it would not tolerate Anabap-

---

[3] "Zu solhem tauff haben sy bewegt die prediger alhie, dann sy sey wol vier jar an ir predig ganngen,
hab ainer das, ain ander ain annders gepredigt, ainer im Sacrament ain zaichen, der ander flaisch und
plut wellen haben, Also wider ain annder gepredigt, unnd sy ganntz irr gemacht, da sy nit gewißt,
was sy glauben solle, und deßhalben begert die anndern auch zuhoren," StadtAA, Reichsstadt,
Urg. 14 May 1528, Agnes Vogel.

tists. From that perspective the situation of Anabaptists living in the religiously diverse city of Augsburg presents a unique and fascinating case for the study of relations between radical and more conventional Christians. A closer look at the Anabaptist community in Augsburg raises questions, however, about how special the Anabaptists were. In many ways they resembled their non-Anabaptist neighbors, both in religious and social practices.

In studies of the Anabaptist movement, the question of why this particular group was denounced by all other religious parties, all over the Holy Roman Empire, has often been posed and answered.[4] The answers range from the theological to the political. First and most importantly, the Anabaptists' rejection of infant baptism was considered heretical by the traditional Catholic Church and by virtually all evangelical reformers, and the Anabaptists' refusal to allow their children to be baptized, in an age when infants were so vulnerable, was considered to be a reprehensible threat to their souls. Infant baptism was one of two Christian sacraments which other Protestants continued to practice. In contrast, Anabaptists discounted the baptism they had received in infancy as worthless. Considering only the baptism to which they were called as adults to be real, they also saw this baptism as bonding them in a special way with their fellow brethren, while setting them apart spiritually from the rest of society. Lee Palmer Wandel points out that it was the common bond of baptism which united Christians before the Reformation,[5] so the rejection of that baptism and the undertaking of a new one could certainly be interpreted by contemporaries as a severing of ties with the rest of the Christian community. Second, the refusal to carry weapons, swear oaths, pay taxes, and otherwise fulfill the duties of an early modern citizen, was anti-social and threatening to society as a whole. Guderian argues that concerns about unrest and uprisings motivated Augsburg's council to regulate Anabaptists more than concern over matters of faith.[6] While not all Anabaptists subscribed to these

---

[4] For general studies of Anabaptists in Augsburg and southern Germany, see Hans Guderian, *Die Täufer in Augsburg: Ihre Geschichte und ihr Erbe*, (Pfaffenhofen: Ludwig Verlag, 1984); Werner O. Packull, *Mysticism and the Early South German-Austrian Anabaptist Movement 1525–31* (Scottdale, PA: Herald Press, 1977); Claus-Peter Clasen, *Anabaptism: a Social History, 1525–1618: Switzerland, Austria, Moravia, South and Central Germany* (Ithaca: Cornell University Press, 1972); and Friedwart Uhland, *Täufertum und Obrigkeit in Augsburg im 16. Jahrhundert* (Diss. University of Tübingen, 1972).

[5] Wandel, *Eucharist*, 46.

[6] Guderian, *Die Täufer in Augsburg*, 82–83.

rules for behavior, it was common knowledge that many Anabaptist preachers promoted them, and some followers attempted to observe them. Furthermore, some Anabaptist ministers preached the holding of goods in common, with the implicit threat to redistribute wealth by force. They sanctioned it with Biblical promises of a reckoning at the coming of the Apocalypse, which was not so far off; some predicted it for Pentecost of 1528. The revolutionary implications of this message inspired among many authorities a deep and abiding distrust of Anabaptist activities.

The Anabaptist community in Augsburg subscribed to few of these doctrines which so alarmed the authorities. They disapproved of Hans Hut's apocalyptic predictions and even forbade him to talk about it.[7] They continued to carry weapons and pay taxes, as responsible citizens. According to one Augsburg Anabaptist, they had considered not carrying weapons as a sign of their faith, but nothing ever came of it.[8] They cared for their poorer brethren; many testified to giving or receiving charity in the form of money, food, or work, but they made no attempt to communalize their property. Nonetheless, like other cities and princes, Augsburg proceeded to forbid Anabaptism beginning in late 1527 and to arrest and punish Anabaptists sporadically throughout the 1520s and 30s. Banned from public pulpits and meeting places, Anabaptists were then held suspect for meeting in secret. By the 1540s the furor had died down, and the council even employed a noted Anabaptist, Pilgram Marbeck, as a civil engineer, on the condition that he practice his faith privately and not preach or publish his beliefs.

The picture of the Anabaptist movement in the late 1520s and early 1530s, revealed in the interrogation records, shows a community that does not fit easily into typical descriptions of their activities and membership. Earlier examinations of the Anabaptist movement in southern Germany have focused on issues, such as its theological framework, the biographies of its leaders, the appeal of the movement for the lower classes, and its suppression by religious and political authorities.[9] As a result, Anabaptists tend to be portrayed either as idealistic ministers or as pious and extremely zealous believers, ready for martyrdom if need

---

[7] Packull, *Mysticism*, 92–99.
[8] "*es sey wol davon geredt worden, dann die bruder die wöre hinder sich solten legen, damit man sy bei dem selben kennet, aber es sei nit bescheen,*" ibid., Martin Schad, 14 April 1528.
[9] See Note 4 above.

be. This has led to a glorification of individual cases of courageous defiance in the face of torture, exile, or execution. At the same time, there is also an understandable note of sympathy for a movement that, despite its good intentions, received nothing but condemnation and in some places disappeared under the pressure of persecution. As appealing as this picture may be—and anyone who reads the interrogation accounts today cannot help but be moved by the plight of those who were persecuted for their faith—it is not the whole picture.

This vision neglects the story of the ordinary follower for whom religious faith was only one facet of life, albeit an important one. In most studies of Anabaptism, the largest portion of the movement, the ordinary followers, remain frustratingly anonymous and one dimensional. This chapter offers a new perspective on the Anabaptists by re-locating the movement in the setting of the early Reformation city and shifting the focus to other aspects of the movement, such as how people came to join the Anabaptists and how they interacted with others. A study of Anabaptists not in isolation but in the urban setting in which they really lived has much to teach us about communal interactions in a time of religious upheaval. Therefore, this chapter focuses on the members themselves, their relations with each other and with other citizens, and gives a sense of how religious communities form and how individual members interact with each other and with non-members. Some aspects of their behavior might be comparable to the situation of the more popular traditional and evangelical religious groups in places where they were illegal.

Three observations become clear. First, people associated with or disassociated themselves from Anabaptists to varying degrees. All was not as black and white as it has usually been portrayed. Rather there was a whole range of degrees to which people could be connected with Anabaptism. Second, the social networks of the early modern city shaped and nourished the Anabaptist movement. The movement relied on interaction with others not isolation from them and grew out of ordinary daily activities. Third, the relationship between the city government and the movement reveals the former's surprising hesitancy to condemn despite the apparent harshness of its prosecution in 1528. It seems that the Anabaptists and the city council generally preferred to ignore each other whenever possible.

Degrees of Association

Identifying a person's religious affiliation was not always a simple matter during the early Reformation, either for the believer himself or for his family and neighbors.[10] The ambiguity of distinctions between faiths, the overlapping of doctrines, the ambivalence of policy-makers, the sheer novelty of it all, are all probable explanations for this phenomenon. The Anabaptists, for all the often-proclaimed uniqueness of their case, fit quite well into this picture. They shared the evangelical reformers' universal emphasis on reading the Bible. The movement seems to have begun in the early to mid-1520s with people meeting in small groups to read the Bible aloud and discuss their interpretations. Some of whom came to feel the need to pursue a Christian life more closely in tune with the Bible than even Luther or Zwingli proclaimed. At that time, they had much in common with Zwinglian theology and united with Zwinglians in the latter's dispute with Lutherans about the Eucharist.[11] Somewhat like Zwingli, they believed that Christ was not physically present in the Eucharist, and they believed that sharing bread and wine together had symbolic meaning only. In the early years, many Anabaptist ministers came from similar backgrounds to the leaders of other movements. Like many evangelical ministers, the Anabaptist preacher Jacob Dachser began his spiritual career as a Catholic priest. He became an Anabaptist, later reconciled with the Zwinglians, and eventually became a minister at St. Georg in Augsburg. Other ministers, such as Bonafacius Wolfart, attempted to convert arrested Anabaptists in prison, believing that they were not beyond persuasion. In addition, it has sometimes been asserted that Anabaptism had the greatest appeal for the disenfranchised, the poorer classes, and women. Hans Guderian, however, has shown that Anabaptists closely mirrored the stratification of society as a whole. In fact, according to his study of Augsburg's tax records, the property-less class was slightly under-represented in comparison to their numbers in the city, while the portion of small- to middling-property holders were over-represented among Anabaptists. In addition, Augsburg's interrogation records contain equal numbers of men and women Anabaptists.

---

[10] See discussions of the Germair household in Chapter One or the Zeindelweber-Meckenloher case in Chapter Two for examples.

[11] Hans Guderian, *Die Täufer in Augsburg*, 30.

The largest volume of legal records on Anabaptists in Augsburg comes from a raid on Easter Sunday, 12 April 1528, at the home of Susanna Taucher, wife of the famous Augsburg sculptor, Adolf Taucher (or Daucher).[12] This investigation led to over one hundred arrests beginning that day and lasting into the following weeks. After overlooking many smaller gatherings, the council finally responded to the large gathering of Anabaptists on Easter Sunday, arresting those who could or would not flee in time and rounding up additional suspects as interrogations revealed other names. Other interrogations of Anabaptists exist from the previous summer and following years, but none of them rival the extensiveness and thoroughness of the investigations from April to May of 1528. The testimonies preserved in the 1528 transcripts have several significant features. For one, they were all recorded by the same scribe. Secondly, they were all guided by the same set of questions, yet each person answered those questions differently. In spite or because of using identical questions, it becomes clear that each interrogation record reflects a unique perspective, that of the defendant. The transcripts reveal differences between male and female speakers, those who co-operated and those who resisted, those who were fearful and those who were bold, those who gave simple answers and those who show more sophisticated thinking. Variations in attitude and behavior appear, and it becomes clear that there is no predictable reaction to interrogation. While we must take into account the agendas of both the interrogators and the interrogated, the diversity of responses to identical questions indicates the potential for recognizing individuals from among the data.

Perhaps the single most important observation to make from reading the transcripts is that people had a great variety of types of relationships with and degrees of involvement in the Anabaptist movement. This is an important point to keep in mind when considering what it means to be identified as a member of a particular religious group. Two general types appear, which will be referred to as the associates and the members. Associates were not baptized and could be either hostile or sympathetic to the movement. Members, who were baptized, could be passive or active participants.

Hostile associates are easy to identify but difficult to evaluate. They found themselves connected to the Anabaptist world against their will

---

[12] Adolf Daucher, *Augsburger Stadtlexicon.*

through the participation of their relatives, neighbors, or servants. While some family members might turn a blind eye to their activities, others disapproved vocally and even violently. Most of those who disapproved remain enigmas. Since hostile associates were not Anabaptists, they were not arrested and interrogated, leaving behind no testimony in their own words. It is difficult to assess their beliefs and opinions beyond the references made to them by their Anabaptist relatives. What we know about them comes second-hand and may have been intended to protect them. Several women testified that their husbands had forbidden them to be baptized or threatened them with violence if they were baptized[13]—important to note is that the threats failed to dissuade in their cases. Agnes Vogel's husband did not like the Anabaptists and had not approved of visits from their landlady, who was an Anabaptist. According to Agnes, her husband would have thrown the Anabaptist minister down the steps if he had found him in the house. She, like other women, avoided a confrontation by simply not telling her husband she had been baptized. In Barbara Näßlin's case,[14] her husband had beaten her first but then accompanied her to meetings and even let her host them in their home in an effort to keep her from leaving him, which she later did anyway.

In other cases, defendants acknowledged that a spouse, parent, or sibling disapproved of their joining the movement. Anna Gablerin, for example, testified that her mother was very unhappy when she and her brother became involved with the Anabaptists. Her sister-in-law, who was not baptized, claimed that although she witnessed her husband's baptism, she had very little understanding of the matter.[15] One man who had attended meetings mentioned that his wife had not wanted him to go. Another woman mentioned that her husband wanted her to recant. In these cases we do not know on what grounds or how strongly their family members objected. Did they disagree with Anabaptist theology or did they fear repercussions from the authorities? Matheis Hieber told the councilors about conversations he had had with a friend, Hans Bollinger. Bollinger was not a "brother" and had often told Hieber that he would like to understand why so many people were drawn to Anabaptism. Bollinger also advised him more

---

[13] Ibid., March–April, Anna Malchingerin, 14 April 1528.
[14] Chapter One.
[15] Ibid., May, Afra Gablerin, 12 May 1528.

than once to abandon the business, and Hieber now regretted not listening to him. Similarly, a number of Anabaptists mentioned that their landlords would not allow them to hold meetings in their houses. So, their landlords knew they were Anabaptists and, although they did not want them to hold illegal meetings on the premises, they apparently did not object to having them as tenants. This leads us to the issue of more sympathetic associates.

Sympathetic associates include both people who supported the Anabaptist movement through various forms of assistance or tolerance and people who attended meetings without committing themselves through baptism. The first type of sympathizer knew about members and their meetings, although they apparently did not attend or participate in them. Defendants alluded to the distinction between sympathizers and true Anabaptists in their testimony. For example, Anna Kochin had learned about a meeting from a woman who knew she would be interested, yet Kochin did not know if the woman was a "sister" or not. Another woman testified that "Clement Kicklingerin" had attended a meeting in her home, "but was not a sister."[16] Nonetheless, Kicklingerin provided vital support for people who were interested in or intimately involved in Anabaptism. At least one of her tenants had also attended meetings without being baptized, and Kicklingerin had provided employment for an Anabaptist woman by letting her do some sewing in her home. People such as Kicklingerin aided the Anabaptist movement by supporting individual members without making a spiritual commitment themselves. Elizabeth Hegenmillerin's husband was not an Anabaptist, but he knew that she was and apparently supported her acts of charity to other Anabaptists. An outspoken woman, Elizabeth declared to the interrogators that if her husband had followed her, he would have become a brother and been baptized as well.[17]

Many family members and neighbors knew of the meetings their relatives and friends attended, despite the supposed secretiveness of the assemblies. People came to know of the meetings through routine daily contact. The council asked Anabaptists how they communicated

---

[16] "*Clement Kicklingerin sei aber kein schwester*," StadtAA, Reichstadt, Lit. 1528, March–April, Dorothea Frolichin, 15 April 1528.

[17] Ibid., Elisabeth Hegenmillerin, 16 April 1528, f. 326–39. She was exiled from Augsburg after having her tongue cut out for blasphemy against the Eucharist. She had repeated what a minister had told her, that the Eucharist was "*gotzenbrot*," or idol's bread.

with each other about their meetings. They wondered if there was a
special sign or greeting, like a secret handshake, or if they used a special
messenger to notify all the members. The evidence shows that the news
actually spread very casually. Sometimes the same person always made
sure to let his or her neighbors know, in other cases in was a different
person every time. A maid might overhear someone telling her mistress
about a meeting, a person might come to someone's shop to invite him
or coax him into coming, or someone would seek out a friend to ask if
she knew when and where the next meeting would take place. Given
the informal means of communicating among interested parties, it
should come as no surprise that many non-members knew about the
Anabaptists' activities. What may be more surprising is that it does not
seem to have created problems outside of the immediate family, if then.
It should be noted that there is not a single case in Augsburg's records
from the first half of the sixteenth century of an Anabaptist ever coming into conflict with a neighbor about religion. Many people seemed
to sympathize with or simply not care about Anabaptists meeting to
read and discuss the Bible, even if they did not share their beliefs or
their level of enthusiasm. This finding agrees with Guderian's claim
that some people rejected the more popular evangelical movements
but did not necessarily join the Anabaptists. Quite a few Anabaptists
mentioned that they participated in Bible reading groups that included
both baptized members and non-baptized friends.

The painter Hans Beck, son of painter Leonhard Beck, provides an
example of the other type of sympathetic associate, the curious. He
had not been baptized, but he had attended two meetings before the
prohibition against Anabaptism was published.[18] After that he stopped
going to meetings until the one on Easter Sunday. As he stated, "he
wasn't even thinking about the prohibition at the time."[19] He was
soon released after swearing an oath not to attend any Anabaptist
assemblies in the future. Of the eighty-eight people arrested on April
12, he was one of four whom the council described as having been
there in innocence or naiveté ("*auß ainfalt*").[20] The council's decision to
release or retain prisoners provides an indication of the validity of their

---

[18] The fact that he attended meetings before the decree and not after was very
important, because it meant he had not broken the law, since one cannot violate a
law not yet enacted.

[19] StadtAA, Reichsstadt, Lit. 1528, March–April, Hans Beck, 13 April 1528.

[20] StadtAA, Reichsstadt, Ratsbuch 1520–1529, 16 April 1528.

testimony. In that period of anxiety, the council only dismissed those who it was sure did not pose a threat. They could confirm a prisoner's testimony by comparing it with statements from others; that was part of the reason why the councilors asked them for the names of people who attended meetings with them.

One of the others quickly released for having become innocently involved in Anabaptism was Dorothea Duchschererin. She gave the following explanation for her presence at the Easter Sunday gathering.

> On Easter Sunday she wanted to go to the service at Holy Cross. On her way there she ran into the maid of Widenman the shoemaker. [The maid] asked her where she was going, and she told her. The maid informed her that there would be an assembly, and she should go with her, she would hear some really neat stuff (*sy wurde gar hupsch ding horen*). As a result, the maid talked her into it, so that she went with her and left her prayer stool in the Widenman's store.[21]

Dorothea Duchschererin informed the interrogators that she had neither been rebaptized, nor had she ever attended another Anabaptist meeting before. She added that, "she didn't think she was doing anything wrong or that it was forbidden." The interrogators, members of the city council, who typically showed tenacity in their prosecution of suspected Anabaptists, released her without further questioning. They were convinced of her innocence or at least satisfied with her demonstration of indifference towards Anabaptism, and no one else mentioned seeing her at meetings before. Several people testified that they were persuaded to attend meetings by friends. Before running into Dorothea Duchschererin, the Widenman's maid had already persuaded her master's daughter to go with, and on the way there they ran into Dorothea, on her way to church, and convinced her to come with them too. After all, the maid promised they would hear "some really neat stuff."

Martin Erhart, a glazier, had attended one meeting during Pentecost in 1527 but no other gatherings until Easter Sunday in 1528.[22] He explained to the interrogators that he had gone there with some good

---

[21] "*Am Ostertag were sy des willens gewesen, gem Heiligen Creutz an die predig zu geen, were sy unnder wegen, zu des Widenmans schuchsters magt komen, die hette sy gefragt, wa sy hinwolt, das sy ir gesagt, hette ir die magt anzaigt, es wurde ain versamblung, unnd sy solt mit ir geen, sy wurde gar hupsch ding horen, Also hette sy die magt uberredt, das sy mit ir were gangen, und hette iren predig stul in des Widenmans laden gelassen, Aber sy sei sonnst nye bey kainer versamblung gewesen, hab auch nit vermaint, das sy an solhen unrecht thue, oder das solhs auch verpoten sei,*" StadtAA, Lit. 1528, March–April, Dorothea Duchschererin.

[22] Martin Erhart was one of Clement Kicklingerin's tenants.

friends, "without thinking much about it."[23] According to Erhart, one of his companions, Leonhart Bienz, was also no longer interested in Anabaptism. Like Dorothea Duchschererin, Erhart claimed that he had been on his way to Holy Cross on Easter Sunday, when he ran into a friend, a fellow glazier from Aalen. Erhart claimed that this friend had convinced him to the meeting by grabbing some of his things so that he had to go after him.[24] According to his story, it was just bad luck that he was arrested half an hour after arriving at Susanna Taucher's house for the fateful meeting. The council must have found Erhart convincing, because they released him without further questioning. The council had the discernment to recognize that not all persons attending Anabaptist meetings were necessarily baptized members, though they might one day have reached that step if they had continued. The council was interested solely in baptized followers, but taking a look at various associates who did not receive baptism adds greatly to our understanding of how religious movements grow and how people became involved in them. Despite the apparently conclusive litmus test of what makes one an Anabaptist—adult baptism—there do not seem to have any boundaries between members and non-members. Even among the baptized there was great variety in the degrees to which they committed themselves to the faith.

Of the baptized followers, the term passive denotes members who did not participate actively in meetings or otherwise support the community after their baptism. Martha Beckin, for example, was baptized in late September of 1527, around the traditional Christian holiday of Michaelmas, and attended no other meeting until Easter Sunday 1528. A friend brought her there but then left.[25] Even after torture with thumbscrews she swore that she knew nothing else to tell them. She could name no other members, because she had not associated with them. She had neither housed nor fed anyone, had neither held nor attended any other assemblies. A few days later Martha Beckin "obediently" took the oath to leave the city, unlike three other women

---

[23] StadtAA, Reichsstadt, Lit. 1528, March–April, Martin Erhart, 12 April 1528.

[24] *"Jetzt am Ostertag seie der glaser von Alenn...Alls er gem Hailigen Creutz zur predig wellen geen, zu ime komen und gesagt lieber laßt uns mit ein ander gienn, man hat mir zu einer versamblung gesagt wol auff mit mir, inn dem er mit ime gangen zu der versamlung,...er seye der sach nit nachgangen der Glaser hab allerlay zeug von ime genomen und also uberredt, mit ime zu geen"* StadtAA, Reichsstadt, Lit. 1528, March–April, Martin Erhart, 12 April 1528.

[25] StadtAA, Reichsstadt, Lit. 1528, March–April, 13 and 15 April 1528.

who were beaten out when they refused to go voluntarily.[26] Similarly,
Anna Graber attended only one meeting after her baptism in August
of 1527. No one came to her house and she never went to meetings
at other houses. She testified that she had held herself back after the
council prohibited Anabaptist activities, because she did not want to get
in trouble. One man had forbidden his wife to have Anabaptists in the
house, yet he had been baptized, while she had not.[27] In such cases, the
council could corroborate the defendant's testimony by comparing them
with evidence from other defendants who gave names of people who
attended or hosted meetings. Naturally, it is difficult to know whether
a lack of involvement after baptism indicates a lack of devotion or a
just fear of getting in trouble, as Graber admitted. One suspects that
their more enthusiastic brethren would have considered it one and the
same. A number of Anabaptists who avoided large gatherings testified
that they were not only invited but pressured to attend meetings by
others.[28]

Some members, who allowed themselves to be baptized, showed
doubts about their choice afterwards. For example, Apollonia Thomas
told her interrogators what she had done with a letter placed in her
keeping by an Anabaptist minister, a former priest of the Teutonic
Order, who had been executed in Rothenburg. Although Apollonia
could not read, she knew the letter had to do with baptism, because
a fellow Anabaptist had read it out-loud. Several prominent women
Anabaptists wanted to have the letter from her for their own edifica-
tion, but Apollonia Thomas held onto to it as long as she could. She
took it to her cousin, the wife of Peter Hainzlin, because she trusted
her and always went to her when she needed advice. Hainzlinin told
Apollonia that she liked what was in the letter, except for the part
about baptism, which she said was not right. When Apollonia asked
if she had done right by joining the Anabaptists, her cousin laughed
and asked why she had not come to her sooner.[29] In the interrogation
record for Apollonia's husband, the scribe noted that "he does nothing but cry." Hans Gabler, who had forbidden his un-baptized wife to

---

[26] Ibid., Ratsbuch, 16 April 1528.
[27] Ibid., Lit. 1528, March–April, Affra Gablerin, 12 April 1528.
[28] Ibid., Reichsstadt, Lit. 1528, March–April 1528, Simprecht Widenman, 20 and
28 April 1528.
[29] Ibid., Apollonia Thomas, 28 April 1528.

host meetings, also paints a picture of regret in his testimony. A friend had talked him into being baptized, and he did not want to be a follower anymore. He actually claimed that he was drunk when he was baptized.[30] Whether this was just an excuse for the council or not, he clearly was not willing to stand by his "faith."

In contrast, there were also many active members who attended meetings whenever they could or held them in their own homes, encouraged others to join them, housed and fed travelling Anabaptists, both ministers and followers, and were not ashamed to admit it. For example, when asked how many meetings she had attended, Margaretha Berchtold, wife of a weaver, responded matter-of-factly that, "she couldn't say how many meetings she had attended; when she knew of one, she went."[31] Dorothea Frolichin said virtually the same, having attended as many meetings as she could, so that she could no longer count them.[32] Many people who were arrested identified Dorothea Frolichin as the person who told them about the meetings. She seems to have been very active in the role of communicating the meetings to interested members. In addition, she held two meetings in her home, with eighteen and ten people respectively. Beyond that she contributed to the movement by hosting at least two Anabaptist women who needed places to stay in town, Scholastica Stierpaurin who was a relative,[33] and Veronica Gross, the wife of an Anabaptist minister. She, like many others, refused to recant even after undergoing several interrogations and suffering torture to extract more information from her.

Many apparently wished to participate actively but proceed cautiously to avoid putting themselves in a dangerous situation. They never attended large meetings, held meetings in their own homes, or housed anyone, however, they would continue to meet in small groups (which was permissible), give traveling Anabaptists work to do, or perhaps gave a few pennies to a poorer brother or sister. For example, the Widenman family provided a haven for Anabaptists to meet informally and in small groups on a daily basis. Travelling Anabaptists would stop to buy shoes from Simprecht Widenman and would read with a minister while they

---

[30] Ibid., March–April, Hans Gabler, 24 April 1528.

[31] "*Sie konnde nit sagen wie offt sy bei den versamblungen gewesen sei, wa sy aine gewist sei sy darzu gangen,*" ibid., Margaretha Berchtold, 13 April 1528.

[32] "*Sie wiß nit wie offt sy bei der versamblungen gewesen sei, so offt sy die erfaren sei sy darzu gangen,*" ibid., Dorothea Frolichin, 13 April 1528.

[33] She also stayed with Clement Kicklingerin.

waited. Anabaptist women would meet with Katharina Widenman to sew and listen while someone read aloud to them. The Widenmans, carefully avoided hosting or attending meetings with more than a few people. On a smaller scale, Anna Malchingerin also tried to contribute prudently. She hosted no meetings and attended only meetings held outside the city limits in the woods near St. Radegunda. Her husband, a launderer, had forbidden her to hold meetings, but she washed shirts for some of the brethren without his knowledge.[34] She added that she could not go to many meetings because she had too much work to do, by which she inadvertently implied that she might have attended more, if she had been able.

Many active members changed their behavior substantially after a brush with the law. The lacemaker Conrad Huber testified that he had frequently held meetings in his home and attended them in other houses until August 1527. After that, he stopped going to meetings and holding them, but he gave food and drink to those who stopped in his house, if God instructed him to do so.[35] Although Conrad had not been arrested in the summer of 1527, his wife Felicitas had, along with many other Anabaptists, who had participated in the large gathering known as the Martyrs' Synod.[36] On 17 September 1527, Felicitas had taken an oath not to attend any more Anabaptist sermons and to confine her activities to reading in small groups of two or three.[37] From that time on, she and her husband restricted their activities.

One of the most eloquent testimonies evoked by the 1528 investigations captures the essence of the conflict faced by Anabaptists who wished to follow their faith and yet remain at peace with their city. Ulrich Rot, a grocer, was one of many devout followers who tailored his religious activities to satisfy the council. In the more than one hundred hearings from the spring of 1528, no one described his case as articulately and explicitly as Rot. First, he readily acknowledged that he had broken the law by being baptized *after* the city's prohibition was declared. Then, even though he was frequently invited to attend meetings, he had attended none of them, because he knew that they

---

[34] Ibid., Anna Malchingerin, 14 April 1528.

[35] Ibid., Conrad Huber, 24 April 1528.

[36] A large gathering of Anabaptists from southern Germany and Switzerland took place on St. Bartholomew's Day in 1527. It became known as the Martyrs' Synod because so many of the leaders who attended the meeting were later executed in other places.

[37] Ibid., Ratsbuch 1520–29, 17 September 1527.

were illegal. Instead, he maintained his faith by reading on his own and keeping his affairs to himself. As a result of his lack of participation, he knew very little about the Anabaptists' business, but steadfastly rejected any notion of seditious behavior. He declared that if he had known of any plan to act against the government, he would have come and told the council himself, rather than waiting to be arrested. He testified to this "as a citizen, because he was an Augsburger and a child of the city,"[38] Throughout his interrogation, Rot conveys a deferential attitude and shows respect for the concerns of the authorities. Nevertheless, in the final statement of his testimony, Rot declared that he did not consider himself to have acted against the council by allowing himself to be baptized, even after the council prohibited it. Rot's sensitive statements highlight the complexity and difficulty of his situation. Rot distinguished between his devotion to his faith and his obligation to his city while denying any contradiction between them. Although Ulrich Rot wished to obey the council and serve his city, he drew the line at sacrificing his soul.

The variety of association and commitment seen in the examples above highlights several important points. First, these diverse cases reflect the various influences at work in the religious movements, loosely grouped together under the name Anabaptist. The openness and fluidity allowed for many people to be exposed to or involved in similar Bible reading groups with or without committing themselves through baptism. The wide range of kinds and degrees of participation in the movement also confirms the porous structure of the organization and its peripatetic followers. Their experiences were shared by many people in the first half of the sixteenth century, who were trying to find their place in the midst of sometimes inspiring and sometimes bewildering changes. In an attempt to make sense of it all, many people attended sermons by different preachers with different religious beliefs, leading their listeners in various directions. Their listeners' decisions about whom to follow, what to believe, or where to attend services were based on all kinds of factors, many of which are not predictable and cannot be accounted for automatically by arguments of appeal by economic status, occupation, geography, or gender. Naturally, factors which encouraged one's exposure to religious ideas were crucial, but, ultimately, one's faith remained a very personal and inscrutable matter.

---

[38] Ibid., Lit. 1528, March–April, Ulrich Rot, 14 May 1528, f. 83–7.

SOCIAL NETWORKS

The intricate overlapping of social and religious life in the early modern city made possible the varied constellation of association within the Anabaptist movement. People came into contact with the Anabaptist message through friends or relatives who shared what they had learned and invited them to go with them to gatherings. In turn, people responded in a variety of degrees of interest, approval, and rejection. In these interrogation records we see the close interaction between the social and religious worlds of the Anabaptists. Many people became involved in the movement through the influence of household members or neighbors. Parents and children, spouses, siblings and in-laws, masters, servants and apprentices would encourage each other to be baptized and attend gatherings. Sometimes the support took the form of active persuasion, and sometimes it was merely the passing on of information, when and where the next meeting would take place. The following example shows how easily everyday social interaction could assist the growth of the Anabaptist community.

Apollonia Widholzin was the wife of Andreas Widholz, a master of the grocers' guild, who had already been exiled for Anabaptism in late summer 1527. Her sister and brother-in-law, Felicitas and Hans Lauterwein, were also Anabaptists. Apollonia was arrested in the fall 1527, along with her husband and two maids. Unlike her husband, Apollonia and her maids avoided exile by swearing to shun all Anabaptist activities. They also had to recant officially and admit that they had erred. In that same oath, she agreed to confine her religious activities to meeting in small groups of no more than two or three people. Although she did not attend the Easter meeting in April 1528, she was arrested afterwards as part of the subsequent investigation into Anabaptist activities and membership in Augsburg.

In her interrogation on 18 May 1528, Apollonia Widholzin described an impromptu Anabaptist encounter which took place in her home.[39] One day not long before her second arrest, while she was still lying in childbed from the recent birth of a daughter, her sister Felicitas Lauterwein paid her a visit. Apollonia's son Berchtold, who was also an Anabaptist, happened to be meeting with the Anabaptist minister Georg von Passau at the same time. Her sister, finding the minister in

---

[39] Ibid., May, Apollonia Widholzin, 18 May 1528.

the house, asked Georg to read her "something good" from the Bible.
He and Felicitas sat together and read, while Apollonia rested in a
separate room set aside for her lying-in period. Later, another visitor,
Magdalena Merzin, came to visit her and then joined Felicitas and
Georg in the other room. Felicitas told her afterwards that Magdalena
wanted very much to be baptized, and when she saw Georg there she
pleaded with him until he baptized her right then and there. Without
being asked, Apollonia also told her interrogators that her mother had
had the new baby baptized at the Cathedral (as a Catholic?).

This case shows how casually contacts among Anabaptists could
take place. The essence of their faith was coming together to read, to
discuss and teach, and to baptize new brethren. They were forbidden
to hold church services, but they did not need them. It was as easy as
visiting a sister or a neighbor. Despite their casual nature, the encounters
had significance for the people involved. The example also shows how
Anabaptism added a new spiritual bond of brother- or sisterhood to
people who were already related through marriage, blood, or service.

As Georg Mair revealed in his testimony, many Anabaptist activities occurred on a small and informal basis rather than on the large,
organized level feared by the authorities. He had been baptized before
the decree in October 1527, attended several meetings up until then,
after which he stopped going to them. He explained that, since then
he often read out-loud from the Bible to visitors who came to see him.
He also read to his own household and in the houses of friends. Caspar
Schlosser also read frequently for his neighbors, and the son of one of
his neighbors also read for visitors, not all of whom were Anabaptists.[40]
In addition, many women gathered in sewing groups at which someone
might read aloud or a minister might stop by to talk with them for a
while. Felicitas Hüberin testified that she met a couple of times with
other women to sew. Once the minister Hans Leupold came to teach
them, and the other time they were alone, at the Widenman's house.[41]
Katherina Widenman, wife of Simprecht, told of another gathering at
Anna Voglin's house. She and several other women Anabaptists came
not to read but to bake and drink together. Each brought a contribu-
tion, such as eggs or lard.[42] One cannot tell whether a shared social life

---

[40] Ibid., March–April, Caspar Schlosser, 16 April 1528.
[41] Ibid., May, Felicitas Hieberin.
[42] Ibid., March–April, Katherina Widenman, 19 April 1528.

led people to become Anabaptists, or whether being Anabaptists then brought them together socially, probably some of each.

Various types of networks which connected Anabaptists to each other, professional, neighborly, and familial, often overlapped. They provided each other with financial and emotional support and encouragement. For example, the shoemaker Simprecht Widenman made shoes for visiting Anabaptists who passed through his house. Most were Anabaptists traveling through Augsburg on their way to another destination, looking for a safe haven after exile elsewhere. Visitors might stay for a day or two with the Widenman family, meet with fellow Anabaptists or even a minister, and Simprecht would make them shoes.[43] Having shoes made may have been a convenient cover to explain their presence there, but it was also a practical way of taking care of necessary business (getting new shoes for a long journey) while receiving spiritual solace and companionship all at once. It is very telling that travelling Anabaptists knew which shoemaker to visit in Augsburg. Clearly a network of communication existed that let them know which houses and businesses were safe and would welcome them for a short time. Local people also passed through the Widenmans' house, including the minister Hans Leupold, whose younger brother Leonhart was one of Simprecht's apprentices. Incidentally, it was the Widenman's maid, Barbara Tetzin, who had encouraged Dorothea Duchschererin to attend the Easter Sunday meeting. Anna Malchingerin sometimes did laundry for Anabaptists, in lieu of actual financial support. She may have done this for Anabaptists who were passing through and had no settled household to carry out such tasks for them.

The Anabaptist dyers Joseph and Apollonia Thomas also received appeals from Anabaptists in need. Anabaptists looking for work sought them out. An older man, a "brother," was sent to them by a woman named Scheuchlerin to do some work, because he was in need of money. As Apollonia reported, they tried to give him some work to do, but he was incapable of it because of some infirmity in his hands, so they eventually had to send him on his way. Apollonia informed the interrogators that they had not hosted any Anabaptists, because their house was so small that the maid had to sleep in the main room. She may have included these details to add verisimilitude, but she also left open the possibility that they might have hosted Anabaptists if their

---

[43] Ibid., Simprecht Widenman, 29 April 1528.

house was larger. The Thomases definitely made an effort to help out
Anabaptists who came to them in need of work. In this way, they provided practical economic support to the movement's followers, whom
they considered to be their brethren.

The Thomases had also employed two foreign Anabaptists as maids,
one of whom came from the Bavarian village of Hirbe. Anna Schuch-
ster had come to Augsburg after she was banished from her home for
being an Anabaptist. Possessing the traditional allure of all big cities,
Augsburg attracted displaced persons looking for a fresh start. Anna
sought an Anabaptist employer who would approve of her beliefs and
not turn her in to the authorities. We do not know how she found the
family, but she probably learned of them through contacts she had
with the extended Anabaptist circle. The Anabaptist community easily
bridged the border between town and country, and their interdependence suggests that those borders were tenuous. The Anabaptists seem
to have crossed the boundaries easily and frequently in both directions. City-dwelling Anabaptists would often gather in gardens outside
the city walls, in a small community, such as St. Radegunda, or even
out in the woods, hence the common appellation of garden-brother
or garden-sister. They were joined by villagers or peasants of similar
sympathies, which is probably how foreigners would know whom to
turn to in Augsburg in times of need.

Connections which spanned town and country also spilled over
into households within Augsburg and further supported the spread of
Anabaptism. Margareta Widenman, the daughter of a baker, learned
about the Easter meeting from the family's maid, Lucy. As Margareta
told her interrogators, Lucy had already been baptized, arrested, and
banished from some other place before, although Margareta did not
know where. Lucy had been with them about three weeks and worked
for Margareta's father to earn bread. According to Margareta, it was
Lucy who talked her into going to the meeting on Easter Sunday. On
their way, they stopped at the house of Lucas Fischer, master of the
Potters' Guild, to ask his maid, Radigunda Raiserin for directions.
Radigunda Raiserin came from Veyenhofen but was no transient, like
Lucy of unknown origins; she claimed that Lucas Fischer had practi-
cally raised her. Radigunda and her surrogate family, the Fischers,
were Anabaptists and had connections to other Anabaptist families.[44]

---

[44] Agnes Vogel was the Fischers' tenant.

Radigunda's mistress, Anna Fischer, was sister-in-law to the shoemaker, Simprecht Widenman, which means that she and Katharina Widenman were probably sisters. It is possible that Margareta Widenman's father was also related to Simprecht.

Many examples show the significance of familial connections in the spread and practice of Anabaptism. Although some families experienced differences of opinion between spouses or between parents and children, most of the defendants interrogated were related to other Anabaptists, as spouses, parents, children, siblings, in-laws, servants, or tenants. The Widenman-Fischer-Widenman circle includes all of those. The Widholzes provide another excellent example of people who made joining Anabaptism a family venture. In the Widholz family alone we know that the guildmaster Andreas and his wife Apollonia both joined, along with at least one grown son, Berchtold, and two maids, Apollonia and Katherina. Moreover, Apollonia's sister Felicitas and her husband Hans Lauterwein were also Anabaptists.

A few more examples illustrate how common it was for people to become Anabaptists as part of a family, in the Heises family the mother and both grown sons became Anabaptists. The brothers Hans and Ulrich Awrbach were Anabaptists, along with Ulrich's wife and her mother Elisabeth Knollin. Anna Gabler and her brother Hans were baptized together. Two pairs of sisters, Elisabeth Hegenmillerin and Regina Weißhaupt, and Susanna Taucher[45] and Maxencia Wisingerin, followed Anabaptism and often attended meetings together. Hans Butz was baptized in his mother's house. Caspar Schlosser, his mother, his stepfather, his sister, and his brother-in-law were all members. The Schleiffer family also included several members and sympathizers, including the mother Barbara, her sons Georg[46] and Gall, her daughter Ursula, and Ursula's husband. Lastly, Thomas Paur was brother-in-law to three different Anabaptist ministers.

In the Spring of 1528, Anabaptism was still a relatively new movement in Augsburg, only a few years old, which means that most of these family ties had existed before the development of the sect. Anabaptists

---

[45] Hostess of the 1528 Easter Sunday gathering.

[46] Ursula stated that her brother Georg worked for "*seiner Meisterin der Schmidin Schlayrwirckerin*," who may be Anna Schlayrwirckerin or her mother Anna Bawmenin, who was a veilmaker. Both of them were Anabaptists, which would extend the Schleiffer-Anabaptist connection one step further. StadtAA, Reichsstadt, Lit. 1528, March–April, Ursula Schleiffer, 22 April 1528.

only began appearing around 1524, so we can assume that common
religious interests had not created most of these family relationships,
but rather the other way around. Testimonies also illustrate that
Anabaptists' family connections extended to servants, employees, and
neighbors as well. The interaction of families and neighbors was critical
to the fostering of Anabaptism. Anna Berchtoldmairin was baptized
in the house of her neighbors Crispin and Scolastica Stierpaur. As she
testified, "Stierpaur was her closest neighbor."[47] Family connections
may have fostered the growth of Anabaptism in a variety of ways. To
some extent the support was probably indirect or incidental, through
the simple sharing of ideas and conversations. Their daily interaction
would have encouraged common experiences. Children and live-in
servants or apprentices could hardly help but be present (at least aware)
if their parents or masters invited an Anabaptist minister to read in
the house. Likewise, siblings and neighbors might be among the first
to be invited to join them.

Support could be direct as well, when family members encouraged each other not only to attend meetings together but to take the
crucial step of baptism. Anna Schleichin describes such a connection
explicitly. She was a servant in the house of her brother Simprecht
Schleichen, a baker. Although her brother was not an Anabaptist, she
was baptized in his house while he was away. According to Anna, it
was her sister-in-law, Afra, who was home because of an illness, who
told her she should let herself be baptized.[48] Also, as the opening quote
to this chapter indicates, friends could be very persuasive. According to
Anna Bützin, her neighbor Magdalena Seizin was encouraged to join
by another woman who offered to give her clothing, if she would be
baptized. While the offer has the ring of a bribe, it may have represented the Anabaptists' commitment to caring for each other, indicating
the sort of welcome Seizin would receive from her new brothers and
sisters. Nevertheless, it certainly introduces a motive for joining other
than the purely spiritual.

---

[47] "*Der Stierpaur seie ir nechster nachpaur gewesen,*" ibid., Anna Berchtoldmairin, 12
April 1528.
[48] Ibid., Anna Schleichin, 12 April 1528.

TROUBLE WITH THE LAW

Historians of the Anabaptist movement and of Augsburg generally agree that local authorities were relatively tolerant of Anabaptist activities in comparison with other cities.[49] Although an Imperial decree from Ferdinand had made Anabaptism illegal throughout the Holy Roman Empire in February 1527, Augsburg's council did not issue its own decree outlawing Anabaptism until October. This decree came only after an unusually large gathering, including many ministers, had met just outside Augsburg in August 1527, leading to the council's first arrests of Anabaptists. The meeting in late August became known as the "Martyrs' Synod" because so many of the people involved, especially leaders, were executed in other places after leaving Augsburg. This meeting drew hundreds of people, including many ministers, from all over southern Germany, Switzerland, and Austria, for the purpose of organizing themselves. It was an event which Augsburg' government could not ignore. With the decree, the city council made it illegal to withhold one's child from baptism, to attend Anabaptist sermons, to feed or house Anabaptist leaders, or to have anything at all to do with Anabaptism.[50] Although Augsburg was a major center of Anabaptist activity in southern Germany, only two Anabaptists died in the custody of Augsburg's government; both men were ministers (*Vorsteher*) or leaders of the movement. Hans Hut, a promoter of the Apocalyptic predictions, was an active writer and preacher, who died during a fire in the prison before his scheduled execution, perhaps as part of an escape attempt. Hans Leupold was a minister who had baptized many people. Since he had been arrested once before in Augsburg and recanted, the council considered him to be beyond redemption. He was publicly beheaded after being arrested again on Easter Sunday 1528. Unlike authorities elsewhere who executed people just for having been re-baptized, Augsburg's city council targeted the leaders of the movement, those people who aggravated their offenses by encouraging others to transgress the law. It never imposed corporal or capital punishments on people simply for being followers. On the other hand, the council did use torture routinely to extract information from Anabaptists about meetings and other members, though not to force recantations. It also

---

[49] See, for example, Hans Guderian, *Die Täufer in Augsburg*, 87.
[50] StadtAA, Reichsstadt, Anschläge und Dekrete, 11 October 1527

exiled foreigners and citizens who would not recant and occasionally administered corporal punishment for people who were guilty of additional infractions.

Augsburg's council used the interrogations to find out how deeply involved an Anabaptist was in the movement and to assess how seriously they had violated the law. The questions asked by the interrogators were intended to establish several things about their subjects. In a typical hearing, the interrogators first sought information about the defendant's status in the movement: whether or not he or she had been baptized, when, where, by whom, and in whose company. Then there were questions about how many meetings he or she had attended, where they were, and who else had attended them. This was the point at which many interrogations stalled, because defendants did not want to give incriminating information about other members. The council pursued these questions to discover missing suspects (those Anabaptists who had not attended the Easter Sunday meeting or who had fled the meeting before being arrested) and to identify the leaders among the group. If the interrogation continued, questions then turned to assess the nature of the defendant's involvement, in particular questions about hosting meetings, housing ministers, feeding or giving drink to Anabaptists, giving them financial aid, or otherwise supporting the movement. These questions helped to establish the degree of a person's guilt regarding violations of city statutes. The date when a person had been baptized, therefore, indicated whether or not they had broken the decree against baptism. Those who were baptized before 11 October 1527 were treated more leniently. On the other hand, those who had held meetings in their homes, or housed and fed Anabaptists, were punished more severely than those who had merely attended one or two meetings.

The council made a further distinction between citizens and foreigners. Foreign Anabaptists were often banished without being interrogated or otherwise punished. For example, when the large 1528 Easter gathering was arrested, officials wrote down the names and places of origin of the foreign Anabaptists on a sheet of paper and then escorted them out of town soon afterwards. Several important ministers, such as Georg von Passau, escaped prosecution in this way. Most of the foreigners were only recent arrivals in Augsburg, after being banished from their own villages, or came solely for the Easter meeting and planned to go home afterwards. Citizens of Augsburg who were baptized and attended a few meetings were given a chance to recant, which meant that they would not be exiled. They might then be penalized with temporary restrictions on their civic privileges, such as voting, or with loss of government employment but otherwise were untouched. Citizens who refused to recant would be banished, though not usually for life. This would explain why people who might sympathize with Anabaptist ideas would try to prevent their spouses or other relatives from joining, because they feared the consequences from civic authorities. Those who had eagerly and unrepentantly supported the movement by hosting meetings and providing other crucial assistance would not only be banished but could suffer additional punishment such as being whipped or branded before being escorted out of town. While exile could place a great strain on individuals and their families, especially if it interfered with their ability to support themselves financially, the council's policy was remarkably lenient for the times.

Ministers were targeted, naturally, because they spread the Anabaptist message and encouraged people to join the movement and performed the baptisms. When Hans Leupold was arrested in April of 1528, not only was he an active preacher and baptizer, but he had broken an earlier oath to recant and abstain from Anabaptist involvement which he made in August of 1527. In addition, the ministers were usually foreigners and, therefore, not as deeply rooted in the community. It was a common practice for Anabaptists periodically to elect new leaders and then send them away to other places. Perhaps, like prophets in their own land, they were expected to be more effective elsewhere.

Augsburg, like other communities, seemed to fear the anti-social and anti-authoritarian message of the Anabaptist movement more than the religious aspects. The council's reasoning appears very clear in the decree which states that the Anabaptist sect

> [is] against God, Christian order, good customs, honorable policy and favors division, schism, dissension, uprising, the downfall of authority (which is instituted by God), also disruption and destruction of brotherly love, and basically leads to nothing good.[51]

As hostile as this statement is, the council's description of Catholicism issued about a decade later, when it declared Catholicism illegal in Augsburg, would be much harsher. This October 1527 decree briefly refers to unchristian behavior, while the rest focuses on the social and political dangers which authorities feared from Anabaptists.

---

[51] Ibid.

From this decree and the legal records of interrogations and sentencings, we know that Augsburg's council forbade Anabaptism and periodically arrested and punished Anabaptists. Some followers were beaten or whipped while others suffered permanent physical disfigurement, such as branding through the cheeks. One woman had her tongue cut out for the additional crime of having blasphemed against the Eucharist. Many households were split up when family members were banished from the city for an indeterminate time. Yet, despite this record of persecution, Augsburg's government retains a reputation with historians for tolerance towards Anabaptists. This reputation must be understood in comparison with other authorities. A most immediate and glaring contrast can be made with the methods of the Swabian League which controlled most of the territory surrounding the city of Augsburg. The Swabian League actively pursued the capture and destruction of Anabaptists as a central goal. The league's provost, Peter Aichellin, became infamous as an executioner of Anabaptists.[52] In 1528, the Swabian League declared that Anabaptists who did not recant would be burned, while those who recanted would receive mercy: men who recanted would be beheaded, and women who recanted would be drowned.[53] This policy applied to anyone associated with the Anabaptist movement, not just the leaders. Eitelhans Langenmantel, an Augsburg patrician who was banished from the city because he refused to recant, took up residence outside the city, where he occasionally met with sympathetic friends. When he was arrested by the Swabian League, he and his servants were executed.

In contrast to the Swabian League, not only did Augsburg actually allow former Anabaptists (who had recanted) to live and remain in the city, they permitted them to continue to meet in small groups to read or talk about the Bible. According to Anna Fischer, the council made this concession in 1527 when Anna Regel, a wealthy citizen, refused to take an oath not to meet with anyone at all.[54] In fact, the council agreed to permit small gatherings of a few people; Anna Fischer claimed that they were allowed to meet with six or eight, but the council records

---

[52] See Chapter Two, in the Zeindelweber-Meckenloher case.
[53] Clasen, 380.
[54] "...hab vermaint solhs sei nit unrecht noch wider ainen Erbern Rat, dann als sy von ainem Erbern Rat abgeschiden were inen irs enthalts anzaigt worden, sie solten der grossen versamblungen muessig steen, Aber wa 6 oder 8 personen zusamen giengen, wurde es kain irrung haben, dann die Reglin hette nit wellen schworen, gar jedermann muessig zusteen," StadtAA, Reichsstadt, Lit. 1528, March-April, Anna Fischer (aka. Hafnerin) fol. 88–99.

from 17 September 1527 actually stated that two or three could read and discuss the Bible together.[55] As a result, defendants in later cases often claimed that they were not breaking the law, because they only met in a small group. Ursula Germairin used this defense to no avail during her interrogation in 1533, but then, she was a foreigner who refused to recant.

Although the Anabaptists present a special case in Augsburg's legal history by being the only group to be systematically prosecuted for religious activities, they had more in common with the experiences of other religious groups in the city than usually assumed. People learned about various reform movements through reading or listening to ministers or lay readers, talking with friends, family, and work associates, and perhaps, like Peter Hainzlin's wife, approving the messages they received selectively. The most significant differences stem from the degree of prosecution the Anabaptists faced. At the same time, they shared much with other groups, in terms of their religious beliefs, such as their views on the Eucharist. The government's interest in their movement reflected the same kinds of concerns they expressed about Catholics and evangelical reformers in the 1520s, mainly a fear of the impact that dissent would have on the community and the possibility of rebellion. Despite those concerns, women such as Anna Regel managed to gain concessions from the city council to preserve the right of people to meet privately to read and discuss the Bible on their own. In addition, the social networks that played such an important role in the Anabaptist movement indicate that Anabaptists were not nearly as isolated as their history might suggest. Rather they were very much a part of the urban community. Finally, just like other Augsburgers, they reveal a wide variety of influences which encouraged the development of their convictions. They provide a perfect example of religious beliefs developing under circumstances independent of the auspices of secular or spiritual authorities. They may serve as a model for how confessional groups might develop later without official involvement or despite official opposition.

---

[55] "*woll mogen zwen oder trey das gotz wort lesen und davon reden, doch kain versamblung noch rottieren furnemen machen und thun,*" ibid., Ratsbuch 1520–29, 17 September 1527.

CHAPTER FOUR

MAGISTERIAL REFORM AND RELIGIOUS DEVIANCE

She likes the evangelical sermons just as much, and she listens to them as gladly as to the others,[1]

He knows nothing bad about the preachers, but then he doesn't know them all,[2]

The nuances concealed in these statements suggest how difficult it could be for civic authorities to shape the religious beliefs of their citizens, as they began to do in the late 1530s. In 1537 Augsburg's government abolished the clergy and ceremonies of the old faith and attempted to make a thorough reformation of the city's churches. Many records indicate that the city council faced obstacles to this endeavor, and that there may have been some uncertainty about how strenuously the council intended to enforce its reformation of worship. The council faced opposition from various sides, not always easy to categorize as for or against reform or a particular type of reform. While evangelical reform seems to have been generally popular in Augsburg, evidence shows that many people in Augsburg followed their own guidance when it came to their religious life.

During the 1530s Augsburg's guilds elected council members who enthusiastically supported reform. Led by avidly Protestant mayors, such as Mang Seitz, Ulrich Rehlinger, Georg Herwart, and Jakob Herbrot, the city council finally gave up its strategy of neutrality and took a stand for the evangelical Reformation. The council had taken several partial steps towards reform in the past without committing itself completely. Beginning in 1534 the council had employed exclusively evangelical ministers in the city-controlled churches, such as St. Anna and the Franciscan churches, as well as the preaching houses of Catholic churches, such as St. Ulrich and Holy Cross. This left the Cathedral and seven other churches under the authority of the bishop of Augsburg who

---

[1] "*...dann die predig des Evangeliums sei ir gleich als lieb, und hoer die als gern, als ander,*" StadtAA, Reichsstadt, Urg. 20 May 1539, Barbara Hertnitin.

[2] "*Den Andern, er wiß nichts weder ubels noch args von den predicanten dan er kenn sie doch nit alle,*" ibid., 13 August 1539, Wilhelm Gemelich.

maintained the Catholic Mass.[3] Despite the council's open support for evangelical preaching, Catholics and Protestants continued to exist side-by-side, though not without occasional friction.[4] In addition, reforming ministers struggled for control over the nature of reform in Augsburg. Supporters of Luther found themselves siding with the Catholics on some issues in order to oppose the more extreme changes proposed by the Zwinglians. According to historian Friedrich Roth, the Lutherans on the city council did not want to prohibit the Catholic clergy and their ceremonies for fear of losing a counterweight to the more radical [Zwinglian] reformers.[5] Three years later, on 21 January 1537, under the leadership of newly elected mayors, the council finally undertook the decisive step of reforming all worship in the city, by forbidding the Catholic Mass in all of Augsburg's churches and expelling the clergy who would not conform to the new church ordinance.

Although the city was overwhelmingly in favor of reform, the Reformation in Augsburg was not universally welcomed by its population. There were still a number of people who preferred the Catholic faith, including the members of several wealthy and influential families, including the Fugger,[6] the Baumgartner, Peutinger, and a branch of the Rehlinger family.[7] Many people of little means and influence also remained loyal to the old church, but they remain unidentified, except for the few who appeared in legal disputes. Although exact numbers are not known,[8] Friedrich Roth asserts that in the early 1530s the council feared an uprising if it forbade the Catholic Mass outright, indicating an appreciable number of Catholic supporters within the city and not just the influence of a few powerful families. Many Lutheran Protestants also opposed Augsburg's Reformation, which was significantly influenced by ministers, such as Michael Keller, Bonifacius Wolfart, and Wolfgang Musculus, who favored Zwingli in debates on the Eucharist. Both Luther

---

[3] These churches included Sts. Ulrich & Afra, St. Georg, St. Moritz, Holy Cross, St. Stefan, St. Peter, St. Ursula, and the Cathedral. Roth, *Augsburgs Reformationsgeschichte*, Bd. II, 110.

[4] For an example of Holy Cross where Catholics and Lutherans worshiped in close proximity to each other, see Gray, *Good Neighbors*.

[5] Ibid., p. 107.

[6] Anthony, Raymond, and Hieronymus Fugger were all Catholic.

[7] The Rehlingers had family members in every major confession in Augsburg; the Catholic Johann, Lutherans Conrad and Wolfgang, and Zwinglian Ulrich.

[8] According to a letter written by a visiting Italian merchant, the Catholics comprised the smallest confessional group, the Lutherans a slightly larger one, and the Zwinglians by far the largest group. Roth, 7–8.

and Zwingli rejected the Catholic Mass, but Luther still believed that Christ was present in the bread and wine, while Zwingli maintained that his presence was purely spiritual. The Eucharist described in Augsburg's church ordinance was closer to Zwingli's conception than Luther's, when it emphasized Christ's presence in the community of believers.[9] In the 1530s, when the council suppressed Lutheran preaching, Martin Luther advised his followers in Augsburg to practice their faith in secret or at least receive the Sacraments from Catholic priests in their homes rather than attend Zwinglian services.[10] As seen in the previous chapter, Anabaptists also provided an obstacle to religious consensus in Augsburg in the 1530s. The ordinance of 1537 was meant to change all that, through some force and much persuasion. By unifying the message preached in all of Augsburg's churches, the council hoped to create agreement where it had not previously existed while conflicting voices had rung from the pulpits.

In addition to regulating the liturgy and clergy in the city, the council's new church ordinance of 1537 also forbade Augsburgers to attend Catholic services outside of Augsburg's walls. Nearby towns, such as Lechhausen, Oberhausen, Friedberg, and others, offered Catholic worship within a tempting distance of the city for those willing to risk the journey. On 27 March the council ordered the city's gatekeepers to watch for people leaving the city to attend Mass or participate in other Catholic services in the countryside. A short time later, on 7 April, an unidentified group of people were admonished by the council not to attend Mass or other Catholic services in or outside the city. The entry in the council records describes these people as behaving, "as if the council had erred and not acted properly" regarding its religious ordinance.[11] Those who were caught leaving the city illicitly for Catholic ceremonies could face punishment, but their situation differed dramatically from that of the Anabaptists who were also forbidden to worship according to their faith. In the 7 April incident no punishment was recorded. Crypto-Catholics were not hunted out nor systematically prosecuted as were the Anabaptists. Their interrogations were less formal and their punishments—when given at all—were far milder. Although both faiths were illegal in Augsburg at this time, they were not treated as equally

---

[9] Wandel, *The Eucharist*, 88–92.
[10] Roth, 51–2.
[11] "…*alß ob ain Rat geirrt, unnd nit wol gehanndelt hette*," StadtAA, Reichsstadt, Ratsbuch 1520–29, 7 April 1537.

undesirable. Then again, Catholicism was the religion of the Emperor Charles V and his brother and heir, King Ferdinand; Anabaptism, on the other hand, had been universally condemned and expressly forbidden by Ferdinand since 1527.

In the records of interrogations and punishments in Augsburg, there are only a couple of incidents of Catholics being arrested for violating the 1537 Church Ordinance. This small number could result either from the low incidence of offenses or a lack of interest on the part of the city council. The most significant cases happened in the years immediately following the ordinance, none appear after 1539. A few other cases involved Protestants, such as one arrested for criticizing the city's preachers, which shows that resistance could come from within the ranks, as well. Citizens in favor of reform did not necessarily accept the settlement reached by Augsburg's evangelical preachers. The existing cases give us a sense of how the city council treated these offenders and, consequently, how it viewed its role in supporting the Reformation and enforcing uniformity.

Two cases involving Catholics deal with people seeking Catholic sacraments outside the city walls, in one case for marriage and in the other baptism. People also went outside the city walls to receive the Eucharist, but that could more easily be kept secret than the events of marriage and baptism which were not just spiritual events effecting the individual soul but also rites of passage with significance for the social community. In both recorded instances, the destination was Lechhausen, a small Bavarian village which lies close to the eastern gate of the Jakob's Quarter and is now a suburb of Augsburg. The Bavarian dukes held firmly for Catholicism and lent support to the Catholics in Augsburg, a policy which only aggravated the rivalry which had existed for centuries between the duchy and the imperial city. Altogether, Bavaria, the bishopric (*Hochstift*) of Augsburg and the Habsburg county of Burgau surrounded the city of Augsburg on all sides and served as havens for Augsburg's Catholics.

In May of 1539, Barbara Hertnitin, attended her maid's Catholic wedding ceremony, which took place in Lechhausen, and then hosted the wedding party at her tavern.[12] This was no clandestine affair of religious defiance; the wedding party brashly played drums and pipes

---

[12] Barbara Hertnitin also appears in Chapter One.

both on the way out of Augsburg and on the way back into town.[13] Hertnitin, her husband Ulrich Hertnit, and two musicians were subsequently arrested. There is no interrogation record for the bride and groom (the Hertnits' maid and her soldier husband), so we have little information on them.[14] Hertnitin claims that she never knew the soldier's name and only remembered that he had said he came from Aachen.[15] The Hertnits' maid and her new husband were not from Augsburg, and it seems they either left the city immediately after the wedding to avoid prosecution, or they may have been summarily exiled without an interrogation, as foreigners often were. A few days before Hertnitin's arrest, entries in the council records and the Punishment Book show that a Margaretha Raunerin of Inningen and Melchior Kag of Offingen were banished for having married against the council's decree.[16] As foreigners, they could readily be disposed of through banishment, without the fuss of lengthy interrogations. Since the maid and soldier are never identified by name in the course of Hertnit's interrogation, we do not know if they were the same couple or if they represent another illegal Catholic wedding.

The city council focused on Barbara Hertnitin, a citizen of Augsburg and the maid's mistress, as the responsible and punishable party. She was charged with accompanying the couple to Lechhausen for the ceremony and then holding the celebration in her house, thereby countenancing their violation of the ordinance. In turn, her husband, Ulrich Hertnit, was punished for having permitted his wife's activities, and the piper and drummer were punished for having provided musical accompaniment for the crime. A number of decrees in the 1530s and 1540s prohibited piping and drumming in the city, along with sled-riding and mummery, as disturbances to the peace and danger to decorum. An ordinance from 1541 forbade piping and drumming at weddings, while a previous ordinance from 1536 excluded weddings from the general proscription

---

[13] Lyndal Roper, "Going to Church and Street: Weddings in Reformation Augsburg," 98.

[14] In February 1540, a man named only as Dietel was to be banished for having been married outside the city. StadtAA, Reichsstadt, Geheimeratsprotokolle, 3 February 1540.

[15] "*Sy wiß nit wie der Lanndtsknecht haÿß, . . . hab sych von Ach genennet,*" ibid., Urg. 15 May 1539, Barbara Hertnitin.

[16] Ibid., Protokolle der Dreizehn, 7 May 1539; and ibid., Strafbuch, 10 May 1539.

against piping and drumming.[17] It is possible that piping and drumming were still legal at weddings in Augsburg in 1539—Hernitin's maid
claimed it was the custom—but the wedding itself was illegal because
of being performed in Catholic Lechhausen.

The bulk of Barbara Hertnitin's testimony is straighforward and
predictable. She claimed that she had not planned to attend the
wedding, but had been talked into it against her judgment, thereby
showing the interrogators her good intentions. Nonetheless, we do
not get a sense that she felt she had done anything wrong, although
she recognized that it was a mistake. Hertnitin stated that she had not
wanted or intended to go to her maid's wedding in Lechhausen, but
that her maid had begged her to come, since she had no other family
in Augsburg. In was customary for servants in Augsburg, who might
be foreigners with no relatives within the city, to invite the members
of their households to their weddings.[18] As the result of overwhelming
entreaties from her maid and the other guests, Hertnitin, therefore, was
persuaded to join them.

Barbara Hertnitin also denied having given the couple any advice
or encouragement to go to Lechhausen for the wedding. According
to her story, they did not necessarily go to Lechhausen for religious
reasons, and yet by going there they made it a religious issue for the
council. On the contrary, she testified that her maid had explained
the choice of Lechhausen in terms of time constraints. In Augsburg it
would take three days to announce the banns in church, and, according
to the maid, her prospective husband did not have enough money to
stay in Augsburg that long. Hertnitin's maid confided to her that she
was worried that if they were not married quickly, the soldier would
kidnap her and take her away with him. Because her maid was "a
pious person," Hertnitin says she took pity on her and agreed to all
their plans.[19] In this way, Hertnitin offered what she must have believed
would be a plausible explanation for her role. Nonetheless, Hertnitin
acknowledged that while she did not advise them on the wedding she
did not discourage them either, which is a surprising admission. She

---

[17] StAA, Schätze 16, fo. 24.
[18] Roper, 79 and 94.
[19] *"und das sy besorgt hab, wa sy nit eingesegnet, es wurde sy der Lanndtsknecht also mit im weckhfueren, dann ir magt als ain from mensch, hab sy erbarmet,"* StadtAA, Reichsstadt, Urg. 15 May 1539, Barbara Hertnitin.

does not seem to have tried to clear herself of blame as strenuously as she might have.

Barbara's husband, Ulrich Hertnit, who served as one of four city bailiffs, in addition to owning a tavern, was suspended from his office when his wife was arrested.[20] Although his involvement in the affair was not yet clear, he was immediately held suspect for permitting his wife to attend the wedding and host the subsequent celebration in their tavern. According to Barbara Hertnitin, the wedding took place without his knowledge or blessing, because he had concerns about the soldier's marital status, not his religion. Hertnitin attempted to clear her husband's name by denying his involvement rather picturesquely. "[Ulrich] would rather have beaten them out of the house with the drums and pipes, but she was entreated to go with them."[21] Regarding the musicians, who accompanied the party as it progressed in and out of town, Hertnitin explained that she had not wanted to allow them to play. The bride and her friends had insisted that it was the custom for drums and pipes to play from the house to the church and then home again. Once again, Hertnitin's maid convinced her to agree, after pleading three times with Hertnitin, "as her mother."[22]

Hertnitin repeatedly denied any wrong-doing, claiming that her only motivation was to support her maid and that she had only agreed after being beseeched not only by the maid but by many of her wedding party. Hernitin's defense consisted, then, not in denying her participation but in justifying it as the result of overwhelming persuasion for what she still insisted were just grounds. Hertnitin speaks in terms of honor (the maid's), expediency, affection, and custom, which together outweighed her misgivings and any fear she might have had of violating the council's right to enforce religious behavior. She explained that she did it not out of disrespect but on the "high pleading" of her

---

[20] Ulrich Hertnit was suspended from his office on 15 May 1539 because he allowed a papist wedding celebration to be held in his house and to go to Mass in Lechhausen with piping and drumming. "*Ulrich Hernit waibel und wirt ist darumb seins ampts entsetzt, das er ain un[u]tze Babsts hochzeit inn seinem hauß halten unnd mit drumel und pfeiffen gen Lechhausen zur Meß hat geen laßen,*" ibid., Protokolle der Dreizehn, vol. 5, 15 May 1539.

[21] "*...es sei mit irs manns wissen und willen nit beschehn, er hette sy lieber mit pfeiffen und trumen auß dem hauß geschlagen, aber sy sey dahin erbethen worden,*" ibid., Urg. 15 May 1539, Barbara Hertnitin.

[22] "*aber die selben anzaigt, es were der gebrauch hie das man von hauß auß die Trumel und pfeiffen biß fur die kirchen, unnd wider anhaimbs gebrauchen mochte, auff solhs hette sy es lassen beschehen, unnd hab solhs auß kainer verachtnus gethan, sonnder auff ir bethe, das zum drittenmal von ir magt an sy als ir mutter beschehen sei,*" ibid.

maid.[23] The maid and her guests at the wedding ceremony (*Kirchgang*) insisted that "it was an honorable thing [Barbara] did."[24] In Barbara Hertnitin's mind it may have been a bad thing to disobey the council's prohibition against attending Catholic ceremonies, but an even worse thing to deny the bride the honor of her mistress' presence at the most important social event of her life.

Despite the apparent defiance shown in disregarding the council's ordinance by attending and celebrating an illegal marriage, there is at first little evidence of religious conviction involved. That is not to say that Hertnitin did not have religious convictions but merely that they are underplayed, despite the council's leading questions. The interrogators referred insultingly to the Catholic wedding ceremony several times, but they never actually asked her what her beliefs were, and Hertnitin made no direct response to the accusations. According to Hertnitin, her reasons for going along with her maid's wishes were personal in nature and not religious. Question Three asked her, "why she had gone with the wedding party and assisted in the *godless work of the papacy;*" (my emphasis). Not rising to the bait, Hertnitin responded simply that her maid had asked her to do so.[25] She gave a similar answer to Question Six, which asked her "why she had *scorned the Christian community* and authority by aiding such *despicable priests' work.*"[26] Hertnitin replied that she had meant no disrespect but only wanted to please her maid and the guests on her wedding day. The interrogators' leading questions produced no protestation and no real sense of what this woman's religious beliefs were.

What were Barbara Hertnitin's true religious preferences? If she was Protestant, her convictions certainly did not deter her from supporting her maid's Catholic wedding. Although she had ample opportunity to defend herself in the interrogation, none of the objections she had made against participating in the wedding were based on religious grounds. The only real objection she claimed to have made was a concern that the soldier might not have been free to marry because of already having a wife, and she claimed that her husband had disapproved of the

---

[23] "*sy sei aus kainer verachtnus, sonder auff das hoch erbitten irer magt zum einsegnen ganngen*," ibid.

[24] "*und gesagt wie sy thut, were es doch ain Eerliche sach*," ibid., 20 May 1539.

[25] "*3 Uß was ursachen sie mit dem kirchgang ganngen unnd zu dem gotlosen werckh des Babstumbs geholffen hab*," ibid., 15 May 1539 (Fragstück).

[26] "*6 Warumb sie zuwerachtung der Christenlichen gemain und Oberkait alhie zu solchen schuoden pfaffen werckh helffen dorffe*," ibid.

marriage for the same reason. Hertnitin testified that she had asked the soldier about it, and he had denied having any previous ties, so her worries on that count were allayed. Actually, the Hertnits most likely had no religious objections to participating in a Catholic wedding, except for the risk of getting into trouble. The strongest evidence for their religious affiliation appears in a case from six years earlier, in which the Hertnits appear in an incidental reference. This case indicates that Barbara Hertnitin and her husband were almost certainly Catholic. In 1533, a tavernkeeper named Hertnit had fired Elizabeth Schenk from her job as a barmaid, for refusing to attend Catholic services at the Cathedral of Our Lady.[27] Between 1533 and 1539 there were no other Hertnits in Augsburg besides Ulrich and Barbara, and we know that they owned a tavern. As a Catholic, Barbara Hertnitin had good reasons to hide her true religious feelings from the council.

Either way, one would expect Hertnitin's defense of her spiritual position to be rather more convincing than it was. On the one hand, as an apparently loyal Catholic, she might defend her faith when the interrogators spoke of it critically. On the other hand, frightened by interrogators—who we can assume might be somewhat intimidating—it would be prudent for her to champion the Gospel, as proof of Protestant sympathy. Other suspects in similar situations defended themselves in a more adamant manner than Barbara Hernitin. Defendants whose religious allegiance was questioned tended to use some variation of, "I hold the Gospel to be right" (*ich halt den Evangelion fur Recht*) to show their support of the new faith, but Hertnitin never made her commitment explicit despite her arrest. She never tries to convince the interrogators that she opposed the wedding on religious grounds, which they clearly wanted to hear. Instead she merely explained that, "if she had known that [her actions] were offensive to the honorable council *to that extent*, she would have refused, because she likes the evangelical sermons just as much, and she listens to them as gladly as to the others."[28] Not exactly an inspiring testimony of faith. The term "to that extent" (*dermassen*), suggests that she had not expected the council to object as strongly as it did to her participation in the wedding, even though she obviously knew it was inappropriate if not downright illegal. While she tried to

---

[27] See Chapter One.

[28] "*wan sy aber gewußt, das solhs wider ain Erbernn Rath dermassen gewesen were, wolt sy solhs wol underlassen haben, dann die predig des Evangeliums sei ir gleich als lieb, und hoer die als gern, als ander,*" ibid. (emphasis mine)

explain that her actions were not based on a rejection of the Protestant faith, she clearly admits, like others before her, to keeping her options open, listening to evangelical sermons as gladly as to Catholic ones. Her case provides an excellent illustration of how people developed their faith by sampling different sermons and shows that they may not have felt the need to make a choice among them.

In her second hearing, Barbara Hertnit answered further questions which aimed at the extent of her disobedience rather than at her motives in supporting the wedding. She never denied attending the wedding in Lechhausen and hosting the celebration in her home, instead she provided viable explanations for her behavior, based on social responsibilities, as surrogate mother, to her maid. Nevertheless, she had raised the council's curiosity about her faith; they pursued the case, with a second interrogation, to establish whether or not she was a crypto-Catholic. Two points in particular are telling. The second question asked her, "where else she attended church until now and heard the Word of God."[29] She responded that "since they had abolished the Mass, she went to no church but St. Moritz. There she heard the Word of God from the minister Herr Bonifacius [Wolfart], whom she praised for having first made a righteous person out of her."[30] The place where one attended sermons gave the most accurate indication of one's beliefs at this time.[31] While confessional names had little meaning or use in this period, the church one attended reflected a choice about whose preaching one wanted to hear or in whose company one wanted to attend services, presumably with like-minded people. The council's question about where Hertnitin attended church reflects their recognition that the location where a person worships was the best sign of her religious affiliation. Hertnitin readily acknowledged that it was the council's ban on Catholic services that persuaded her to attend evangelical sermons. She also admitted that she had not gone to

---

[29] "2 Wo sie sunst bishere zu kirchen gangen und das wort gottis gehoret hab," ibid., 17 May 1539 (Fragstück).
[30] "Sagt sy sey seidther man die mes abgethan hab, in kain kirchen ganngen, dann geen Sannt Moritzen, daselbs hab sy von Herrn Bonofacius predigkanndten das gots wort gehort, dem sy auch das lob gebe, das er erst ain Recht mensch auß ir gemacht hab, Aber sy sey ettlich wuchen krannckhait halben irs leibs, an kainer predig gewest," ibid. Bonifacius Wohlfart was pastor at St. Anna's church, on the recommendation of Martin Bucer, until it was closed in 1534 by the city council and then at St. Moritz from 1534 to 1543, Augsburger Stadtlexikon.
[31] The importance of locating the site of one's religious worship is exemplified in the Germair-household case, discussed in Chapter One.

church for several weeks because of an illness (an illness that was not severe enough to keep her from going to Lechhausen). When she was asked if she had previously attended Mass in Lechhausen, how often, and on which days, Hertnitin stated that she had not attended Mass in Lechhausen or anywhere else and did not ask about it. However, she did admit that she had recently gone to a Catholic church-festival (*Kirchweih*) in Derching, beyond Lechhausen.

Barbara Hertnitin explained that her decisions to attend the Catholic affairs mentioned in her interrogation—the wedding and the *Kirch-weih*—were motivated by social events rather than routine religious devotion. At least, her preference for Catholic worship does not seem to have been compelling enough for her to risk defying the council on a regular basis. Her responses to the interrogation reflect her accommodation with the new order: she had been a follower of the old faith until it was forbidden in 1537 and then attended evangelical services from that point on. Although she indicated a special appreciation for the preaching of Bonifacius Wolfart, she never claimed to be a supporter of the Gospel or reform. Rather, she demonstrated a willingness to go along with the religious changes outwardly at least. Her religious practices showed both deference to the law and open-mindedness to different kinds of sermons; she liked the Protestant sermons just as much as the Catholic ones.

Hertnitin based her defense on the social bonds within a household, which carried obligations for a mistress towards her maid. She proposed that her maid's officially marrying in some church with the presence and support of her mistress (as the closest thing to kin in the city) was more important than loyalty to a new religion or obedience to a two-year old statute, which had included the concession that it might change when a national church council took place. Barbara Hertnitin clearly expected the council to understand her position and to appreciate the social value of the marriage. To some extent she was right; in the midst of investigating her religious transgressions, the interrogators asked about the groom's marital status. In this way both mistress and council tried to make sure the marriage would be legitimate regardless of where the wedding was held.

In the first years following the new Church Ordinance of 1537, it may have been unclear to Augsburgers just how seriously the council would prosecute violators. People like Barbara Hertnitin, who tested the new order, apparently expected a certain degree of tolerance or understanding from the authorities. In addition, the vague statement regarding which sermons she preferred—the evangelical sermons being as good as any other—would not seem to be the most useful or compelling defense, but perhaps her apparent candor had resonance with the interrogators. A willingness to attend the officially sanctioned sermons may have been all they expected or required. Nonetheless, her lack of commitment is noteworthy, given the extensive proselytizing efforts of Augsburg's evangelical preachers in the 1530s. Her case confirms the uphill battle that councils and ministers faced trying to convince people to make exclusive religious commitments.

In a last vain effort to coerce more information from Barbara Hertnitin, the interrogators threatened her with the application of thumbscrews. A note in the accompanying list of questions (*Fragstück*) gave the interrogators permission to place the thumbscrews on her, if she would not answer willingly, but not to tighten them. This restraint on behalf of the council indicates that they did not consider the matter serious enough for extreme measures or perhaps they had no wish to create a Catholic martyr. This is a striking difference from the situation of women Anabaptists, who were routinely subjected to torture with thumbscrews if they refused to answer questions about accomplices. In response to this threat of torture, Hertnitin reiterated once more that she had not been thinking of the Mass, and what she had done was for honor's sake and for the good of her maid.[32] Regardless of her private faith—whatever that may have been—or her public accommodation, Hertnitin utilized the notion of honor as a defense for her violation of the city's religious settlement. She, and those who went with her to Lechhausen, chose to see her maid's wedding carried out in an honorable and timely fashion rather than obey the council's church ordinance.

Barbara Hertnitin was held in prison in chains for several days and then remanded to the council for a lecture. Her husband Ulrich and the musicians, none of whom were interrogated, were each sentenced to three days in the tower.[33] Although an entry in the council minutes indicated that Ulrich Hertnit was to be removed from his office, as a

---

[32] "*sy habe nit vermaint noch gedacht, das sy darmit wider ain Erbern Rath hanndeln solte, dann es sey ir bey hochster warhait die meß in ir gedanncken nit komen, unnd was sy gethan hab sey von Eeren wegen, irer magt zu gutem beschehen,*" StadtAA, Reichsstadt, Urg. 17 May 1539, Barbara Hertnit.

[33] Ibid., Strafbuch 1533–39, 22 May 1539 (Barbara Hörtnitin and Ulrich Hörtnit) and 29 May 1539 (Paul Koler piper and Georg Graw drummer).

result of this incident, that never happened. Hertnit received all four of his quarterly payments for his services that year in full and continued to do so into the next decade.[34]

Three days after Barbara Hertnitin's punishment was recorded in the Punishment Book, the city council issued a decree against "Foreign Ceremonies." In this decree, the council stated that "men and women, in no small number, were despising the preaching of the pure Word of God [in Augsburg] and pursuing foreign teaching and ceremonies in the countryside," which happened, as the council noted, "undoubtedly more out of disrespect for the council than Christian devotion."[35] Consequently,

> it [was] the council's earnest desire and command of each and every male and female citizen, resident, and subject, young or old, of whatever condition or status they might be, that from now on no one from within [Augsburg] will go, ride, or drive, or in any other way visit or make use of the teaching, preaching, Sacraments, and church services within a mile radius around the city,[36]

Did the council have Barbara Hernitin in mind? Undoubtedly, and apparently she was not alone. Despite the threats of serious punishment, from which no one was to be excluded, the council faced a violation of this new decree just a few weeks later.

In this next case, a group of women took a baby to Lechhausen for a Catholic baptism. The party included the baby's aunts, a nurse, another woman, and a male servant. The affair was arranged by the baby's maternal grandmother, Helena Meutingin. Although Meutingin, a wealthy Augsburg citizen, did not accompany the group, it was clearly under her direction and command that the baptism was carried out. In her place she had sent two of her daughters, Ursula Ehingerin and Anna Weissenprunnerin, presumably to serve as godparents, which

---

[34] According to the Strafbuch on 22 May 1539, Ulrich Hertnit's only punishment was to spend three days in a tower, with no mention of losing his office. See also the Baumeisterbuch for 1539.

[35] "*Allso das manns unnd weibs personen nit inn geringer anzal, die predig des Rainen götlichenn worts alhie verachtenn unnd frembder Lere unnd Ceremonien uff dem Lannd nachlauffen, ungezweifellt mer aus verachtung der oberkait dan Christennlicher andacht,*" ibid., Schätze 16, 25 May 1539.

[36] "*So ist ains Erbarn Rats ernnstlicher will unnd gepeüt hiemit allenn unnd ÿedenn irn Burgern, Burgerin, inwonern unnd unnderthanen Jung unnd allt, was wesenns oder Stannds die seÿenn, das fürohin nÿemannd von hinnen aus inn ainer gannzen meil wegs die negst, rings umb dise Stat, die widerwerttige Lere, Predigenn, Sacrament unnd kirchenndiennst weder mit geen, Reitenn, farn, noch in ainig annder weis besuchenn, oder sich derselbenn geprauchen soll,*" ibid.

means that the infant was most likely female. The baby's nursemaid, Ännli, another woman named only as Dichtlin from Munich, and a male servant completed the group.

Sibilla Schrenckin, the baby's mother, did not accompany them to Lechhausen. If the baptism took place shortly after the birth, she was probably still in childbed and not able to travel. She was not interrogated, and there is no indication of her role in planning the baptism, nor is there any sign that she was punished in any way. Likewise, the child's father, Bartholomäus Schrenck from Notzingen, is not mentioned at all in the case records.[37] It seems odd that the parents were not questioned about the matter by the council. In fact, they are conspicuously absent from the legal proceedings regarding their daughter's baptism. From other sources we know that Schrenck was not an Augsburger and that he was in the service of the dukes of Bavaria, which means not only that he was Catholic—and presumably supported the undertaking—but also that he was beyond the council's jurisdiction.

It is unclear how the council became aware of the incident. The group might have drawn someone's attention while passing through the city gate, a neighbor might have informed on them, or perhaps they aroused suspicion by not having the child baptized in one of the city churches. After all this was not the child of some anonymous vagrant but the offspring of a well-to-do family. There is no official interrogation record for this case, and it seems probable that there never was one. Instead, references to the case appear in notes of business discussed by the Small Council on 17 and 19 June 1539 and in entries of the book where the punishments were recorded. Thus, the council seems to have handled the case rather informally, perhaps to avoid scandal. Either the magistrates did not want to publicize yet another transgression of their religious settlement or the offenders' social status made it wise to handle the matter more diplomatically. The only people questioned in the case appear to have been the nursemaid and Gertrud Plaphartin, who was in the city's employ as midwife, though she did not participate in the baptism. Their answers agreed regarding who had participated in the baptism. The nursemaid testified that it was Helena Meutingin, the maternal grandmother, who had ordered that the child be baptized outside the city, and she revealed to the council that the household

---

[37] Bartholomäus Schrenck was a noble and the ducal Bavarian Rentmeister in Munich and Pfleger zu Eckmühl. Seifert *Genealogischer Stammtafel*, SStBA.

had actually discussed the fact that it was forbidden to take the baby to Lechhausen.[38] As a result, they could hardly plead ignorance of the council's decree.

The grandmother, Helena Meutingin, and the nursemaid, Ännli, were punished for pursuing the forbidden sacrament on the child's behalf. Meutingin had directed the plot, and Ännli had carried the child to the baptism. If she served as a wetnurse to the baby, her participation would have been crucial to making the trip feasible. The council recorded the women's punishments in their minutes. Meutingin was to be sentenced to three weeks in the tower; the nursemaid received three days, the same as Barbara Hertnitin's accomplices, her husband Ulrich and the musicians. Alternatively, Meutingin was to be offered the option of paying three gulden in exchange for each day in the tower. This concession was probably offered out of consideration both for her social position and her age, which might have made an extended stay in the tower dangerous to her health. Helena Adlerin had married Lucas Meuting thirty-seven years earlier in 1502, which meant that she could have been about sixty. The Punishment Book records that Meutingin paid thirty gulden into the Poor Relief Fund (*Almosenseckel*) rather than spending time in the tower, while Ännli spent the required three days "willingly and obediently."

The punishment of the nursemaid seems rather unfair and even uncharacteristic of the council's usual rationale. She was clearly in a dependent position, following the orders of her employers, which the council would usually take into account. However, the council may have seen her assistance as a violation of the decree from March of 1537 which forbade midwives to perform baptisms themselves, except in the case of emergencies, and instead ordered them to carry the infants to baptism and not hinder the baptism in anyway.[39] This decree was intended to ensure that baptisms were carried out by the proper authorities, the evangelical ministers, and not administered by unqualified lay people or in prohibited ceremonies, such as Catholic rites. It also attempted to ensure that Anabaptists did not withhold their children from infant baptism. By carrying the infant to a Catholic baptism in

---

[38] "*Das Ennli zaigt an, die Meutingin habs haißen das kynd daußen tauffen, es sei im hauß davon geredt das es verpotten sei,*" StadtAA, Reichsstadt, Lit. 17 July 1539.

[39] "*Eodem die [27 March 1537], erkennt, das den hebamen ernnstlich gesagt, und verpoten werden sölle, das sie hinfüro kain kind mer, annderst dann in der Noth, tauffen, sonnder zur tauff tragen unnd daran kains wegs verhindern sollen,*" ibid., Ratsbuch 1529–40, 27 March 1537.

Lechhausen, the nursemaid, Ännli, directly flouted the spirit, if not the letter, of this ordinance.

The infant's two aunts, Ursula Ehingerin and Anna Weissenbrun-nerin, who presumably served as godparents in Lechhausen, received nothing more than a visit from the mayors.[40] On 19 June, the Council of Thirteen noted that Ulrich Rehlinger and Georg Wieland would instruct the two women that the council was very offended by their going to Lechhausen, and that if they wanted to remain in Augsburg, they would have to obey the council's ordinance. One reason for this restrained treatment appears in the directions for the reprimand, which defined their offense as "having allowed the child to be baptized in Lechhausen."[41] On the other hand, the matriarch of the family, Helena Meutingin, had not only, "allowed her daughter's child to be taken out of Augsburg and baptized in Lechhausen," but had also, "com-manded, ordered, and directed it to happen."[42] Therefore, although Meutingin had not gone out to Lechhausen in person, she earned the severest punishment by having been the mastermind and compelling force behind the entire affair. Having her sentence commuted to a fine, however, must have taken the sting out of the sentence for the affluent Meutingin.

One reason for the council's leniency may have been the Meuting family's influence in the political, social, and financial worlds of Augs-burg and Europe. Helena Meutingin was the widow of Lucas Meuting, a wealthy Augsburg merchant and former Fugger agent with connections, through marriage, to the Welser, Fugger, and von Stetten families.[43] One branch of the Meuting family joined the patriciate and had recently provided a bishop to the see of Chiemsee. Helena's father, Philip Adler, had served as a courtier to Emperor Maximilian I and counted among the ten wealthiest families in Augsburg. Her sister's marriages connected her to future-emperor King Ferdinand's financial ministers,[44] as well

---

[40] Ulrich Rehlinger was Zwinglian; Georg Wieland was Eitelhans Langenmantel's brother-in-law and had business connections in Salzburg.

[41] *"Darumb das sie der Schrenckin kynd zu Lachhausen tauffen laßen wider ains Rats verbott,"* ibid., Lit. 19 June 1539.

[42] *"Umb das sie über ains erbern Rats beruęff irer tochter der Schrenckin kind von Augspurg ausfueren unnd zu Leechhausen tauffen lassen hat, dasselbig also zugeschehen bevolhen, gehaissen, und angeordnet,"* ibid., Strafbuch 17 June 1539.

[43] See the *Augsburger Stadtlexikon* for more information on the Meuting, Adler, and Ehinger families.

[44] Ursula Adlerin had married first Jacob Villinger and later Johann Löblin, both financial ministers of King Ferdinand.

as the Welser and Höchstetter families.[45] Her daughters, Ursula and Anna, who stood as godmothers to the infant, were well-married to men with connections in Spain and Salzburg.[46] Her son, Jakob Meuting lent great sums of money to King Ferdinand. Thus, Helena Meutingin was connected through blood, marriage or business to Augsburg's elite families.[47] Ties to the Emperor and his brother provided Meutingin and her daughters with the most influential Catholic patronage.[48] Marital connections to powerful families in Augsburg would also have provided a considerable degree of security from prosecution one can assume. One almost wonders that she was punished at all. Her connections and status in Augsburg society explain the relatively light punishment and the absence of any formal interrogation records. Without those records we know, perhaps, why Meutingin felt it was safe to risk violating the law but not her motivation for defying the council so purposefully.

Augsburg's council attempted to restrict their citizens' access to Catholic services in the years immediately following the prohibition of the Mass and expulsion of Catholic clergy in 1537. Clearly some people felt the risk of punishment was worth the benefit of Catholic ceremonies for rites of passage such as marriage and baptism. It is difficult to assess how many might have violated the council's church ordinance, but the absence of many arrests, when the records for this period are otherwise extant, indicate that either the numbers were not high or the council chose not to pursue them, at least not as vigorously as they sometimes prosecuted Anabaptists. For example, the council did

---

[45] Of Helena's half-sisters, Anna had married Franz Welser (Anna and Franz were the parents of Philippine Welser who married Archduke Ferdinand in 1557), brother of the devoted Catholic Bartholome V Welser; Barbara had married their cousin, Hans Welser; and Benigna had married Joseph Höchstetter.

[46] Ursula and Anna were married to Augsburger Ulrich Ehinger and Salzburger Georg Weissenbrunner, respectively. Ehinger was among the most important German merchants in Spain and was knighted by Emperor Charles V in the Order of Santiago. According to the 1539 *Steuerbuch*, Jerg Weissenbrunner lived in a wealthy quarter known as "Von Sant Anthonino," with notables such as the Welsers, Rehlingers, Peutingers, and so on, as neighbors. Likewise, Ulrich Ehinger, lived near the Shoemakers' House, with neighbors Bernhard Rehlinger and Jorg von Stetten.

[47] A granddaughter, her namesake Helena, married Claudius Eusebius Peutinger, grandson of Augsburg's famous humanist, Conrad Peutinger, who was city scribe (*Ratschreiber*) and legal advisor. Marriages to other important families in Augsburg, included the Rehlinger, Vetter, Langenmantel, and Arzt

[48] Helena's brother-in-law, Johann Löblin, royal financier to King Ferdinand, had interceded with the council for her daughter Felicitas and her new husband, Dr. Johann Veit, when they secretly held a Catholic wedding Mass in 1534. StadtAA, Reichsstadt, Protokolle der Dreizehn, 12 September 1534.

not ask anyone in the Hertnitin or Meutingin cases who else attended
Catholic services with them. The existence, however, of decrees chas-
tising people for leaving the city for Catholic services and occasional
references to such transgressions in the council minutes, though not
in interrogation records, suggests that there was a definite element of
defiance from Catholics in the city.

Later in the summer of 1539, the council continued to encounter
affronts to the new religious order, but of a different sort. On 13 August
Wilhelm Gemelich was arrested and interrogated for criticizing the
city's preachers and, by implication, the city council. The records of
the Small Council state that, because of several speeches he had made
against the preachers, Gemelich was put in irons and should appear
before the council.[49] The first answer in his interrogation indicates
that Gemelich had insulted the preachers as a group. Unfortunately,
no one particular preacher is named in either the council's records or
the interrogation record, and there is no List of Questions. Nor do we
know what exactly Gemelich had said about them. In his interrogation,
Gemelich stated that "he neither opposed nor hated the preachers. He
treated everyone as he was treated." Referring to how one was "treated"
suggests that he may have had personal rather than theological differences with some of the preachers.

Continuing his defense, Gemelich stated, "he also went to their
sermons and had a brother-in-law who was a preacher at St. Stefan's,
to whom he had recently given thirty gulden."[50] Johann Ehinger, the
preacher at St. Stefan, was married to Wilhelm's sister, Anna Gemelich.
Ehinger had formerly been an assistant to Wolfgang Musculus, the
evangelical minister at Holy Cross, until he got his own parish in 1537.[51]
Thirty gulden was quite a hefty sum to give as a gift, but Gemelich,
who was a goldsmith, was probably rather well-to-do. In any case, he
mentioned it to give evidence of his support and approval of the city's
ministers in general.

---

[49] "*Wilhelm Gemelich von wegen etlicher reden wider die predicanten geubt, in eisen gelegen, und sol sich fur Rath stellen,*" ibid., 14 August 1539.

[50] "*Den Erstenn, er seie ine weder feind noch hessig sonder gonne jedem was ime gonne er gee auch an ir predig hab ein schwager der seie auch ain predicant alhie zue Sant Steffann, dem hab er neulich xxx guldin geschenckt,*" ibid., Urg., 13 August 1539, Wilhelm Gemelich.

[51] Johann Ehinger was also brother-in-law to Bernhard Unsynn, a Schwenkfeldian, who may or may not have been related to Gemelich as well. For more on Ehinger, see the *Augsburger Stadtlexicon.*

Regarding the critical speech itself, which, unfortunately, is not recorded, Gemelich flatly denied having said anything of the sort, adding emphatically, that if he had said it, he had no knowledge of it, and if the speech was from him, then he was truly sorry. Such all-encompassing denials are common from defendants, especially in cases involving critical speeches or public insults, for which there could be no evidence except witness testimony. This attempt to cover all grounds, making one's responses conditional on the evidence found against him, almost suggests that the defendant was unsure of his own actions. More likely it stemmed from knowing that witnesses could be produced who could testify to the council that he had made the statements, even if they were not true, and one did not want to be accused of lying, in addition to everything else.

Besides having offended the preachers, Gemelich was also accused of having criticized the city council. Again, we do not know what Gemelich may have said about the council, but criticism of the preachers would have indirectly implied criticism of the authority that hired them for office. He added that he had said nothing against the Gospel, because he knew the Gospel was right.[52] Supporting the Gospel was a way for Gemelich to express general support for evangelical preaching, which received this name from professing to teach from it alone. Gemelich was released the next day on the strength of a petition without any further punishment. Unlike Barbara Hertnitin, Gemelich readily claimed to support Protestantism. However, we do not know what type of Protestantism he preferred nor with which ministers he had had a falling out. At the very least, the case shows that a Protestant could also run into trouble with Augsburg's religious regime, but Gemelich had seen trouble before.

Sixteen years earlier, almost to the day, Wilhelm Gemelich had been arrested and interrogated extensively regarding a vast number of offenses. By 1523 some Augsburgers had begun aggressively demanding church reform, and the city council feared disgruntled citizens would plot an uprising. In fact, that summer a group of men gathered one evening in St. Moritz to make plans for approaching the council with a

---

[52] *"wider ain erbern Rat hab er gar nichts geredt, deßgleichen wider das Evanglion auch dann er wiß das des Evangelion gerecht seie,"* StadtAA, Reichsstadt, Urg. 13 August 1539, Wilhelm Gemelich.

list of grievances.[53] In August of 1523 Wilhelm Gemelich, like several others, was arrested by a rather nervous council and interrogated about his involvement in those plans and any other potential plans to attack the city and council. The breadth of issues touched on in Gemelich's 1523 interrogation suggests that the council did not know exactly what it was looking for but was examining all suspicious persons.

Gemelich's testimony reveals something about where his sympathies lay then. On his way out of St. Anna on 12 August, where he had attended services, Gemelich was invited to join the men meeting in St. Moritz. Although he seems not to have participated actively in the events of 1523, at least not as one of the organizers, Gemelich was probably a supporter of the new evangelical faith. The Carmelite monks at St. Anna were some of the earliest supporters of Luther in Augsburg. St. Anna's prior, Johann Frosch, was an old friend of Luther's and one of the first priests to be married in Augsburg. Gemelich was friends with several of the other men who were arrested in 1523, including Sixtus Saur, who was also a supporter of the evangelical Franciscan monk Johann Schilling in 1524.[54]

Gemelich's allegedly offensive statements in 1539, were probably not motivated by loyalty to the Catholic church. Rather, they may have stemmed from some kind of theological dispute which occurred among evangelical reformers. In the 1530s Zwinglian, Lutheran and other ministers fought zealously for control of the Reformation in Augsburg. Gemelich might have disagreed with a minister on a doctrinal issue, or he might have had a personal difference with one of the preachers. Many initial supporters of the Reformation were unhappy that the Protestant churches did not make significant changes in morality and in other areas. Gemelich's objections could have been based any of a number of issues, moral, political, financial, and so on. In one of his answers, Gemelich claimed rather flippantly that "he knew nothing either evil or bad about the preachers, but then he did not know them

---

[53] Soon after, there was an incident at the Franciscan church (Barfüßer), where a Mass book was taken from a monk and thrown in a basin of holy water. Many of the same men were involved. See Chapter Two for a discussion of this incident.

[54] Johann Schilling was the lector (Leßmeister) at the Franciscan (Barfüßer) Church. When the city council secretly forced him into exile, a mob of people gathered on the city hall square threatening to storm the city hall, if Schilling was not returned. Sixt Saur received a substantial annual salary of 136 gulden from the city, as a civil servant (Ratsdiener).

all."[55] Reserving judgment? Just being honest? Certainly he would not ally the council's concerns this way. His statement makes the case seem to be an issue of reputation, which suggests that he had insulted them on a point of honor rather than of religion.

Gemelich's case and the cases of Barbara Hertnitin and Meutingin show that the council was dedicated to policing offensives against the new religious order, whether material or verbal, from Catholics and Protestants. They also show the persistence of Augsburg's citizens in forming their own opinions about their religious beliefs and practices. In the preface to the 1539 decree regarding foreign ceremonies, the Augsburg council explained its position. "Thus, the honorable council, as a Christian and proper authority, finds itself responsible to preserve and maintain this wholesome instruction (*hailwerttig Lere*) as much as possible."[56] As a result of asserting its right and responsibility to determine the religious character of Augsburg's population, the council encountered opposition to its authority. Even in a time of official religious unity, with much popular support for the legal faith, the city contained elements of disobedience. At the same time, the council seems to have treated the offenders rather mildly. The authorities and the citizens were measuring the limits of each other's resolve and of the new order's viability in an age of changing religious norms. The ordinance of 1537, which established the new church in Augsburg, took the precaution of suggesting that it was merely provisional, until a nation-wide church council could make a final decision on the religious issues. In addition, the city's elite families, who ruled the council, were very much divided.

In the course of the following decade, other Augsburgers met with difficulties accommodating themselves to the city's new religious order, because their faith deviated from the legally prescribed norms. It was not always a matter of confessional differences *per se* but sometimes of theological nuances. In May 1541, Katharina Kunigin was arrested and questioned regarding the overdue baptism of her youngest child. Kunigin's decision to postpone the child's baptism led to suspicions that she was an Anabaptist. Although her position on baptism suggested

---

[55] "*Den Andern, er wiß nichts weder ubels noch args von den predicanten dan er kenn sie doch nit alle,*" StadtAA, Reichsstadt, Urg. 13 August 1539, Wilhelm Gemelich.

[56] "*So befindt sich ain Erber Rath als ain christennliche ordennliche oberkait, schulldig dieselbig hailwerttig Lere sovil muglich zuerhallttenn unnd zuhanndthabenn,*" ibid., Schätze 16, 25 May 1539.

some similarity to Anabaptist views, she did not describe herself as belonging to a distinct sect or even being at odds with her fellow Christians in Augsburg; she never referred to brethren or spoke of herself as a "sister," a common sign of an Anabaptist at that time. Nonetheless she held certain views that made her religious position unique and reveal that she was influenced by forces other than the preachers she heard in church.

First, on the issue of her son's baptism, Kunigin told the interrogators that she had been prompted to have her son baptized when he expressed a wish to receive the Eucharist with her. Through this Kunigin realized that God had called him, so she decided to let him be baptized. She told her son that he had already been baptized with the blood of Christ but had not yet received the baptism of water. Kunigin stated that until that time she had not seen any need for it.[57] Kunigin described her understanding of baptism as having two aspects: a baptism by blood, which had already occurred through Christ's sacrifice, and one by water, which occurred when the individual felt the call to do so. She explained that the Lord's suffering had erased both original sin and all the sins of the world for those who believed and repented. According to her belief, "from the moment a child is born it sees and hears God and his Word in an internal spiritual way."[58] Kunigin held out the possibility that she might be persuaded to believe otherwise, if anyone could instruct her; yet she clearly stated that she had "observed God's command," suggesting tacitly that it superseded the council's command, which she had neglected. Her other children, two daughters and another son, had already been baptized as children, but we do not know if they were infants at their baptisms, because the interrogators did not ask her to give their ages.

Kunigin's view of baptism as something one did after being called by God to receive the sign was a belief held by the Anabaptists. They also shared the belief that Christ's sacrifice on the cross had wiped away original sin for believers (making infant baptism for the saving of

---

[57] "... *Sie hab uff den beruff gottes gemerckht, dann als neulicher zeit der knab sie angesprochenn hab ob sie ine nit mit ir zum nachtmal fürn wollt, hab sie ime angezaigt, wie das er noch nit mit dem wassertauff sonnder mit dem plut Christi getaufft sey, Also hab sie ine volgennd uß schickhunng unnd beruff Gottes tauffenn lassenn unnd vermerckht das er ainen guten willen zu Got hab*," ibid., Urg. 6 May 1541, Katharina Kunigin.

[58] "*Allso das sie acht wann ain kinndlein geborn werde, sehe unnd höre es alßbald Got unnd sein wort doch innerlicher gaistlicher weis, wiß sie aber yemann mit grunnd annders zuberichtenn es wöll sie sich weisenn lassenn*," ibid.

souls unnecessary), which was a position that Catholics and Protestants both rejected. Naturally the city council wondered about Kunigin's connection to Anabaptism. When asked if she had not once been an Anabaptist, Kunigin informed them that she had indeed "a long time ago given the brethren an accounting of her faith and thereupon received the sign on her brow, as the Prophet Esaias prescribed."[59] In fact, Katharina Kunigin had been baptized by Sigmund Salminger, an Anabaptist minister who was active in Augsburg in Spring 1527. Kunigin had been arrested in September of 1527, along with other Anabaptists from in- and outside of Augsburg. As a result of this prosecution, she and about thirty other Augsburgers took an oath to abandon Anabaptism and stay away from their meetings. The following year, in May 1528, Katharina Kunigin was arrested once again in an attempt to round up all remaining followers in the city, who had been missing from the major gathering on Easter Sunday.[60] At that time, Kunigin was quickly released by the council and described as being, "not in her right senses."[61]

When the council interrogated her thirteen years later about her son's baptism, they made no mention of any mental infirmity. We can assume, therefore, that it had been a temporary condition or at least that it did not interfere with her giving testimony in 1541. Like other incidents from the post-1537 period, Kunigin received relative leniency from the council. The list of questions for her interrogation indicates that she was to be asked "earnestly but not with force or torture."[62] In 1541, she was pardoned and then lectured by the council but received no other punishment. Although her beliefs were hardly orthodox, the council apparently considered her to be harmless. As far as they were concerned, Kunigin was a former Anabaptist who had been rather successfully integrated into Augsburg's legal religious community. She attended church services in Augsburg, but she still reserved her own opinions on particular issues like baptism. Her testimony reveals that

---

[59] "Zum 6ten Sie hab den Brüdern langst verganngner zeit rechenschafft irs glaubenns gebenn unnd nachvolgennd die bezaichtunng an ir stirn vonn inenn daruff genommen wie der Prophet Esaias darvon schreibe," ibid.

[60] See Chapter Three for more information on the Anabaptist prosecutions surrounding Easter Sunday, 12 April 1528.

[61] "Ist nicht bei synnenn unnd ferrer nicht gefragt worden," ibid., 16 May 1528, Katharina Stainmutzlin [Kunigin].

[62] "Soll um alles ernstlich doch nit peinlich oder mit dem daumenstokh gefragt oder angesprochen werden," ibid., 6 May 1541.

she was able to retain a considerable degree of independence in her belief system.

When asked how long she had remained "in this error [of Anabaptism],"[63] Kunigin responded that "she believed herself not to be in error but in the proper faith." She justified her position with a lengthy description of a vision she had had in which Christ spoke to her.

> She saw Christ as he had once been among humans on earth. In this vision, Kunigin's hands were bound, and she had a weight on her back, so she asked him for forgiveness of her sins. He turned to her right away and offered her his hand, at which the ropes and the burden fell from her, and she was released. Christ then disappeared, and a fountain flowing with grace and mercy appeared. After this Christ reappeared to her, carrying a cross in his hand, and spoke to her, saying he loved her so much that he had suffered death on the cross for her and asked her how much she loved him. To this Kunigin answered that she loved him enough that she would also go on the cross for him. He answered, then you love me enough. When he asked how much she loved her neighbor, she answered that she would give her life that her neighbor might be saved.[64]

After this Kunigin received an instruction from God according to which she was supposed to go through all the streets and call out, "improve yourselves, or God will punish the world!" However, since this command

---

[63] "*Wie lanng sie inn solchem irrtumb verjart,*" ibid. (Fragstück).

[64] "*Zum 7ten, Si verhoff si sey inn khainem irrthumb sonder im rechtenn glaubenn, Dann sie hab ains mals Christu wie der seiner zeit uff erdenn unnder den mennschen gewanndlet hab gesehenn nachdem sie aber gepunden gewesen unnd ain purd uff irem ruckh gehabt hab sie ine umb verzeyhunng irer sunnd gebettenn, hab ersich zustundan zu ir gewanndt ir die hannd pettenn, Alßballd sey die pürd vonn irem ruckhenn unnd auch die pannd vonn ir gefallen allso das sie der pannd unnd purde erledigt gewest, sey er vor ir verschwunden, darnach hab sie ainen prunnen gemes ainem schalprunnen vol gnad und barmhertzigkait fliessen sehen. Nachdem aber derselb auch verschwunden sey Christus ir abermals inn vorgemelltter gestalt ain Creutz inn seiner hannd habennd, erschinnen ir das Creutz zaigt unnd mit menschlicher stimm zu ir geredt, Wie das er sie so lieb gehabt das er auch den tod am kreutz für sie gelittenn hette, Wie lieb dann sie ine habenn wollte, dem sie geanntwurt, Herr so lieb will ich dich habenn das ich umb deinetwillen auch an das kreutz will, der ir geanntwurt, so hastu mich gnug lieb. Darauff er weitter zu ir geredt wie lieb sie dann iren negstenn habenn wollt, hab sie geantwurt, Herr so lieb will ich ine habenn, das ich mein lebenn für ine lassen will, damit er genese unnd selig werde. Nachvolgend sey ir ain eingebunng vonn Got kommen, das sie in alle gassenn lauffenn unnd rueffenn sollt, pessert Euch, dann Got will die wellt straffenn. Nachdem ir aber solchs durch vorgesehnen Christum nit mundtlich bevolhen wurdenn hab sie geacht wo sie solchs thette, Si wurd für sie ain thörin gehalltenn werdenn unnd Got us solchem kain lob erwachsenn, sie hab es aber dannoch etlichen predicanten angezaigt das sie solchs thun solltten damit es dannocht inn all gassenn kome. Mer hab sie sollenn schreyenn, wer die gnad gottes nit annemen wölle unnd sich pessern, uber die werde die gerechtigkait Gottes kommen. Letzlich hab sie schreye sollenn. Es werde groß plutvergiessenn in unnd usserhalb diser Stat Augspurg unnd im ganntzen Teutschlannd von Gottes wort wegen sich erheben dahin dann nit lang sey wo man sich nit pessere unnd pus thue das sey ir alles vonn Got eingegen worden,*" ibid., 6 May 1541.

was given to her silently and not orally by Christ, Kunigin interpreted that to mean that if she did such a thing, she would be considered crazy, in which case, God would gain no glory. Instead she told several preachers that they should deliver this message in order for it to reach all the streets. Moreover, she was supposed to call out, "whoever does not accept the grace of God and improve himself, will be judged by God," and "there will be great bloodshed in- and outside of the city of Augsburg and in all of Germany because of God's word, and it will not be far off if people do not amend their ways and repent."

The aspect of this vision which might have intrigued the city council the most, because of the potential for disturbing the peace or causing a public quarrel, was God's command that Katharina call out His message in the streets of Augsburg. In addition, the preachers would have been displeased at the idea of a woman taking on the[ir] role of messenger from God. However, Katharina Kunigin, despite her visions and her alleged mental incapacity (probably one and the same thing to the council members), very astutely allayed the authorities' fears by having decided—as she explained in the course of her story—not to undertake this task herself but to leave it to the officially appointed ministers. She explained that she did not want people to think she was a crazy woman (*"ain Thörin"*), because it would not help God's cause. Kunigin was probably sensitive to this possibility after being described as not in her right senses (*"nit bey sinnen"*) by the council in 1528. She surely also realized that it would relieve the council to hear that she did not intend to take her cause to the streets. She may have remained steadfast in her private beliefs, as her description of her position on baptism revealed, but she was no longer willing to display it as openly as she did a decade earlier. Like many Anabaptists faced with over-whelming persecution, in the form of imprisonment, exile or death, and deprivation of communal spiritual comfort, in the form of assemblies and ministers, she adapted to the world in which she found herself, as far as her conscience would allow, not unlike Barbara Hertnitin.

In 1544 another case showed the limits of the council's ability to control religious activities in Augsburg and the variety of activities that needed to be policed. If anything, it would have confirmed the need for watchfulness. In this case it was not an issue of criticizing the ministers, pursuing illegal sacraments or missing legal ones but a matter of using religious attributes sacred to the Catholic faith for illicit and supersti-tious purposes. A group of men and women were observed digging in a garden, reading from an unknown book, drawing symbols in the earth and generally acting mysteriously. An unusually high number of witnesses, forty in all, were questioned about what they had seen in Regina Kochin's garden. Regina Kochin was a mason's widow who supported herself and her young son Hennsle by selling vegetables, herbs, and even trees from her garden. From the questions posed in the list of questions, we can see that the council initially suspected Kochin of encouraging immoral sexual behavior in her house, in addition to the other charges of suspicious activities. The breadth of the questions in the list provided indicates that the council was not exactly sure what it was after. For example, they asked if she had heard ghosts in the house, but they pursued the charge of procuring as far they could.

The council was aware, probably through a neighbor who had complained, that two unfamiliar women had been staying in Kochin's house, which in itself was a violation of council policy against the unreported housing of foreigners. When a number of men subsequently came to the house for unknown purposes, they were immediately suspected of carrying on adultery and possibly prostitution. As a result, Kochin was interrogated three times and tortured twice, without success, to elicit information from her about her visitors' business. As the owner of the house, Regina Kochin could be held responsible for permitting them to use her home to commit adultery especially if she received payment in return. Although the council was not inclined to believe her statements, the testimony of the numerous witnesses, most of whom were neighbors who had known her for years, confirmed that she was not involved in any sexual wrong-doing. What Kochin's neighbors found most puzzling were the goings-on in her garden. The almost comically ineffectual efforts to keep the business secret—waving away the spectators, throwing dirt at them, and finally hanging up sheets to block their view—failed to keep the neighbors from seeing or hearing what the strangers were doing: they were digging for buried treasure. It was the odd behavior which accompanied the digging that mystified Kochin's neighbors and inspired the council's investigation.

When Otilia Wolkenstein from Nuremberg first approached Regina Kochin on Good Friday, 11 April 1544, about looking in her garden for a treasure, Kochin was skeptical and dismissed it as nonsense. She testified that Wolkenstein claimed the treasure, a whole pot full of money (*ain gannzer khessel vol gellts*), had been left to her eighteen years earlier by the house's former owner, a woman identified only as "Grissin."[65]

---

[65] StadtAA, Reichsstadt, Urg. 27 May 1544, Regina Kochin.

Kochin had never heard of the treasure and did not believe it would be found, but Wolkenstein insisted that she knew of a woman who could find the treasure for them. Six weeks later, on 21 May, Wolkenstein came to Kochin's house again, this time with Sophia Voitin, a friend from Nuremberg. Kochin admitted to her interrogators that she was finally persuaded to let them dig, although she still did not believe they would find anything. They had at last won her over to the plan with promises for how they would spend the money; one quarter would go to the hospital, a second would go to the poor, the third would go to the diggers, and the last quarter would go to Regina Kochin, as the owner of the house. She said that she did not worry about doing anything wrong since the garden was hers.[66]

Once plans for the digging were underway, Sophia Voitin took charge, while Kochin remained aloof, usually inside the house with Wolkenstein. To get started, Voitin required men to dig, and the women turned first to Wolkenstein's brother-in-law, Hans Meichsner. Meichsner was a cabinet-maker, married to a daughter of the Augsburger tavern-keeper Utz Menhart, Wolkenstein's father. Meichsner, in turn, sought out his good friend, shoemaker Georg Näßlin[67] to help with the digging. Näßlin brought along the weaver Claus Schmid. Finally the three men were joined by Jorg Weber, also known as Klein Jorg, who was Kochin's tenant. Known to the neighbors as "the Hessian," Jorg Weber agreed to help them because, he declared simply, "he had that day off anyway."[68] In addition to these men, engaged to dig in exchange for a piece of the treasure, Voitin needed one more thing for the operation: a priest. She asked Näßlin if he knew of a priest, and he immediately volunteered a man named Herr Hans (Johann Summerman), pastor of Täfertingen, a small village northwest of the city. According to Näßlin, Herr Hans was already in Augsburg anyway, and he joined them willingly.[69]

---

[66] "*Auf des hab sies inen vergunt zu graben, hab aber doch selbs nichts darvon gehalten, und gar nit gefurht noch besorgt, das sie daran unrecht thue, die weils in dem iren beschehe,*" ibid.

[67] He is undoubtedly the son of the shoemaker Georg Näßlin, who was arrested with his wife, Barbara, for iconoclasm in 1524 and Anabaptism in 1533. It is probably he (then a boy) who reportedly fetched the blood which his father's servant Leonhart had used to vandalize the Cathedral.

[68] "*weil er one das desselben tags gefeirt,*" ibid., 31 May 1544, Jorg Weber.

[69] "*habe ine di groß frau angesprochen, ob er in ain pfaffen wiß, des dorfft sie auch hierzu, hab er Hannsen pfaffer zu Deferdingen, der one das hie gewest, anzaigt… der auch gutwillig gewest,*" ibid., 31 May 1544, Jorg Näßlin.

Having gathered the necessary workforce, Sophia Voitin proceeded with her operation. With the combined testimonies of witnesses and suspects, we can reconstruct the following scene. Voitin, described by most of the witnesses as tall and by some as pretty, began by drawing a circle in the ground with a drawn sword. According to Walpurg Thenn, wife of the butcher Matheis Thenn, Voitin then sprinkled water on the circle, as if she were holding a holy water font and then drew four strokes inside the circle with a hoe.[70] A number of neighbors also saw a cross stuck in the ground and then covered with a cloth. Others observed Voitin walking around the circle with wax candles and reading from a book. One neighbor, Martha Paurenfeindin, actually claimed to have heard a few words, as Voitin sat in the circle and read from her book, "I beg you or I give you by the power of God," she was not sure which.[71] Voitin wore glasses while reading for some time and then passed the unidentified book on to the priest. The priest was also seen circling around the site, alternately reading and burning incense from a thurifier. Andreas Schmid, a baker, claimed to have seen the priest hold in his hand a plate, on which figures had been drawn in chalk, and then throw it down onto the ground, thereby indicating where they should dig.[72]

The men who took part in the excavation claimed not to know what the book was or not to understand it. Most likely the book was in Latin, containing prayers or psalms, which might explain why they did not understand or at least recognize it. A couple of decades of vernacular preaching may have made Latin a less familiar language to most citizens in Augsburg. A number of contemporary books were considered to hold the secrets to magical powers, including a so-called Sixth Book of Moses and the books of Sts. Christopher and Walburga. It is possible that the diggers did not want to admit to having understood it, if it was a forbidden Catholic text or something more

---

[70] "*mit ainem plossen schwerdt ain kraiß gemacht, in wellichem die fraw mit ainem wedelin gesprentzt gleich alls ob es weichtprunnen sey, unnd volgennd mit ainer hauen, vier straich in den kraiß gethan,*" ibid., 29 May 1544, Walpurg Thenn.

[71] "*unnd die hupscher frau, mitten in krayß gesessen ain puech uff der schoß gehabt darinn gelesen aber sy Zeugin nichtz annderst horn khonnden dann das sy die frau gesagt, Ich bitt dich oder ich beut dir bei der Crafft Gottes, (wiß nit weders)*" ibid., Martha Paurenfeindin.

[72] "*darnach sey ain man khomen den er fur ain Pfaffen angesehen, der hab ain Theller in der hanndt getragen mit kreiden uberschriben, in den grub dann ganngen unnd dasselbig Teller, uf die erdt geschlagen, innen damit gedeudet, wohin sy graben sollen,*" ibid., Andreas Schmidt.

nefarious, or they may simply have been too busy with the exertion of digging to pay attention.

The priest, Johann Summerman, was hardly a mysterious figure to the witnesses. What was he doing in Augsburg in 1544 when not digging for buried treasure? The witnesses who did not recognize him personally were still able to identify him readily as a priest by his clothing. Michael Widenman, horse-seller, saw "a man wearing an overgarment just like a priest."[73] The linen vestment he wore gave him away, which indicates that he did not try to hide his vocation. Some of the witnesses were actually able to identify him specifically as the pastor of Täfertingen or had at least heard that it was he. The diggers Hans Meichsner and Georg Näßlin confirmed this identification and added that he had carried an incense burner with glowing coals at the site. Moreover, the two men explained that they had said prayers with the priest before they began digging—giving the whole thing an air of religious ceremony or at least divine blessing. They said several psalms, the Our Father, and the Creed (unspecified), and then they were forbidden to speak as they proceeded to dig.

Oddly enough, the center of all this effort, the treasure, never surfaces in the course of the many interrogations, suggesting that it was never found. Instead, the conclusion to the case, described in the punishment of the suspects, addresses above all the crimes of superstition and the abuse of God's name for the purpose of finding gold. After interrogating Regina Kochin and forty witnesses (an unusually high number), the council lost interest in the issue of licentious behavior, due to a lack of evidence. When questioning the digging crew, they relegated the question of Kochin's being a procurer to one single inquiry which was saved until the end, almost as an afterthought. All of the diggers, including Kochin's tenant and her young son Hennsle, denied any knowledge of disreputable behavior on her part or any scandalous activities in her house. Her tenant Jorg Weber said, "he had neither seen nor perceived any dishonorable doings in his landlady's house; she's not that type." The council dropped the matter and did not refer to it in Kochin's sentence, which concentrated on the housing foreigners and permitting superstitious activities in her garden.

In this case, the council punished everyone involved, unlike other cases, where the punishments appear to have been more selective.

---

[73] "*ainer in ainem leibkitelin ainem pfaffen gleich,*" ibid., Michael Widenman.

The two Nurembergers, Sophia Voitin and Otilia Wolkenstainin, were banished on 29 May, before the other interrogations were finished. There is no interrogation record for either of them. Specific orders aimed to remove them from the city as speedily as possible; two city guards were directed to escort them immediately to their quarters to pack their things and leave. The sentence listed Voitin's many nefarious activities as follows,

> Sophia Voitin... drew a circle, walked around it carrying candles,... took a naked sword and marked the ground where one should dig, sat down in the circle, placed a crucifix and covered it with a cloth, read aloud from a book, where the village priest also sat and read, both drew crosses and other symbols, in short, they tried to find a treasure, and along with these superstitious deeds and aims, they also abused the name and Word of God.[74]

In short, they were punished for superstitious and irreverent behavior.

Regina Kochin and the diggers received their sentences on 3 June. Kochin had been held in prison since 27 May but was subsequently released because of a submissive petition. She was also lectured by the council for having housed foreigners without reporting it to the council and for having permitted her guests to dig for treasure in her garden without the knowledge of the authorities and consequently "to do all sorts of diabolical, supernatural, and superstitious works."[75] Of the four diggers, Hans Meichsner received the heaviest sentence for having incited the others to join him in "letting themselves be used"[76] for diabolical work (*Teuffelsgespennst*) and treasure-digging. As a result, he was sentenced to eight days and nights in a tower, while the others, Georg Näßlin, Claus Schmid, and Jorg Weber, each were sentenced to four. Even the priest, who was not from Augsburg, eventually received

---

[74] "*daselbst gedachte Sophia Voitin ain craiß oder zirkhel gemacht, mit wachs liechtern herumb ganngen, von ainem knecht ain plosse wöhr genomen und ain ort damit ausbezaichnet, da man graben sollt, darnach ist sie inn den craiß gesessenn, hat ain creutz oder crucifix uff ain wasen gestekht, unnd ain tuchlin daruber gelegt, darbei aus ainem puchlin gelesen, alda auch obgedachter dorffpfaff gesessen unnd inn ainem puchlin gelesen, haben baide creutz unnd caractares gemacht, unnd inn summa ain schatz graben wollen, unnd bey solchen aberglaubischen werkh unnd furnemen den namen unnd das wort Gottis großlich misbraucht*," ibid., Strafbuch 29 May 1544.

[75] "*Regina Kochin hat Sophia Voitin unnd Otilia Wolkhenstainin von Nurmberg, uber unnd wider ains Ersamen Rats satzung und gebet unangezaigt, behauset unnd behoft, auch denselben gestattet, inn irem garten on vorwissen der oberkait ain schatz zugraben, unnd dabey allerlay teuffels gespennst unnd aberglaubische werkh zutreiben*," ibid., 3 June 1544.

[76] "*...nachdem sich Hanns Meichsner, Jorg Näßlin schuster, Clauß Schmidt weber, unnd Jorg Weber, sonnst Clain Jorg genannt zu solchem teuffelsgespennst unnd schatz graben brauchen lassen*," ibid.

his punishment on 9 August, as recorded in the Punishment Book. (He was not interrogated in May.) For having "agreed to treasure-digging and all sorts of diabolical magic and superstition, which is against God and our holy faith,"[77] Johann Summerman was forbidden to enter the city and the surrounding area.

Regina Kochin does not appear in the tax records of 1544, which indicates that she may have died within months of her release, before taxes were collected in October. The suffering of a week-long stay in prison, the physical abuse of being tortured twice with the thumb-screws, the stress of being under the suspicion of the city council, and the betrayal of neighbors who testified against her might have had a cumulative and fatal effect on her health.[78] Releasing her from prison on the strength of a petition, with no further punishment than a warning, suggests that the council was aware of endangering her health.

Although this case does not address issues of religious belief or dispute explicitly, it does reveal an instance of citizens and magistrates coming into conflict over the superstitious use of forbidden religious objects and rites. Significantly, the question of religious affiliation never arose in the course of the interrogations; none of the suspects was questioned about his or her faith or participation in other Catholic rites (as Barbara Hertnitin was in 1539). It does not appear to have concerned the council in this case, and I would suggest that it was irrelevant to the crime. They were trying to rein in superstition and the abuse of God's name. In addition to supporting and protecting the Protestant faith, in this case the council also demonstrated its right to police piety, which had a long tradition extending back to the Middle Ages.

The case also sheds light on the lingering trust, even among urban citizens of large Protestant metropolises like Augsburg and Nuremberg, in the magical power of traditional Catholic instruments, such as holy water, candles, incense, and Latin prayers, and in the efficacy of a priest to wield them. The church ordinance banning what reformers called the superstitious practice of Catholic Mass had not banished faith in the efficacy of its attributes. For unearthing a lost treasure a Catholic priest, not a Protestant minister, was absolutely essential. Yet the Nuremberger,

---

[77] "*Johannes Summerman pfarrer zu Taffertingen..., das er sich...understanden...ain schatz zugraben, unnd allerlay teuffelsgespennst unnd aberglaubische werkh, die wider Got unnd unnsern heiligen glauben synnd zutreiben,*" ibid.

[78] Conditions in the city's holding cells could be so miserable as to constitute a form of corporal punishment. Schorer, *Strafgerichtsbarkeit*, 177.

Sophia Voitin, was in charge of the digging enterprise. Otilia Wolkenstein relied on her as someone who possessed specialized knowledge
about how to find a lost treasure. Her authority was undisputed; the
diggers deferred to her and willingly followed her instructions. Voitin
was obviously a literate and educated woman with sufficient resources
to have both the need and the means for reading glasses. She read from
the mysterious book and sprinkled holy water, but she still required a
priest to provide a special connection to the spiritual world. An evangelical preacher might offer instruction about the Gospels, but he had
no authority to use incense or bless holy water, which were essential
for seeking divine assistance in a search for a buried legacy.

The cases in this chapter illustrate the limitations of the council's
ability to police religious beliefs and practices. People continued to
exercise their own judgment in pursuing their spiritual life, and the
council showed noticeable restraint in handling incidents of deviance
from its new church ordinance. Arrests of Catholics leaving the city for
sacraments did not lead to further investigations of Catholic worship,
a woman announcing a clearly Anabaptist objection to infant baptism
was not punished in any way, and a superstitious hunt for treasure did
not unleash a trial for witchcraft. These cases and the council's treatment of them add some complexity to our picture of the course of
the Reformation, the spread of ideas, adaptation of new practices, and
the removal of old habits and beliefs. The fact that Augsburg instituted
a reformation of the city's churches in 1537 should not be equated
with the establishment of religious uniformity among the population.
Even with a consensus achieved amongst Augsburg's ministers, and
approximate consistency of preaching and practice, the reformation
of the people was not quick, easy, or complete. The council had to
deal with non-conformity, active and passive resistance, criticism, and
superstition.

CHAPTER FIVE

MAKING THE BI-CONFESSIONAL CITY:
POLITICAL ENCOUNTERS

A mutiny might have arisen, and the community might have struck the council dead![1]

In the late 1540s tensions flared when the Schmalkaldic War ended Augsburg's decade-long experiment with religious uniformity. In 1537 a reforming council had attempted to silence debate and controversy in the city by establishing a new religious order, but its fall revealed the vulnerability of the city's policy. In 1536, a year before issuing the new church ordinance, Augsburg had joined the Schmalkaldic League of Protestant princes and cities.[2] After years of hesitating, this decision had signaled the council's readiness to support reform openly. Persuaded by influential leaders Georg Herwart and Jakob Herbrot, Augsburg made the fateful decision to side with the Protestant princes against the emperor when war broke out in 1546.[3] One of the city's great mercenary generals, Captain Schertlin von Burtenbach, served with Philip of Hesse in the war. After a few initial victories, the Schmalkaldic League was strategically weakened when Duke Moritz of Saxony, a Lutheran, invaded the lands of one of its leaders, his cousin, Elector Johann Friedrich. On 24 April 1547, Charles V defeated Johann Friedrich at Mühlberg, and Philip of Hesse soon capitulated as well. They, and other members of the league, such as Augsburg, faced the consequences of rebellion. In the fall of 1547 Charles convened an imperial diet in Augsburg to assert his authority and consolidate his victory with a resolution of the religious divisions in his empire.

The Diet of Augsburg caused a significant transformation in the political and religious history of the city of Augsburg. The eight-year

---

[1] *"Darumb mocht ainmall ain meutterey entsteen, unnd die gemaind ain Rat zu todt schlagen,"* StadtAA, Reichsstadt, Strafbuch, 16 April 1547.

[2] The League of Schmalkalden was founded in 1530 by signers of the Augsburg Confession for mutual support in case the emperor took action against any of the members.

[3] Georg Herwart, one of the mayors, and Jakob Herbrot, the Furriers' guildmaster, were both avid Zwinglians, and Jakob Herbrot had important business connections to the league's leading members, Philip of Hesse and Ottheinrich of the Palatinate.

period between the imperial diets of 1547 and 1555 comprises not only a transition but a time of great upheaval in the life of Augsburg's citizens. It marked the removal of the centuries-old guild organization from civic government and the return of the Catholic clergy and Catholic ceremonies to the city after a decade of exile. Once again the old and new faiths were practiced openly side by side, but imperial intervention in the city's government now made it difficult for Protestants to view Catholics without suspicion or resentment. Guild members resented the loss of their political representation and influence in city government at the hands of the emperor. Consequently, the city began a new era as a *de facto* bi-confessional city. These changes caused a great deal of consternation amongst the populace, as familiar institutions and practices were threatened, and some even disappeared. Augsburg's new government oversaw a city in turmoil after the war and in doubt about its religious future.

In the fall of 1547, the emperor and estates gathered in Augsburg to address once more the religious conflict that had been plaguing the empire's German lands for the last three decades. The diet established a provisional peace agreement, which became known as the Augsburg Interim. Among other things, the diet implemented a new statement of faith, which all Protestants in the empire were supposed to obey. It included a few concessions, such as clerical marriage and communion in two forms, but not enough to please most evangelical reformers. It was too close to Catholicism to please the Protestants, but not close enough to satisfy followers of the old church. Since the Interim was only intended as a temporary settlement for Protestants, and Catholics did not have to follow the new statement of faith, the Interim did not lead to any sort of reconciliation or unification in the empire or the city of Augsburg. The Interim delegated that task to the Council of Trent, which met intermittently from 1545 to 1563.

Before leaving Augsburg in 1548, Charles V turned his attention to the cities who had supported his opponents in the Schmalkaldic War. Along with hefty indemnities, the emperor determined to impose constitutional changes on the cities' governments. An opportunity like this for close imperial scrutiny was just what Augsburg's magistrates had feared and why they had hoped to avoid hosting an imperial diet ever since they reformed the city in 1537.[4] Augsburg, home to wealthy financiers,

---

[4] See Roth, *Augsburgs Reformationsgeschichte*, vol. 3, Chapter Two, especially 42.

such as the Fuggers and Welsers, had often provided comfortable and gracious hospitality to the Holy Roman emperors in the past, especially Charles' grandfather, Maximilian I. The city, whose business interests, as well as prestige, relied so heavily on imperial favor, had proved to be a dependable financial supporter of Charles V's ventures, such as his wars with France and the Ottoman Empire. Throughout the 1530s the city had attempted to assure the emperor of its firm loyalty to him, despite its prohibition of Catholicism. Hopes of staying on friendly terms were, of course, dashed by siding with the Schmalkaldic League in a losing war.

At the conclusion of the diet in 1548, Charles V set about ensuring that his once reliable city of Augsburg would remain a trustworthy ally in the future. He believed that the guilds were responsible for the city's disloyalty. After all, guild masters had led the government that banished the Catholic clergy, forbidden the Mass, and instituted a Protestant church ordinance. Therefore, Charles decided to eliminate the guilds' influence in the government. He dissolved the guilds as political units and installed new magistrates, giving precedence to patricians in the most important offices. The elected mayors (*Bürgermeister*) were super-seded by hand-picked governors (*Stadtpfleger*), and so on. In this way Charles V guaranteed that Catholics held a majority in the highest governing bodies—far out of proportion to their numbers in the city as a whole. Among the patrician class Charles V could expect to find, if not Catholics, then at least tractable Protestants who would be loyal to the emperor. Up until 1537, some Protestant magistrates on the City council had actually opposed creating a new church ordinance, though that was as much to preclude a Zwinglian takeover as to avoid angering the emperor.[5] During his residence in the city, the emperor also banished Augsburg's Protestant clergy, who had supported the decision to join the Schmalkaldic League. Thus, he forced into exile ministers who had been preaching in Augsburg for decades, such as Michael Keller. In their place, only Protestant ministers who took an oath to accept the Interim were to be permitted to preach. The Interim's terms were much too restrictive for most of Augsburg's ministers, who in the past had frequently had difficulties with Luther and his circle in Wittenberg because they disagreed with him on the Eucharist, on which they tended to side with Zwingli. Most of the ministers refused

---

[5] Roth, vol. 2, Chapter Five, especially 107.

to take the oath and subsequently left the city. Moreover, and most galling of all for ardent Protestants, the Catholic clergy returned to the city. They reclaimed their churches, relegating Protestant ministers and their listeners back to the smaller meeting houses, and began saying Mass again. With their return came not just the old ceremonies and individual priests but numerous clergy with administrative, judicial, and property claims. Most prominent among these was the cathedral chapter. The chapter consisted exclusively of landed nobles from the countryside around Augsburg who administrated the bishopric's vast properties and parishes; they represented everything the Protestants (and even reform-minded Catholics) despised about the wealth and power of the Catholic Church.

Thus, after a decade of supporting religious unity in order to stifle dissent and keep the peace, Augsburg's magistrates saw their work come undone. Moreover, the populace felt their trust violated, as they were forced to surrender both their religious institutions and political voices. In this period religious affiliations began to generate more attention, because they appeared to be linked to political policies. One can see similar trends in the 1520s, when magistrates feared radical reformers, such as Johann Schilling, would inspire a rebellion against the council, but there seemed to be more at stake in the late 1540s. Reconciliation no longer seemed possible and each side feared suppression of its beliefs, if the other dominated the government. Protestants could not know if the emperor would abolish evangelical reforms entirely, and Catholics must suspect that worship in the old faith would once again be banned, if Protestants reclaimed the council.

In the years after 1548, the Protestant princes struggle to assert their independence from the emperor. Duke Moritz of Saxony had sided with the Catholic emperor in the Schmalkaldic War in order to gain electoral title in Saxony for his family line and other territorial prizes. Charles granted him the electoral title but denied him the lands he coveted. When Charles V attempted to strengthen imperial authority after his victory, Duke Moritz rallied against his one-time ally with the support of the French king—Charles V's frequent rival. In April of 1552, Moritz' Protestant forces occupied Augsburg, which led to another dramatic reversal of fortune. With Jakob Herbrot returned to power, a new government restored the political and religious institutions that had been abolished by Charles V in 1548. They reinstated the guild-led government and once again banned Catholic clergy and worship. In August 1552, after several tense months, Charles V occupied the city once more, abolished the guilds, and brought back Catholic worship. The atmosphere in the community naturally reflected the tensions and anxieties of this period, as evangelical ministers and Catholic priests alternately gained control of the pulpits in tandem with fluctuations in leadership.

New concerns and problems arose with the disturbing changes in government and the return of religious discord to the city after 1548. Many residents felt betrayed by the council, whom they blamed for not protecting the Protestant faith. They also felt disadvantaged by the power given to the wealthy patriciate and resented the loss of the guilds' prestige and influence in civic affairs. After years of aggressive preaching against Catholicism, anti-clericalism reared its ugly head again, as the presence of Catholic clergy and ceremonies irritated already aggrieved evangelical sensibilities. Moreover, many people despised the Protestant ministers who cooperated with the Interim for compromising their principles and sacrificing beliefs and practices that had been promoted in Augsburg for the past decade. The newly-installed council felt the insecurity of its position deeply, and it nervously sought to suppress dissension and protect the new clergy.

The cases that came before the council in these Interim years, 1547–1555, reflect the instability and unease of the era. They fall roughly under the following headings: offensive publications, critical speeches, attacks on clergy, and religious deviance. This chapter addresses the first two groups of censored printing and speech. The next chapter addresses the incidents that evoked religious issues more explicitly. Censorship of offensive printed materials, which was not exactly a new issue, increased in volume and significance in these years. More printers and booksellers faced charges for producing or distributing the wrong materials, including books, pamphlets, songs, and pictures. The "wrong" materials could be anything that criticized the political or religious authorities and anything which might lead to conflict in the community by offending either Catholics or Protestants or which spread illegal religious beliefs, such as Schwenkfeldian or anti-trinitarian tracts.

The council also tried to silence people who publicly criticized authorities, including the council and the emperor, in speech. The censorship of outspoken critics became a bigger problem than in the past. The government arrested people for expressing dissent or criticism of the council, which could target its policies or individual magistrates, because of the potential for causing unrest, therefore, the more witnesses who heard it the more dangerous the speech. These "critical

speeches" did not always involve criticism of the government, nor did
the speechmakers always intend to rouse dissent, therefore the terms
sedition or treason seem too extreme to describe these incidents. To
refer to all of the cases inclusively as seditious or treasonous assumes
too much about the motivations of the defendants and places too much
emphasis on the council's viewpoint.

Renewed attacks on clergy evoked the anti-clericalism that had
appeared in the early years of reform and took up a considerable
amount of the court's time. Those who insulted or threatened priests,
even clergy from outside Augsburg, and especially the well-connected
cathedral chapter, would face stern reprisals. The category of anti-
clerical attacks contains a number of relatively minor incidents that
show the council's sensitivity to potential violence against the clergy.
The late 1540s and early 1550s also saw a variation on the old theme
of anti-clericalism. The council now found itself in the curious position of having to defend Protestant clergy as well, namely those who
collaborated with the unpopular Interim.

Religious deviance also remained a concern for the authorities.
Anabaptists, Schwenkfeldians, Arians (anti-trinitarians), and even the
occasional Cathar appeared in the city hall's prison cells. All of these
sects, which were illegal not only in Augsburg but throughout the
Empire, defied the authorities' attempts to extinguish them by exile or
conversion. Forced by imperial decree to find a way to handle Protestants and Catholics living and worshipping openly in one city, the
magistrates were not inclined, nor authorized, to extend their narrow
framework of toleration to any other religious groups. Lastly, a few other
significant incidents cannot easily be grouped under any other heading than miscellaneous. One involved an exchange of religious insults
between neighbors who were also colleagues, and another concerned
a beggar who tried to win alms by using his alleged connections to the
Franciscan monk Johann Schilling.[6] These last two cases illustrate the
development of religious sensibilities in the first half of the sixteenth
century by reflecting the continuities and departures from the early
years of reform.

The nature of the crimes which occurred in Augsburg in this period,
1547 to 1555, remind one of the cases which appeared in the mid to

---

[6] In 1524 citizens had protested when the city council forced Johann Schilling to
leave the city for inflammatory preaching.

late 1520s. At that time the Reformation was gaining momentum in the city, but the council still had to protect the rights of the Catholic Church, and unrest threatened to break out. In both periods magistrates focused their efforts on similar concerns, printed or spoken criticism of authorities, anti-clericalism, and fear of rebellion. The atmosphere of anxiety and insecurity on the part of the council, as it trod new territory, pervades the interrogations in both periods. Yet the similarities should not be exaggerated. The situations were not identical. Having had their fingers burnt in 1548, the councilors had more experience than in the early days of the Reformation. Fear of the unknown became fear of the known. One sees from the council both a sense of resignation to what could no longer be avoided (religious diversity within the city) and a vigorous determination to eliminate anyone and anything that threatened to upset the fragile peace. In the years 1522 to 1530 there were four arrests for anti-clerical behavior, but seven between 1547 and 1555. Likewise, two cases of censorship compared to nine after 1547, and eight critical speeches compared to thirteen in the later period. Virtually no incidents of these sorts appear in the years between 1530 and 1547, despite the completeness of the records. The increase in the number of cases does not reflect an increase in record-keeping over three decades, as the overall numbers of cases heard remains the same, but it shows a noticeable concentration on certain types of incidents which demanded the council's attention.

The defendants interrogated during the Interim seem to have been in a state of shock, a sort of delayed recognition of the changes that had taken place. After ten years of rabidly anti-Catholic propaganda, preached from the pulpits, distributed in printed matter, and sanctioned by the government, people were suddenly getting into trouble for insulting priests. They were expressing opinions which had been not only acceptable but popularly and officially approved just a year or two before. Booksellers and printers almost uniformly claimed in their defense to have been distributing materials that had been approved in the past and which they did not know were forbidden. If they violated current prohibitions deliberately to express their resistance to change rather than through ignorance, the numbers of cases and gravity with which they were handled suggest that either the defendants were willing to risk quite a lot or that they had no idea how seriously their offenses would be taken. In many cases, it seems to have been the latter: they simply did not realize where the council stood now. The types of cases discussed in this section may seem to indicate a greater interest

nite

in the council's perspective than the book has pursued so far. In part this emphasis reflects the sources, which include more cases of conflict between the government and individual citizens rather than interaction among citizens. However, the goal is to gauge the reactions of the community to changing circumstances; some reactions were directed at the authorities (secular and spiritual), some towards other citizens. Government and citizenry alike were trying to come to terms with the legal coexistence of competing faiths.

CENSORSHIP OF PRINTING

A brief discussion of censorship in this period aims to uncover the government's motivation in suppressing dissent and the nature of defendants' efforts to justify their actions. This section does not intend to examine printed materials or the printing trade in Augsburg but rather the individual printers who came into conflict with their community or authorities because of their religious beliefs or the beliefs expressed in the materials they produced.[7] Printers were not publishing their own writings, and many of the authors whose works appeared in the illegal printed materials were not Augsburgers. Nor does the printing or distribution of them for sale necessarily indicate any religious affiliation on the part of the printers or booksellers; often they were just trying to earn a living. In addition, many copies of the materials that were produced by printers in Augsburg were actually intended for sale in foreign markets. An attempt to reconstruct the buyers of these materials in Augsburg, as a sign of the populace's interests, is also beyond the scope of this project. Though interesting, it would also be very difficult to do, given the lack of sources beyond a few elite libraries. Instead this discussion focuses on what we can learn from interrogation records about the atmosphere in the city, by looking at the occasions of tension and how defendants explained their actions.

Narciß Raminger, who came from a well-established printing family in Augsburg, was one of the printers arrested in August of 1549.

---

[7] For more information on printing and propaganda in the Reformation see Hans-Jorg Künast, *'Getruckt zu Augspurg:' Buchdruck und Buchhandel in Augsburg zwischen 1468 und 1555.* (Tubingen: Max Niemeyer Verlag, 1997); Miriam Usher Chrisman, *Conflicting Visions of Reform: German Lay Propaganda Pamphlets, 1519–1530,* (Atlantic Highlands, NJ: Humanities Press, 1996); and Robert Scribner, *For the Sake of Simple Folk,* (New York: Cambridge University Press, 1981).

He and his journeyman, Marcus Fischer, were arrested for printing a libelous song about "König Antiocho,"[8] who kills a woman with seven sons because of God's law. It is difficult to tell how contemporaries understood the song in the context of 1549. Did the song allude to Protestant victims being abused by a powerful ruler? Did it advocate using force to carry out divine justice? Raminger denied any knowledge about the printing of the song, which had been done by his subordinate. The journeyman, Fischer, corroborated this statement, admitting that "he did not know if his master knew about it, since he printed only with the help of his wife and a female servant."[9] On the other hand, he asserted that he had merely behaved as an obedient servant, because Raminger had told him to print anything that Hans Westermair brought him, so long as it was not libelous or offensive. The master, Raminger, stated that he had originally received this song for printing in 1538, at which time Ulrich Rehlinger, the Zwinglian mayor, had given him permission to print it. He explained that "he thought that anything that was printed here before was not insulting or offensive, and could, therefore, be printed now, just as he had printed [other religious songs]."[10] Raminger's disingenuous explanation is hardly to be believed. It is certainly possible that he did not know specifically about everything being printed by his journeyman, but he could not have been unaware that materials printed eleven years earlier were not automatically permissible after the introduction of the Interim. The council apparently also saw it this way. Both Raminger and Fischer were held in prison. Fischer was soon released in response to a petition. His master, Raminger, was also released but forbidden to print. After about four months, in January of 1550, the council approved Raminger's petition to be allowed to resume printing. Therefore, he experienced only a temporary set-back as the result of violating the prohibition.

Two items from the list of questions reveal the council's concerns in this case. First, Question Two: "Did he not do it [i.e. have the song printed] among other [reasons] in order that the common man would

---

[8] The song related a story about a king who killed a woman with seven sons because of God's command.

[9] "*Er khonne nit wissen, ob er sei maister gewist oder nit, dann nur sein fraw unnd dienerin ime truckhen helfen,*" StadtAA, Reichsstadt, Urg. 27 August 1549, Marcus Fischer.

[10] "*10 Er hab vermaint, was hievor getruckht worden, nit schentlich oder schmehlich sei, das mögen sie wol wider truckhen, wie er dann das lied hilff gott das mir gelinge, den gaistlichen buchsbaum, den passion etc. bißher getruckht,*" ibid., 20 August 1549, Narciß Raminger.

be strengthened against the Interim and be moved to steadfastness?"[11] This very clearly shows that the council believed that the spread of certain documents could lead to resistance or an actual uprising from the population, with whom the Interim was already unpopular. Secondly, Question Four: "Did not some preachers and others on their behalf incite him to do it?"[12] Naturally the council also expected that those Protestant ministers who had lost their positions as a result of the Interim would try to encourage the people to support their cause. Removed from the city's pulpits, they turned to the printed word in order to spread their message. These and similar concerns motivated the council in most of the other arrests of printers and booksellers in this period.

The case of Friedrich Thum stands out among other arrests in the printing trade around this time, especially in contrast with Jorg Willer, who was arrested in the same year. In February of 1551, Friedrich Thum, by trade a bookbinder, had been buying and selling books and illustrations which had been banned by the Interim. The minutes of the council note that many people had petitioned on Thum's behalf and that his activities were not considered a serious offense in other places.[13] The council judged that he should be forbidden to practice his trade and banished from the city, but they decided to hold Thum in prison, until they heard from Emperor Charles V's court in Arras. Through the intervention of the bibliophile Hans Jacob Fugger, then mayor of Augsburg, this punishment was overturned by the emperor. The council received word, through Fugger and Chrisostomus Peutinger, that the emperor was gratified by the council's proposed punishment of Thum. He had, however, decided that the books were not so dangerous, and Thum should be permitted to continue his trade and reside in Augsburg.[14]

In this curious case we see the city of Augsburg eager to demonstrate its loyalty to the emperor and its defense of the Interim. Thus, the defendant Thum had to be rescued from the council's punishment through the intervention of the emperor himself. The intercession on Thum's behalf by Fugger and Peutinger can be easily explained. Fridrich

---

[11] "*2 Ob ers nit under anderm auch darumb gethan das dardurch der gemain mann wider das Interim gesterkht und zu standhafftikhait bewegt wurd,*" ibid., (Fragstück).

[12] "*4 Ob in nit auch ettliche predicanten und welhe derhalb angelangt haben,*" ibid.

[13] Ibid., Ratsbuch 1550–55, 24 February and 5 March 1551.

[14] Ibid., Strafbuch, 1543–53, 7 March 1551.

Thum was the third generation of a prosperous family of bookbind-
ers in Augsburg. In addition to binding books, the Thum's also sold
books to wealthy clients, such as the Fuggers and the humanist Conrad
Peutinger, father of Chrisostomus.

Several months later, in August 1551, the bookseller Jorg Willer had a
very different experience. He had been selling forbidden libelous books.
Like Thum, Willer claimed to be unfamiliar with the contents of the
materials he was selling. Without further ado—or aid from Fugger,
Peutinger, or the emperor—Willer was held in prison and then promptly
put in a tower for four weeks. Although the council was concerned with
punishing the printing of all forbidden materials, it handled cases on
an individual basis.

On 3 October 1552 the lace-maker Lienhart Schondorffer was
arrested for selling *pasquilles* and illustrations. In his hearing, Schondorffer identified the two men who had provided him with various
books, tracts, and pictures. One of his suppliers, a printer named Hans
Zimmerman, was subsequently arrested and brought in for questioning.
The other man, Martin Schrot, does not appear in any of the relevant
legal sources, which suggests that he was not in Augsburg at the time
and therefore could not be arrested. From Schrot, Schondorffer had
received "all sorts of books, pictures, and tracts," and from Zimmerman he had received "songs, one about the expulsion of the preachers
and one about the eagle (a symbol for the emperor), and two pieces
from Meislin". Meislin was the exiled Zwinglian, Wolfgang Musculus,
who had been a preacher in Augsburg from 1531 to 1548.[15] Musculus had expressed his aggressive position even before the Interim was
declared, when he informed the City council, in August 1547, that if
the Catholic clergy were not banished from Augsburg after the imperial diet, he would leave the city.[16] When Schondorffer was arrested in
1552 the emperor had recently returned to Augsburg to reinforce the
Interim's terms.

The bookseller Schondorffer and the printer Zimmerman defended
themselves as Raminger had earlier. Both claimed that they had
assumed that whatever had been printed before could be printed now.
For example, Schondorffer explained that he had not sold the same
pasquille as Willer had "but instead something older which was printed

---

[15] StadtAA, Reichsstadt, Urg. 3 October 1552, Lienhart Schondorffer.
[16] Ibid., Ratsbuch 1540–49, 6 August 1547.

in 1546, so that he figured that since it was an old book it couldn't do
any harm."[17] He also confessed at the beginning of his hearing that,
although he knew of the council's prohibitions regarding *pasquilles*, "he
had not really thought much about it until now."[18] Zimmerman, on the
other hand, also testified that since others were selling similar books,
he thought he could do it too. This traditionally useless excuse, he had
simply been following the crowd, did not carry much weight with the
council; nor did the explanation that he had printed Musculus' letter
because, although the appointed officials (*Schulherren*) had not approved
it for printing, they had not expressly forbidden it.

The council's view of Musculus' writing reflects the changes which
had occurred in Augsburg. Having once been one of Augsburg's most
respected and admired preachers, both for his preaching and his
scholarly accomplishments, Musculus was now considered a dangerous
author. As the council's inquiry indicates, Question Ten: "He knows
well that he should not spread or sell the song about the expulsion of
the preachers" and Question Twelve: "nor Musculus' booklet which
might lead to disunity and antagonism or disobedience."[19] To these
accusations Zimmerman responded, like Schondorffer, "he didn't think
that it would do any harm now because it had been sold before."[20]

The significance of the common explanation in hearings of booksellers and printers—that it had been done in the past—does not
lie in whether or not the council would have believed it. No one in
Augsburg could have failed to be aware of the change in political and
religious power since the Schmalkaldic War. Significantly, none of the
printers or booksellers who were questioned claimed to be ignorant
of the ordinances which required them to seek approval before printing. It is immaterial whether or not they actually believed it would be
okay to print documents which had been acceptable before. What is
interesting is that they all fell back on this explanation at some point

---

[17] "*sonder waß altens im 46ten jar getruckht worden, derhalb er vermaint, so es alte buchlin seind
es sol nit schaden,*" ibid., Urg., 3 October 1552 Lienhart Schondorffer.
[18] "*Erstlichen, er khonn sichs erinnern das schmachbucher fail zehaben, verpotten, er habs aber
gleichwol hievor so wol nit bedacht, derhalb er umb gnad bitt,*" ibid.
[19] "*10 Er wiß wol das er das lied vom ausschaffen der predicanten nit auspraiten oder verkhauffen
soll... 12 Noch auch des meuslins puechle so zw unainikhait und widerwillen oder ungehorsam dienen
mocht,*" ibid. 5 October 1552, Hans Zimmerman (Fragstück).
[20] "*2 Er hab nicht vermaint das es diser zeit schaden sol weil es sonst auch fail gehalten worden,*"
ibid.

in their interrogations. Their defense, that they had not realized these materials were no longer acceptable, highlights the very changes in acceptability of which they were claiming to be unaware. In reminding the council of how recently the same books, pamphlets, and illustrations were approved by the magistrates, they were pointing out the council's failure to maintain Augsburg's religious position and independence. Schondorffer illustrates this poignantly when he admitted that although he knew of the council's prohibition of *pasquilles*, he had not taken it seriously. In other words, Schondorffer did not expect the council to take its defense of the Interim so earnestly. Like Barbara Hertnitin in an earlier period, Schondorffer found himself at odds with the council, having misjudged the new council's commitment to enforcing the Interim's decrees.

Schondorffer, the lacemaker, was sentenced to spend eight days in a tower and forbidden to sell books or pictures in the future, while the printer, Zimmerman, who had supplied him with illegal materials, was banished. The cases of censorship show that the Interim caused a clear lack of harmony between the goals of the new council and the interests of the citizen printers and booksellers, who were responding to a market that the council wanted to suppress.

CRITICAL SPEECHES

The group of cases involving critical speeches includes a variety of offensive statements, not all directed against the council. Some criticized the council as a whole, while others focused on specific members; some criticized the emperor; and some simply raised issues that the council found dangerous. The earliest examples come from the year 1547. Hans Stehelin was disappointed by Augsburg's defeat in the Schmalkaldic War and subsequent submission to the emperor. He criticized the city council with the following "offensive, harmful" words: "the council gave the city over to the emperor without the permission of the community (*Gemeinde*)." Although Stehelin refused to confess to having made this speech, witnesses had provided convincing evidence. It is important to remember that the availability of witnesses made the crime more serious. A man's private thoughts were nowhere near as dangerous as a speech made publicly. When Stehelin was whipped out of the city and banished, the public sentence declared that, "from this a mutiny might

have arisen, and the community might have struck the council dead."[21]
Likewise the recorded judgment in the punishment book (*Strafbuch*)
warned that, "a rebellion and other evil things might have arisen."[22]

A few months later, Michael Kleinheinz made a somewhat similar
complaint against the guildmaster Hans Mair.[23] The only evidence
of Kleinheinz' antagonism toward Mair comes from the relevant
Punishment Book entry. Apparently, Kleinheinz had already pledged
to hold his peace against Mair, "in word and deed," after a previous
incident. In August, Kleinheinz broke this pledge and insulted Mair
once again, accusing him of being a "yes-man". The following speech
from Kleinheinz was recorded in the Punishment Book: "anyone could
be a yes-sir like him, yes my Yessir, you like tipping your hat". He
also accused Mair of saying "the emperor wants to do away with the
guilds, and if he doesn't do it, he's making a mistake."[24] Kleinheinz
insulted Mair by claiming he had cooperated with the emperor's plan
to abolish the political power of Augsburg's guilds. As the result of a
petition, Kleinheinz was released on the condition that he apologize to
Mair in front of the council and then afterwards appear before the six
Discipline Lords (*Zuchtherren*) to receive a reprimand. Thus, Kleinheinz
was punished for violating the previously sworn peace against Mair,
not for criticizing the government.

Both of these cases reveal some of the disappointment which the
people of Augsburg felt in the aftermath of the defeat of the Schmalkaldic League. The magistrates were not willing to tolerate people
who cast aspersions on the means by which the present council had
come into office. Hans Stehelin had raised the dangerous legal issue of
whether or not the magistrates' submission was legitimate without the

---

[21] "*Hanns Stehelin von Augspurg hat sich gegen etlichen personen mit beschwerlichen verletzlichen
reden wider ain Ersamen Rat, unnd ungeverlich mit disen worten vernumen lassen, Ain Rat hab die Stat
der Kay. Mt. on bewilligung der Gemaind ubergeben. Darumb mocht ainmall ain meutterey entsteen,
unnd die gemaind ain Rat zu todt schlagen, unnd wie wol er solcher rede nit genntzlich gestannden,
So ist er doch derselben uberwisen wordenn, Darumb er mit Ruten ausgestrichen, auch der Statt unnd
Etter sein lebenlanng verwisen wordenn,*" ibid., Strafbuch, 16 April 1547.

[22] "*daraus emporung unnd annder ubel entsteen hetten mogenn,*" ibid., Urg, 16 April 1547
(Urteil).

[23] In a register of office-holders, Hans Mair is listed as the guildmaster for the
grocers. Ibid., Ämter-Besetzung 1241–1614 (Register #38), p. 19.

[24] "*Michel Klainheintz hat gegen zunfftmaister Hannsen Mair fridt fur wort unnd werkh angelobt,
welchen er aber nit gehaltenn, sonnder ine ain Juden gescholten, hat auch zu ime gesagt, es konne
ain jeder ain solcher ja herr sein wie er, ja mein Jaherr, du hast gern das man das huetlin [zieh].
Item der Kaiser wölle die zunfften alhie abthun, unnd wann ers nit thue so thue er unrecht,*" ibid.,
Strafbuch, 16 August 1547.

permission of the community (*Gemeinde*). Challenging the legitimacy of the current government's right to rule is a common foundation for revolutionary movements. Whether Stehelin had such a goal in mind (to incite his fellow citizens to rebellion), the council immediately recognized the risk in allowing him to continue spreading his ideas. However, since Michael Kleinheinz's antagonism towards the guildmaster Hans Mair was more isolated and personal in nature, regarding his alleged collusion in the fall of the guilds, it could be dealt with as an issue of honor rather than of sedition.

The next case involved an apparently innocuous speech, but one which nonetheless gave the council cause for concern. The tailor Jeronimus Kunig did not actually criticize the council, but so far as the councilors were concerned, his careless words might have stirred up "trouble" (*Unrad*). According to his interrogation from 2 January 1550, the following events occurred. About a week earlier, Kunig's journeyman, Jorg, had come home and told his master that he had heard some journeymen say that the tailor Lechmair was making five banners, and the council would be hiring soldiers. Kunig then responded to this news, "maybe they will drive the preachers out of the city."[25] This statement caused Kunig to be arrested, held in prison for two days, and then sentenced to spend two weeks in a tower.

Kunig's words were not as harmless as they might first appear. The description of his crime in the Punishment Book reveals the underlying menace perceived by the council.

> Jeronimus Kunig, tailor from Augsburg, has said untrue things and poured out that the tailor Lechmair is making five banners, and an honorable council will hire soldiers, turn the same on the citizenry here, and then drive the preachers out of the city, through which [statement] reckless mischief (*leichtlich unrad*) might have arisen.[26]

The real harm lay in spreading rumors rather than in a direct criticism of the council. By implication Kunig had suggested that the council

---

[25] "*Erstlich, sein gesell Jorg, sey ungeferlich vor 8 tagen haim khomen, unnd gesagt Maister, ich hab davorn, von den gsellen gehort, der Lechmair schneider mache funf fendlin, unnd man werde knecht annemen etc., darauf er one als geferh, unnd unbedacht gesagt, man wurt villeicht die predicanten aus der Statt thun,*" ibid., Urg. 2 January 1550, Jeronimus Kunig.

[26] "*Jeronimus Kunig schneider von Augspurg, hat unwarhaffter ding geredt unnd ausgossen der Lechmair schneider mach funff fendlin unnd ain Ersamer Rate werde knecht annemen, dieselben herein auff die Burgerschaft legen, unnd alsdann die Predicanten hinaus treiben, dardurch leichtlich unrad hett entsteen mogen,*" ibid., Strafbuch 4 January 1550.

might use military force against its own citizens in order to expel the
Protestant preachers, who were supported by the majority of citizens in
Augsburg. If Kunig's statement were repeated and believed, many peo-
ple would be upset and their trust in the council further weakened.

After securing from Kunig a confession of what he had really said
to his journeyman, the council planned in the next two questions to
ascertain who else had heard him and, thereby, to measure the extent
of the damage done. "Where, to whom, and in whose presence did
he make this statement?"[27] When Kunig named only the painter Furtenagel and Furtenagel's journeyman, the interrogators produced evidence
that Furtenagel's wife, servant, and young son were also in the room.
Kunig claimed not to remember if they had been there. Even so, it
was a rather intimate crowd, which means that Kunig had not spoken
at a public gathering.

To establish the full extent of Kunig's guilt, the interrogators asked
him specifically about his motives. "What caused him to say such a
groundless thing? Didn't he, in this way, want to stir up unrest and
rebellion among the common man?"[28] Kunig responded in protest
(several times) that, "he said this speech truly without reflection" (*aus
unverdachten mute*), "without [meaning] anything bad" and "without thinking".[29] The interrogators also asked where he had gotten his information
and who had encouraged him to say such a thing. In response to all
of these questions Kunig could only tell the interrogators what they
already knew of the conversation between him and his journeyman.
The council pursued the hearing no further, though further interrogation could have been conducted with torture if they had thought that
he was withholding the truth. Kunig was punished for his irresponsible
speech and the trouble it might have caused, but the council apparently
found no evidence of a seditious plot.

Similarly critical remarks surfaced through the following years. In
1551, Lienhart Bihelmair reported to the guild lords at the Fishers'
Hall,[30] that a man by the name of Stefan Schot had insulted the
emperor and the mayors of the city. Eight witnesses, including Bihelmair,

---

[27] Ibid., Urg. 2 January 1550, Jeronimus Kunig.
[28] Ibid. (Fragstück).
[29] Ibid.
[30] The fisher and butcher guilds in Augsburg had their own justice system for dealing with minor misdemeanors within their own guilds. More serious offenses, such as
Stefan Schot's would be passed along to the city council for punishment.

described Schot's criticism of the civic authorities, the emperor, and his soldiers. According to the gatekeeper Merat Wiest, Schot had said that "the king[s] of France and England, have accepted the Word of God, but the emperor wants to abolish it, and suppress it".[31] Furthermore, Andreas Orland claimed that Schot said, "he shits on the authorities, he couldn't care less about the emperor, and the same with his lords the mayors, because they gave up the city without the knowledge of the people".[32] In another example, Bernhart Markhauer testified that Schot had said, "the soldiers, as many as they were, were all useless; why do they serve the emperor instead of going home?"[33]

The testimony of eight witnesses sufficed to convince the guild masters that Stefan Schot should be brought in for questioning and punishment. When he did not appear and then fled the city, a general command was given out to look for Schot and put him in chains when he was found. Sometime not long thereafter Schot was found and arrested. The Fishers' guild masters referred the matter to the city council at this point, taking care not to overstep their jurisdiction. In their report to the council, they stated, "…we do not dictate to your noble, steady, careful, honorable, wise[nesses], rather, because he is an old, long-lived man, over eighty years, who is somewhat, due to his age, robbed of his reason, we defer to your graces' and lordships' merciful consideration."[34]

Oddly enough, Schot himself does not appear as a defendant. The report includes the testimony of witnesses and a notice of Schot's incarceration, but there is no indication that the Fishers' Guild interrogated him or any record of what he had to say for himself. Moreover, beyond this report (which lies in the collection of interrogation records but was not written by the city's scribe), there is no record of an interrogation

---

[31] "*Merat Wiest, der thorwart burger alhie, sagt er Steffan Schot, hab gesagt, der kinnig aus Franckhreich, und Engaland, habenn das wort gotes angenumenn, aber der Kaiser welle es ab thonn, und nider thruckhenn,*" StadtAA, Reichsstadt, Urg. 12 January 1551, Stefan Schot (Report).

[32] "*Enderis Orland Rotmaister sagt, bei seinem aidt, das Stefan Schot geret, hab mit Ernn zu schreiben, er scheise ann die obrikait, er frag auch nichts nach denn Kaiser, des gleichenn nach seinen herrn denn burgermaisternn, dan sie heten die stat unne wisen der underthan uff gebenn,*" ibid.

[33] "*Bernnhart Markhauer, von Straubinngenn, sagt wie obgemelter Ennders Orlandt, gesagt hat und das mer die Lantsknecht so vil ir werenn weren al kainn nitz, war um sie dem kaiser denten und nit haim zugenn,*" ibid.

[34] "*dar auf ist gedachter Schot, inn die penn gefallenn darinen wir Eiwer edlen vesten virsichtigen ersamen weishaiten kainn mas geben, sunder die weil er ain alter, bis inn die 80 jar, erlepter man ist, der dan, etwas, seines alters halbenn, seiner vernwnfft beraupt, geben wir Eiwer gnaden und heilikaiten genedigklichen zu bedinckhenn,*" ibid.

by the council and no entry in the council's minutes or the Punishment Book to indicate a decision regarding his case. Because of Schot's
advanced age, the council very likely dismissed him with a lecture on
watching his tongue or may have remanded him to the custody of
the Hospital, as in the case of Leonhard Widenman discussed later.[35]
Despite the council's sensitivity to insults to its own members and the
emperor, a man in Schot's condition could easily be discredited and,
therefore, dismissed as harmless. In fact, his obvious senility would only
make his insults look more ridiculous, and the council that disciplined
him look despicable. In this case, the council's image may have been
better protected by not prosecuting.

In the spring of 1552 Protestant forces under Duke Moritz of Saxony were marching southward; in April they occupied Augsburg and
reinstated the pre-Interim government. This new shift in authority led
to more discontent among Augsburg's citizens. On a June evening the
weaver Hans Streler was drinking with two companions at a tavern on
Perlach Hill by the City Hall. While drinking, his friends Hans Fießler
and Hans Partenschlag, also weavers, began to tease him about being
a Catholic.[36] As the tavernkeeper's wife, Anna Schmid, testified,

> when the people in the tavern teased [Streler] and made fun of the
> priests (and their ceremonies), he would say improper things, especially
> yesterday evening when he said 'that his lords had expelled the previous
> ministers and put other ministers in their place, who preached the word
> of God as wrongly as the previous ones, because it is not possible for
> any human, only God alone.' Otherwise Streler was a good man, if he
> weren't such a big papist.[37]

Likewise, Streler's friend Partenschlag explained that while drinking,
he and his companions had been joking and teasing each other, which
led to some statements, which he no longer remembered, because he

---

[35] Leonhard Widenman's case is discussed in Chapter Six.

[36] The modern German word "*vexieren*" means to tease or annoy, similar to the
English term "to vex". The sixteenth century spelling of the word "*fexieren*", as well
as the noun form "*Fexierung*", also shows similarities to the terms "*fechten*" and "*Fecht*",
for duelling, which suggests a sort of verbal sparring, which also fits the context. See
Grimm's *Wörterbuch*.

[37] "*Wann ine die leut, inn der zech gesatzt, unnd das pfaffenwerckh furgerupfft, hab er sich alsdann
auch zun zeiten ungebürlicher reden hören lassen, sonnderlich hab er gestern gesagt, meine hern heten
die vorigen predicanten hinaus gethon, unnd anndere an die statt auffgestelt, welche das wort gottes
gleich so wenig gerecht wurden sagen, als die vorigen, dann es khainem menschen muglich dann alain
gott alain, Sonnst were er Streler ain frummer mensch, wann er nit so gar ain grosser papstler wer,
etc.*" StadtAA, Reichsstadt, Urg. 15 June 1552, Anna Schmid (witness).

was rather drunk at the time. He also suggested that the city guards, who were sitting at another table and overheard them, may have taken it more seriously and evilly than he did, because otherwise he knew nothing to say about Streler except that he was a good man but a big papist.[38] Lastly, Fießler testified that there had been some teasing about the papacy, but that he knew of nothing improper to say about Streler, except he was a papist through and through and had been since childhood.[39]

The two city guards, Peter Raid and Asam Aman, who had been sitting nearby and overhead the conversation, told a somewhat different story from Streler's friends—the essential difference being that rather than protecting Hans Streler, they had turned him in to the council. While not exactly contradicting Streler's companions, they filled in some of the blanks in the story which the weavers had told. According to the city guards' testimony, after some teasing about the papacy Streler had said, "my lords are false traitors, and he does not owe them obedience. In six weeks we will see what the emperor will do, and he would like to punch the Lords Mayor in the face. Furthermore, no one can tell him what to do, because he has not sworn or pledged to anyone."[40] Another witness, Claus Muckensturm, testified that he had heard the same as the City Guards, "except for the part about wanting to hit the Lord Mayors in the face,"[41] which he had not heard.

The testimony from the guards served as the basis for Hans Streler's interrogation, which shows a distinct trend in the council's concerns. He was asked why he had called the councilors "false traitors" and if he knew of anything "improper or false" about them. Had he sworn the annual oath, especially the most recent one, to the mayors, and

---

[38] "*als er... unnd andern, ... an gestern gezecht, unnd ainer den anndern schertzweise gefexirt, haben sich etliche reden zutragen, die ime furwar nit bewist seien, dann er gar wol bezecht gewest, vermelt auch das... statknecht, so an ainem andern tisch gezecht, solche reden gehört, die es villeicht basser anzezaigen wissen möchten, dann er, sonst wisse er von Hansen Streler nichts zesagen, dann das er ain frummer mann, aber grosser papstler sei,*" ibid., Hans Partenschlag (witness).

[39] "*hab sich ain fexierung deß papstumbs halben zwischen inen zutragen, wisse aber nichts ungebürlichs, von gemelten Streler zesagen, dann das er je unnd allweg, von jugendt auff ain grosser papstler gewest sei,*" ibid., Hans Fießler (witness).

[40] "*si haben... von Hansen Strelern gehört, nachdem er, unnd anndere deß papstumbts halb gefexiert, das er gesagt, meine herrn wern maynaydig laurn, unnd er sei inen nit schuldig unnderthnig zesein, man werde auch innerhalb 6 wochen wol sehen, was der kaiser thun werde, unnd er wolte den Herrn Burgermaistern inn das angesicht thun, es hab ime auch niemandts zubieten, wollt gern sehen wer ims wern dann er niemandts gelobt unnd geschworen sei,*" ibid., Peter Raid und Asam Aman (witnesses).

[41] Ibid., Claus Muckensturm (witness).

why had he said that "he didn't owe them obedience?" What did he know of the emperor's plans that led him to say that "one would see in six weeks what the emperor would do to the city?" What improper things did he know about the former or current ministers? What were his intentions were towards the civic community and the preachers, and "didn't he intend to cause an uprising with his agitating, disrespectful, improper behavior?" Moreover, who encouraged or supported him and what were they plotting? And, lastly—but certainly not least—why had he said that "he would like to hit the mayors in the face?"[42]

In response to these questions, Hans Streler swore he knew of nothing bad to say about the council, the mayors, or the ministers. He meant no harm against anyone, planned no insurrection, had sworn his civic oath this year as always, and considered himself an obedient citizen. In the course of answering a total of nine questions, he took four opportunities to explain that he had been very drunk at the time and, therefore, did not really know what he had said. Nonetheless, he clearly remembered that his companions taunted him about the emperor's retreat to Innsbruck, "So, where did your emperor run away to? Why didn't he stay with his sheep?" To which he had responded, "The emperor hadn't run away from them, he might come too soon for them. One would see within six weeks what would come of it."[43]

The council pursued Streler's case in a second interrogation four days later, on 20 June, in which the interrogators were instructed to threaten Streler with torture if he did not answer their questions honestly. As the second list of questions indicates, they were not going to pardon Streler by letting him excuse his behavior with drunkenness. The second interrogation focused on four main points, which they required Streler to admit: that he had called the councilors "false traitors", that he had said he did not owe them obedience, that he wanted to punch the mayors in the face, and that he was not sworn to anyone. No torture was necessary. Streler admitted to every statement with the repeated explanation that he had been angry and drunk and with a plea for mercy and forgiveness. In his words, "regrettably he did say this but only out of great anger and heat, to which he was incited and provoked by his drinking companions, and also from drunkenness."

---

[42] Ibid., 16 June 1552, Hans Streler.

[43] "Als seine zechgesellen, ine inn der zech gefatzt, mit meldung, wo sein kaiser were hingeflohen, unnd warumb er nit bei sein schaffen pliben, het er gesagt, der kaiser were inen noch nit entrunnen, er möchte inen noch zu frue khommen, man möchte noch inn 6 wochen vil innenwerden," ibid.

At the end of his second interrogation, Streler added a voluntary statement, which defendants occasionally did. In this case, Streler wanted to reassure the lords of his obedience and show that he was aware of his civic duty towards them.

> He had pledged and sworn to his lords, did the civic oath every year, and had comported himself accordingly—so that no human on earth could truthfully say anything against him about this—because he was an obedient citizen and planned to remain so. He asked most heartily for mercy, because what he had done had happened from being angry, heated, irritated, and moved, and, particularly from being inebriated. He hadn't meant anything bad.[44]

The council saw the matter differently. As the verdict against him states, Hans Streler had offended the honorable council, "against God, Honor, and Justice, with libelous, illegal speeches and words." Consequently, Streler was escorted publicly out of town, to make an example of him.

This case raises several issues. For one, it shows a passionate Catholic, whose feelings were well known to his drinking companions who were obviously Protestant. From the testimony of the tavern keeper, Anna Schmid, and the interrogators' questions, we know that these men were friends who often drank together and that the talk frequently led to vexing Streler for the fun of it. Streler apparently took no lasting offense from this, and Partenschlag and Fießler, as well as the tavern keeper, defended him as a "*frommer mann*," a good man. The only thing they could say against him, which they mentioned in order to account for his sensitivity, was that he was very Catholic or "papist."[45] For these men their religious differences were cause for amusement but no reason not to socialize together. Streler's friends did not feel threatened by him, nor he by them.

The problem for Streler arose not from mixing with his Protestant friends but from offending the city council. If he had not insulted the

---

[44] "*Vermelt auch das er meinen Herrn gelobt, unnd geschworn, alle jar den burgerlichen ayde gethon, unnd sich inn allem erzaigt hab, das khain mensch auf erdterich sei, der inn disem, ime etwas zuwider mit der warhait anzezaigen wiste, dann er sich je unnd allweg als ain gehorsamer burger gehalten, wolle es auch noch thun, Bitt uber das alles nochmaln zum höchsten, umb gnad, dann was er verhandlt, sei ainmal nur aus zorn, hitz, anraitzung, unnd bewegung, innsonnderhait auch aus beweinigung beschehen, hab es auch nit arg gemaint, Bitt aber doch derhalb umb gnad,*" ibid., 20 June 1552, Hans Streler.
[45] "*wisse aber nichts ungebürlichs, von gemelten Streler zesagen, dann das er je unnd allweg, von jugendt auff ain grosser papstler gewest sei,*" ibid., 15 June 1552, Hans Fießler.

council, and, more regrettably, if he had not done so in front of two city guards, Streler would have been left in peace, just the butt of his drinking companions' jokes. Religious disputes were not the heart of the issue in their friendship or in the council's prosecution. However, the honor of the council was at stake, and it was the responsibility of every citizen not only to show respect to his lords and mayors but also to uphold his obligation to obey them. Streler had not only called the councilors bad names, he had also denied one of the basic foundations of law and order in the urban community, the citizens' oath to the council. That Streler had been intoxicated or provoked by his companions to make such outrageous and treasonous statements did not appease the council, except to the extent that it might have saved him from a harsher punishment. He could have been whipped before being escorted out publicly.

Two other contemporary themes arise in the course of Streler's interrogation. First, the emperor appears as an ominous figure, one who would soon arrive and do who knows what to the city. Such talk about him reflects the citizens' fear that the emperor would take vengeance again. When Moritz of Saxony had appeared with his troops before the city's walls on 1 April 1552, Augsburg's population had, not surprisingly, offered no resistance.[46] The city's complicity in Moritz's betrayal of the emperor meant that Augsburgers could anticipate another punishment like the Interim in 1548. The interrogators' somewhat nervous question to Streler, "what does the emperor plan to do against the city?" reveals the councilors' anxiety, as if Streler would have been privy to information unknown to the council. The council saw spies and plotters everywhere at this time. Streler's case presents a contrast to the tensions that erupted between Hans Heinisch and his neighbors, which are discussed below. By August, when Heinisch yelled out into the street that his neighbors had threatened the emperor, imperial troops were in Augsburg again, and the atmosphere in the city had changed once more. Streler had the misfortune to speak six weeks too soon. Nonetheless he benefited from the subsequent change in fortune when he was pardoned on 29 August 1552, two months after his arrest.[47]

Second, Streler's comments about the preachers in Augsburg reflect a further source of dissatisfaction in the city. After the emperor had

---

[46] Zorn, *Augsburg*, 225.
[47] Ibid., Ratsbuch, 29 August 1552.

changed the city's constitution in 1548, the council was forced to expel all preachers who would not conform to the Interim. The new preachers were considered to be sort of collaborators, those who would preach anything to please the council and be paid for it. Many Protestants in the city were unhappy with them and the conservative style of the services permitted by the Interim. Streler's case shows that the preachers were also an object of disdain among Catholics. It was just one more sore point with the council on which Streler had so imprudently touched.

Another case further illustrates some of the issues which worried both the populace and the council at large in Augsburg in the summer of 1552. A citizen of Augsburg, Peter Peurer, turned in Valentin Hefelin from Scheppach to the authorities. Peurer reported on 8 August 1552, that Hefelin had come to his home on the previous Saturday, 6 August, and said the following things:

> [Hefelin] had just come from Füssen where he had received four letters from the emperor's chancellor [Granvelle], among which was one letter for my lord Mayor Rudolf...and he knew that when Lord Mayor Rudolf received his letter, he would laugh...Furthermore, 'you Augsburgers think you have a government which the princes gave you, which is for you, but it was never of that opinion, and if I were the emperor and came into the city, I would have [Mayor Herbrot's] and others' heads chopped off, even if they had a hundred, one on top of the other. That would certainly happen when the emperor arrived in the city in three days. Then he would call a diet and persuade and convince the princes to send their soldiers to the Turks, and then the emperor would bring his entire military into this area, reinstate the bishop of Augsburg and the other Electoral Princes, and expel the Lutherans...[48]

Unfortunately, Hefelin's answers to the accusation reveal almost nothing. For the most part, Hefelin simply denied any wrong-doing, claiming that

---

[48] *"Peter Peurer zaigt an das am sambstag verschinen ainer Valtin Hefelin von Scheppach bey Hausstetten zu ime komen unnd sich hette vernemen lassen, wie er von Fuessen herab zuge, unnd hett vier brieff von der kay. mt. canntzler empfanngen, ainer am herrn Burgermaister Rudolff...unnd er wusste wol so er den brieff herrn Burger. Rudolff zugehorig ime uber anntworten, so wurde er lachen, dann er herr Rudolff wer nit haß als er lauset, mit weitterer vermeldung, ir Augspurger mainet ir habt jetze ain oberkait so euch die fursten gesetzt haben, die fur euch sey, aber es hat nit die maynung nit unnd wann ich kaiser were unnd inn die stat keme, so wolt ich dem kursner sambt andern den kopff herab reissen, unnd wenn sie hundert obeinannder hette, dann das wer gewiß so der kaiser, inn diser statt, welchs inner 3 tagen beschehen solt keme, so wurde er ain Reichstag ausschreiben unnd die fursten dahin persnadirn unnd vermogen, das sie ir kriegsfolkh hinab ann Turken schiken wurden, alsdann wurde der kaiser sein gesamlet kriegsfolkh inn dise Lanndsart bringen, den Bischoffen von Augspurg, des gleichen den alten Churfursten wider einsetzen, unnd also die Luterischen widerumb pasca,"* ibid., 8 August 1552, Urg., Peter Peurer (witness).

he had never received any letters, did not know the emperor's plans, and had nothing against Augsburg's authorities. In one or two instances he denied having made the alleged statements at all. Otherwise, he claimed merely to have repeated things he had heard commonly spoken. For example, in the poultry market in Augsburg he had heard news regarding the emperor's alleged location and plans. His statements seem to have come more from boasting than actual involvement in intrigue.

Hefelin did provide some information by giving an alternative interpretation of his statements. Regarding his statement that the authorities were not as they seemed ("you Augsburgers think you have a government which the princes gave you, which is for you, but it was never of that opinion"), Hefelin explained that he had actually been speaking of the bishop of Augsburg, "because he was afraid that if he came back into this land, he might do a lot of violence, as had happened before."[49] This seems to have been a rather obvious attempt to mislead the interrogators, who knew that he meant the recently reinstated Protestant regime. He was interrogated twice, with the same list of questions, and then tortured. As the scribe noted, "when he did not want to confess anymore, he was...pulled up...and spoken to most earnestly. But in spite of all of that, he did not want in the least to reveal or confess anything further or more."[50]

A closer look at the questions which the council posed to Hefelin shows how anxious the council was about the emperor and how uncertain they were of the future. For example, they asked him, where was the emperor now? On what grounds did he know that the emperor would be here in three days? How did he know that the emperor would call an imperial diet, send the princes' soldiers to Turkey, reinstate the Bishop, expel the Lutherans, "and return everything to its previous state?"[51] It seems ludicrous to think that the council might expect to learn more about the imperial court from a poor peasant from Scheppach than they knew from their own ambassadors. On the other hand, the questions reflect the council's uneasiness about the city's situation.

---

[49] "*Er hab dises nit wider ainen Er. Rate alhie sonnder wider sein herrn den Bischofe von Augspurg geredt, Dann er furcht wann er wider inn das land khombt, so möcht er vilen gwalt thun, wie hievor auch beschehen,*" ibid., 9 August 1552, Valentin Hefelin.

[50] "*Alls er nichts weiters bekhennen wollen, ist er gebunden, auffgestelt, unnd mit der alten leeren scheiben auffzogen, unnd zum ernstlichsten angesprochen worden, Aber unangesehen dessen alles, hatt er mit dem wenigsten weiters merers oder annders nit anzaigen noch bekhennen wollen, Dann wie obsteet, unnd er hievor anzaigt hat,*" ibid., 10 August 1552, Valentin Hefelin.

[51] Ibid., (Fragstück). See Questions 2, 10, and 11.

They were determined to pursue any opportunity to gain more information which might help them prevent or prepare for a calamity like the kind Hefelin described.

Immediately following these inquiries, the interrogators also questioned Hefelin about what undertaking he intended to carry out in Augsburg and who had sent him. The council "could well suppose that it was his intention to stir up mutiny and rioting here. How, and with what means did he plan to carry that out?"[52] Hefelin could only deny having had any such plans.

In addition to the threat of imperial forces, the insults to the mayors of Augsburg also aroused concern. A number of the questions in Hefelin's interrogation ask him what he had against the mayors. What did he know about them that led him to say, for example, that if he were the emperor he would chop off Herbrot's head and others, "even if they had a hundred of them, one on top of the other"? Who were the others whose heads he wanted to chop off?[53] Hefelin denied having said these things and added that he would like to confront the people who claimed to have heard it from him. Of all the various issues which worried the council about Hefelin's "critical speech," in the verdict they focused on his offensive comments about the authorities in Augsburg and "certain persons in particular," referring to the two mayors. The man from Scheppach was stood up on the scaffold and publicly led out of town and banished for life.[54]

The case of the helmetsmith, Hans Heinisch, presents an unusual variation on the types of critical speeches discussed above. In those cases, defendants were arrested or reported for criticizing the authorities in some way. In Heinisch's case, he was arrested for having accused his neighbors of criticizing the authorities. Despite the council's thin skin regarding offenses to the honor of the authorities, especially anything which might cause an uprising, Heinisch was the one arrested, not his neighbors. Also, interestingly, his interrogators focused on what he had said about his neighbors and what he meant by it, but they never asked him about what the neighbors had said. Furthermore, the only

---

[52] "*13) Es sey wol zuvermuetten er hab alhie meutterey unnd auffrur erweken wollen, wie unnd durch was mittel er solchs anrichten wollen, das soll er anzaigen,*" ibid.

[53] "*8) Was fell oder mangel er ab dem herrn Burgermaister Horbrod hab, unnd was strefflichs er gehandlet, die weil er sich horen lassen, wann er kaiser were, so wolt er ime herrn Herbrod sambt anndern den kopff herab reissen, unnd wann sie 100 ob ein annder hetten,*" and "*9) Wer die anndern sein, den er also die kopff herab reissen wolt,*" ibid.

[54] Ibid., 11 August 1552 (Urteil).

witnesses who testified in Heinisch's case were his neighbors, the very people who had turned him in. Their testimony focused on illustrating Heinisch's unfriendly words, rather than on defending their own behavior. None of them denied having criticized the emperor, almost certainly because the council never asked if they had done so. The current government under Herbrot led the opposition to the emperor itself. In other words, the interrogators did not view the incident as a case of potential anti-government plotters, as in the previous cases. Instead, they investigated Heinisch for having insulted the honor of his neighbors by accusing them of making critical speeches. By this point, attributing a critical speech to someone had in itself become a crime in the eyes of the city council, a form of libel, and a way to seek revenge against one's neighbors.

On Saturday night, after drinking at home with his wife and companions, the helmetsmith carried on a dispute, through his window, with his neighbors who were out in the street. According to Heinisch, the innkeeper Christof Raiser and his wife had begun the argument by calling Heinisch "a thief and a knave," and "a thief and a traitor," respectively. In response, Heinisch had retorted to Raiser that "you wanted to kill the emperor, why don't you do it now?"[55] When Raiser's wife tried to silence Heinisch, he called her a "brothel keeper and told her she should reprimand her husband [and not him] because [Raiser] and his neighbors had said there would be no peace in the German lands until the emperor was killed…"[56]

In Raiser's testimony, when he filed charges against Heinisch, he naturally failed to mention having insulted Heinisch in any way. Instead he claimed that after Heinisch had accused him and his friends of having insulted the emperor, Raiser went up to Heinisch and spoke to him, "why do [you] publicly yell out falsehoods about [me] and [my] neighbors?"[57] When Heinisch repeated that he had heard Raiser and the others say treasonous things about the emperor, "Raiser excused

---

[55] "*Ei ir habt umb er dar den Kaiser zu todt schlagen wollen, warumb schlagt ir ine jetzt nit zu todt,*" ibid., 25 August 1552, Hans Heinisch.

[56] "*Christof Raisers wurts weib derhalb guetlich angesprochen unnd abweisen wöllen, warumb er gesagt du hürenwürtin, straff deinen mann selbs, dann er unnd seine nachbauern ausgeben es wurd nimmermer gut thun, auch kain frid inn Teutsch Landen bis der Kaiser zu todt geschlagen unnd gar ausgereut werde,*" ibid.

[57] "*nachdem er Raiser solhs gehort sei er zu ime hinab geloffen unnd ine angesprochen warumb er die unwarhait von ime und sein nachbaurn, also offentlich ausschrie,*" ibid., 24 August 1552, Christof Raiser (witness).

himself further by [Heinisch] and stated that [Heinisch] did him wrong and an injustice, as a "desperate scoundrel" and added that "he would have let him have it" if imperial troops had not arrived and separated them.[58]

After this altercation, Christof Raiser spread the story of Heinisch's accusations to the rest of the neighbors whom he had also implicated. On Sunday around midday, two of the neighbors, Martin Schefelin and Hans Hoffmair, went to see Heinisch by direction of their Upper Street Captain, in order to settle the matter out of court. Hoffmair reported that when they approached Heinisch about his false accusations, "Heinisch did not want to answer them, instead remained extremely obstinate and informed them that he…had filed charges against them with the authorities, and so it would remain, also, he had the die in his hand now, so he could say whatever he wanted."[59]

Raiser and his neighbors apparently knew that the best defense is a good offense. On the following Wednesday Raiser, Hoffmair, Schefelin, and Christoff Wibele went to the council and reported the incident, which initially had involved only Raiser and his wife. The next day, Thursday 25 August 1552, Hans Heinisch was arrested and interrogated.

In addition to his testimony against Heinisch, Hoffmair also declared indignantly that Heinisch's wife had not been friendly to him when he was on his way to file charges against her husband. According to Hoffmair,

> as he and his co-witnesses were on their way to the chancellery today to make their statements and were passing by the helmetsmith's house, he greeted the helm-smith's wife, who was sitting by her window. When she didn't thank him, he asked her if he wasn't worth thanking. To which she responded, oh, you're a fine [one], you have a lot to [do], if I wanted to make the 'little horse run' you wouldn't live another year…and made other threats.[60]

---

[58] "*Dagegen er Raiser sich weiter gegen ime entshuldigt, mit anzaig er thet ime als ain verzweifelter böswicht gewalt unnd unrecht, het sich auch derwegen schier gegen ime nit vhed eingelasen, es wern aber etliche kay. trabanten darzu khommen, welche si von einanndern gebracht,*" ibid.

[59] "*sei er unnd Martin Schifelin, aus bevelch irs ober gassen haubtmans, am Suntag vershinen zu mittag zu ime Haubenschmid gangen, unnd ine solcher von inen ausgebner unwahrhafften reden halben guetlich angesprochen, Auf welches er inen khain anntwurt geben wollen, sonnder zum höchsten gebocht, mit meldung er het es selb viert an die oberkhait bracht, dabei belibe es, er het auch jetzt den wurf inn seiner hand derhalben er auch reden möcht was er wolt, etc.*" ibid., 24 August 1552, Hans Hoffmair (witness).

[60] "*als er unnd seine ob unnd nachvermelte mitzeugen, heut herein zu diser sag inn die cantzlei, unnd für sein Haubenschmidts herbrig gangen, hab er sein Haubenschmidts hausfrau so inn irem*

It is hard to imagine that Hoffmair actually expected the wife of the man he was filing charges against to receive his greeting with gratitude. Clearly, Hoffmair was attempting to discredit Heinisch further, by showing that Hoffmair's wife had ungraciously rejected his friendly gesture. It also shows how deeply the antagonism between the parties ran. Perhaps he even hoped to get Heinisch's wife in trouble for making a superstitious threat. To the interrogators' credit, they ignored this matter in their examination of Heinisch.

In his interrogation, Hans Heinisch admitted to having accused his neighbors of saying, "it would do no more good and there would be no peace in the German lands until the emperor was killed and completely done away with".[61] However, he also added that he had said this only in anger and did not mean anyone specifically.[62] Despite this qualification, Heinisch specifically described a treasonous statement about the emperor and the Catholic clergy, which he had "often" heard from his neighbor Master Jörg Zimmerman: "it will do no good if one doesn't kill the emperor's followers and priestly rabble."[63] According to Heinisch, the other neighbors had also heard Zimmerman say this. For the most part, Heinisch qualified his accusations of his neighbors with the explanation that he had spoken in anger, because they had insulted him, but he never said how or when they had insulted him. Again, the council apparently was not interested.

As for Heinisch's allegation that Raiser's wife was a "brothelkeeper", he explained that he had said this because they had housed a prostitute for half a year. Later on in his testimony Heinish explained that he had only said this in anger, because she had called him a knave and a thief, and because she had indeed housed a common prostitute. In other words, although the accusation was not exactly a lie, he would not have had cause to call her names, if she had not insulted him first.

---

venster gelegen gegruest, unnd als sie ime nit gedanckht, er zu ir gesagt ob er nit dannckhens wert were, darauff si geredt, Ei ir seit ain feiner haußwürt, habt vil zu kneten, wann ich das Rößlin lauffen machen wolt, solt ir wol nit ain jar mehr leben, Item er het auch ain heußlin, unnd der teufl khonts bald hinfüeren, etc. mit der gleichen troe worten mehr etc." ibid.

[61] *"Es wurd nimmermer gut thun, auch kain frid inn Teutsch Landen bis der Kaiser zu todt geschlagen unnd gar ausgereut werde,"* ibid.

[62] *"Hab er inn zorn dise rede gethan, hab aber niemandts gemaint,"* ibid.

[63] *"Er hab solche reden von niemandts dann von seinem nachbaurn, Maister Jörgen Zimmerman, zum offtermaln gehört, das er gesagt, es wurde khain gut thun, aldweil man deß kaisers anhang, unnd pfaffengesind nit zu todt schluege, unnd haben sollihs seine nachpaurn den merertail all gehört,"* ibid., 25 August 1552, Hans Heinisch.

Heinisch also had to answer questions about his meeting with Hoff-mair and Schefelin, who had come to his house on Sunday to discuss the matter with him. Why had he been unwilling to make peace with them? Regarding his claim that he had already filed charges against them, Heinisch explained that he had not been stubborn and had only mentioned filing charges in order to scare them so that they would leave him in peace.[64] Likewise, concerning his claim that he "now had the die in his hand and could say whatever he wanted," Heinisch had said this because they made a show of wanting to make peace with him, but "they had called him a knave, a traitor, and a thief and extremely offended his honor, so that he refused and still refuses."[65] In his final statement to the interrogators, in which he made the traditional request for mercy, forgiveness, and release from imprisonment, Heinisch added that everything he had done, "he had done out of great anger, for which he had great cause."[66]

One question, in particular, captures the irony of this interrogation. As in the cases of critical speeches discussed above, the interrogators asked Hans Heinisch, "wasn't it your intention, with such above-mentioned words and expressions, to cause a mutiny, uprising, and blood-shed?"[67] This question reflects a turning point both in the council's approach to such "critical speeches" and in the significance of the speeches themselves. By 1552, accusing someone of uttering treasonous insults had in itself become a dangerous thing to do. As a result, the accusation—not the alleged speech or insult—was the potential disturber of the peace. The question from the council suggests that Heinisch might have caused a riot (or at least a brawl) by giving out that certain citizens in Augsburg had criticized or threatened the emperor. As Raiser stated in his interrogation, imperial guards had appeared to break up the altercation, which indicates that the emperor was currently residing in the city—which may have been what Heinisch meant by having the

---

[64] "*Er hab dise zwen nit gebocht, unnd die wort, das er es selb viert an die Oberkhait gebracht, annderer gestalt nie geredt, dann das er vermaint si damit zeschrecken, damit si ine weiter unbekhumert liessen,*" ibid.

[65] "*Er hab diß darumb gesagt, dhweil sy mit ime tedigen wöllen, aber ine wie obsteet, schelmen lauren unnd dieb unnd also zum höchsten an sein Eeren gescholten, das ers nit thun noch inn khain teding eingeen wöllen,*" ibid.

[66] "*Bitt zum höchsten umb gnad, verzeihung unnd widerledigung seiner venckhnus, dann was er wie obsteet verhanndlt hab er aus grossem zorn, darzu er dann zum hechsten verursacht, gethan,*" ibid.

[67] "*Ob er nit mit sollichen obgemelten worten unnd ausgeben, ain Meiterei, auffrur, unnd plütver-giessen zuerweckhen im synn gehabt,*" ibid. (Fragstück).

die in his hand now. Catholics, hearing of the men's alleged insults and
strengthened by the presence of imperial forces, might have attacked
Raiser and his friends. Or, conversely, Protestants might have found
inspiration in the words and been encouraged to resist the emperor,
thereby embarrassing the council. The magistrates were already in the
awkward position of not wanting to accept the emperor's offers for
military assistance against the defiant population and yet wanting to
use the intractability of the citizens as an excuse for not being able to
enforce his decrees. As a result, the tables were turned in this case, in
which not the critics but their accuser came under attack.

I would also suggest that the council did not pursue Raiser and his
friends because it did not wish to investigate or punish another case
of anti-imperial sentiment. Rather, the council chose to treat it as a
case of libel or personal enmity amongst the neighbors. The incident
shows how accusing someone of making a critical speech could serve
as a weapon to use against people who offended your honor. Despite
his words to them, Heinisch had never actually reported his neighbors
for making critical speeches; he used it as a feint to scare them. It was
not his intention to turn them in as dangerous plotters but rather to
intimidate them into leaving him alone. Unfortunately for Heinisch,
they called his bluff. The tone of the accusations which flew back and
forth between Heinisch and his neighbors suggests that there was a
history of antagonism between them. Some cause for the enmity may
lie in the word traitor (*Laur*) which Raiser, Hoffmair, and Schefelin had
called Heinisch. Heinisch, a smith who specialized in making helmets,
was in service with the imperial troops. His wife petitioned the emperor
for assistance and indicated that her husband was about to leave town
under the command of Captain Franz von Steinbrunnen.

It is very likely that Heinisch and his neighbors were at odds because
of his serving the emperor and that Raiser and the others had indeed
expressed sentiments very similar to the ones which Heinisch had attributed to them. Nonetheless, it did not serve the council's interests at this
time to investigate them and perhaps turn up evidence they would rather
leave concealed, especially if the emperor decided to intervene and make
an example of the men. The council did not care if Heinisch's allegations were accurate or not. Very possibly the council cared less about
insults to the emperor than about its own honor, as long as they were
not expressed in a way which could embarrass the council. Heinisch's
crime in the eyes of the council and his neighbors—which had driven

them to take legal action—was the fact that he had spoken about them "openly." Heinisch's case resembles the other critical speeches in this concern about their public nature.

The council conveniently and quietly disposed of Hans Heinisch by releasing him from prison in order to join his regiment on time. As the scribe noted on the back of his interrogation record, "[Hans Heinisch] has been turned over to his regiment without any action being undertaken."[68]

A few months after the emperor's arrival in Augsburg, another case of derogatory speech arose when some men allegedly called out, "ha, priest!" (*hui pfaff!*) while sleigh-riding through town. Both men, Joachim Elsesser and Philip Gauger insisted that they had not yelled "ha, priest" and Gauger even claimed, "he had absolutely no idea what 'ha, priest' was supposed to mean."[69] Their driver, Jorg Mayer, testified that "he didn't hear that they had yelled 'ha, priest', but he did hear them yell 'ha, cat!' (*hui katz!*) several times."[70] (He did not know what that meant either.) The council suspected that the men had been ridiculing someone, and the interrogators wanted to know who their intended victim was.[71] When the men refused to admit having yelled "ha, priest," the council had them interrogated a second time. The council's information must have been fairly reliable, or have come from an influential source, for them to have pursued the matter further. The list of questions from the second hearing insisted with some frustration, "they would not have yelled 'ha, priest' aimlessly or without reason."[72]

The resulting entry in the punishment book says nothing at all about what the men yelled. Instead it merely states, rather vaguely, that they went sleigh-riding at night, behaved very badly in front of the commander's quarters, and spoke disrespectfully to the soldiers on guard. They were sentenced to four weeks in a tower, after which they

---

[68] "*Ist inns Regiment on furnemung ainicher handlung geanntwort worden,*" ibid., 25 August 1552, Hans Heinisch.

[69] "*Er wiß auch gar mit nichten waß dasselb geschray hui pfaff bedeutten soll,*" ibid., 7 December 1552, Philip Gauger.

[70] "*er hab nit gehort, das sy hui pfaff geschrien haben, aber wol hui khatz hab er sy ettlich mal schreien horen,*" 7 December 1552, Jorg Mayer (witness).

[71] "*Wer sy angelernet zu schreien hui pfaff und ob sy damit den hern obristen ain ersa. rath oder di knecht haben schmehen oder verklainern wollen, und was gestallt,*" ibid., 3 December 1552, Philip Gauger (Frastück).

[72] "*so wurden sy nit vergebens oder on ursach geschrien haben hui pfaff,*" ibid., 7 December 1552 (Fragstück).

were to be released on a written bond, forbidden to enter the taverns for a year or set foot on the imperial highway after curfew, and, lastly, they were to be given no wine while they were in the tower.[73] It seems a rather heavy sentence for unspecified harm aimed at an obscure target. It is unclear which commander's housing is referred to in this statement. It could refer either to the city council's military command or to the command of the emperor, whose troops were still residing in Augsburg. The emperor's presence in 1552 required the city council to enforce the Interim, a policy which was unpopular with many Augsburgers.

As these cases demonstrate, not only did various citizens voice their criticism of the government, but the council responded with an almost irrational fear of insurrection. Both the populace and the city government seem to have been frustrated at their lack of control over the circumstances that guided Augsburg's fate in the 1550s. The religious issues have faded somewhat to the background in this discussion, while political issues have come to the fore. Yet, as seen in several of the cases, such as the Catholic Hans Streler, who criticized the council and preachers, or the men who yelled, "ha, priest!" in front of the commander's house, the religious and political aspects of cases often intertwined themselves in such a way that the attempt to separate them would be artificial. The exploration of tension, which emerged in conflicts over printed and spoken words, shows the existence of genuine dissent amongst the populace, some of which may have arisen from religious opinions but which were often expressed as discontent with the political authorities that determined religious affairs. The emperor's intervention in Augsburg's government and the indisputable linking of the political regime with the religious establishment connected these issues inseparably and added a new facet to relations among Augsburg's citizens. It is in this respect that we begin to see signs of the phenomenon known as confessionalization, in the sense, first of all, that people felt that one's choice of religion reflected one's political

---

[73] "*Philips Gauger unnd Joachim Elsesser, sein bey nechtlicher weil im schlitten gefarn, unnd haben sich vor des obersten herberg unnd sonnst gannz ungeschikt gehalten, auch den lanndsknechten an der wach unbeschaidenlich zugesprochen, Derhalben sie inn fronvest gelegt, unnd volgends vier wochen auff ain thurn geschafft worden, Unnd so sie solche aufferlegte thurnstraff erstattet, sollen sie auff ain geschribne urphed wider herab gelassen und inen aufferlegt werden, die wiertsheuser ain jar lanng zumeiden, unnd zwischen den zwaien hornplasen nit auffs Reichsstraß zukomen inen soll auch kain wein auff den thurn geben werdenn,*" ibid., Strafbuch, 8 December 1552.

allegiance and, secondly, that one ought to take a stand one way or the other, even though the council did not ask them to do so. The linking of religious and political positions seemed to make the need for clarity more important though not yet essential.

CHAPTER SIX

MAKING THE BI-CONFESSIONAL CITY:
RELIGIOUS ENCOUNTERS

What is his confession or belief?[1]

Good question. Or is it? As so many cases have shown, the question of
how to identify one's confession or belief was hardly a straightforward
matter in the sixteenth century. Certainly it could not be answered
with the simple labels given to the many confessions of faith that
would later emerge. The young man to whom this question was posed
responded like so many of his contemporaries by locating the place(s)
where his faith was practiced. Yet something new was revealed in his
interrogation. This question, which appeared in a list of inquiries for
him in 1550, marks the first occasion on which the term "confession"
appeared in one of Augsburg's judicial interrogations. It was also the
first time the council has asked a defendant directly about his beliefs
(*glaub*). The city of Augsburg witnessed many changes after its defeat
in the Schmalkaldic War: the loss of the guilds' political power in
favor of the patricians, the return of Catholicism, and the imposition
of the Interim's controversial form of Protestantism. The presence of
two religions, in a politically divisive period, heightened interests in
identifying religious affiliations.

This chapter focuses on the religious themes that appear prominently
in legal cases from 1548 to 1555. As discussed in the previous chapter,
it is difficult to isolate religious from political or economic aspects in
these cases, since a combination of factors usually motivated people.
Focusing on the religious aspects of the cases allows us to see how and
under what circumstances religion could bring persons into conflict
with one another and with their council. It also gives us an idea of
which problems Augsburg's council viewed as most important and how
it viewed its role in regulating religious life in Augsburg.

---

[1] "*Was sein confeßion oder glaub sei*," StadtAA, Reichsstadt, Urg. 23 June 1550, Thomas
von Löven (Fragstück).

During this period the population responded to the innovations and insecurity that were introduced by the Interim in 1548 and not resolved until Augsburg reconciled itself to being a religiously diverse community in 1555. While the cases examined in this period do show religious conflicts, they also show evidence of harmony, as did the Catholic Hans Streler who socialized regularly with Protestant companions.[2] As did the Germair household, the parties involved had been getting along with each other; the city government did not intervene to settle a conflict among friends or neighbors.[3] The few conflicts that do emerge between citizens, usually close neighbors, clearly demonstrate that it took a combination of factors, not religious differences alone, to motivate hostility. In this period we also see a gradual change in Augsburg, as religious beliefs became linked to particular government policies, introducing a sort of confessionalized age into Augsburg, though—or perhaps because—it embraced two confessions at once. Rather than supporting one faith to the exclusion of others, Augsburgers now had to find ways to accommodate both.

ATTACKS ON THE CLERGY

The first group of cases, which concerns attacks on members of the clergy, includes two general types. The first few cases comprise incidents in which anti-clerical behavior was suspected but remained unproven or unsubstantiated. The very tenuousness of the allegations suggests the elevated sensitivity of the council to anti-clerical sentiments. The second group of cases involves very direct and indisputable, usually verbal, attacks on clergy for a variety of reasons. Most of the attacks were directed specifically against representatives of the Catholic Church, although one targeted Protestants instead. Another incident shows hostility towards Catholic ceremonies conducted by priests. Although some of these cases may reflect a dislike of clergy for reasons other than doctrine (because of their privileges, wealth, authority, or abuse of power) most of the incidents seem to reflect an antipathy for the religion the priests represented. In other words, they are both anti-clerical and anti-Catholic at the same time. One interesting feature

---

[2] Hans Streler's case is discussed in Chapter Five.
[3] The Germair household is discussed in Chapter One.

about these conflicts is that Augsburgers usually expressed religious dissent by attacking church representatives rather than their followers.

The story of Hans Hoffmann, a baker's journeyman from Bamberg, introduces the first group of cases. Hoffmann had been drinking on St. Jacob's Eve at Koch's tavern by Our Lady's Gate. He was so inebriated that he could not recall how much he or his companions had drunk. On the way home, he became involved in an altercation at Bonifacius Wallesser's house. He allegedly "hunted" or chased a monk who had been standing in Wallesser's doorway and then shoved open Wallesser's window twice to challenge him and the others within. The list of questions (*Fragstück*) indicates that Hoffmann called to them, "if you're honorable people, come on out and fight me!"[4] Did Hoffmann really want to attack the monk? Did he know the monk personally or did he just recognize his monastic garb? Did anti-clerical feelings drive him to challenge Wallesser, because he harbored clerics in his home? We have no way of knowing. Hoffmann denied having chased the monk or even having seen a monk that evening.

The few questions in Hoffmann's interrogation indicate that he had undoubtedly displayed unruly behavior. He had "cursed and sworn in an unchristian manner," and he had "yelled at the provost...and behaved very badly."[5] It is quite possible that Hoffmann was too drunk to notice if the man in the doorway were a monk or not. The interesting aspect is that the council thought it worth investigating. Hoffmann had not chased just anyone but he had "hunted a monk." In 1548, monks had reappeared in Augsburg, and the city council tried to discourage displays of disrespect or resentment against them. The punishment book (*Strafbuch*) entry listed Hoffmann's crimes as "being drunk, cursing, chasing a monk, breaking a window, and resisting arrest." After a night in prison, Hoffmann was banished. As a foreigner, Hoffmann was easily disposed of through banishment.

Almost one year later, on 30 July 1549, Heinrich Korn was arrested for an alleged attack on a priest. Korn explains it best in his own words:

---

[4] "*wern sie erlich lewt sollten sie herauß unnd mit ime schlagen*," ibid., 31 July 1548, Hans Hoffmann (Fragstück).

[5] "*3) Warumb er so unchristlich geflucht unnd geschworen hab*" and "*5) Warumb er uber den profosen...geschryen, unnd sich so ungeschickht gehalten*," ibid.

As he came in by [Holy] Cross [Gate], someone came up to him and stood quietly. [Korn] wished him a good evening, but the other didn't thank him. Instead [the other man] pushed him out of the way, drew from his scabbard and attacked him. If Korn had not jumped backwards a step, [the man] probably would have cleaved his shoulders in two. Upon this, Korn drew his dagger, because he had no other weapon on him, and said, 'he should do it properly.' At this, the other—he didn't know if it was a priest or who he was, because it was nine at night and pitch dark—said to him, 'you're not the one I'm waiting for,' and then left abruptly.[6]

Not only did Korn not know that he had drawn his weapon against a priest, but he claimed it was a case of self-defense. The council must have had better information than Korn about his attacker's identity, although it is unclear who reported the matter. The interrogators' questions sought a source for Korn's supposed enmity against the priest. "Why did he throw his dagger at the priest?" "What caused him to bear such a grudge against the clergy?" "Hadn't he made an attack against them?"[7] Korn denied having any "grudge" against the clergy and asserted once more, in his request for mercy and release, that "he came into the matter innocently and had extreme and great cause for how he handled himself."[8] The council saw it that way too in the end. The entry in the punishment book explained that Korn had drawn a dagger on a priest but was shown not to have drawn first. Therefore, although a foreigner like Hoffmann, Korn was released but first sent to appear before the Discipline Lords (*Zuchtherren*).

One would love to know why a priest would be waiting in the dark by Holy Cross Gate to draw his sword on an enemy. What we do know is that Heinrich Korn, a tailor's journeyman from Wembding, happened to be in the wrong place at the wrong time. His alleged anti-clericalism turned out to be specious. Like the previous case, this incident shows that

---

[6] "*Erstlich, als er auffm kreutz herein ganngen, sei ime ainer khomen der still gestanden deme er ainen guten abendt gewunst, der ime aber nit gedanckht, sonnder ine den negsten aus dem weg gestossen, von leder gezuckht unnd auff ine geschlagen, unnd wo er Khorn nit ainen sprung hinder sich gethon, so hette er ime vermutlich den Ruggen von einanndern gespalten etc. darauf er Khorn seinen tolchen, dann er sonst khain wehr gehabt, auch von leder gezuckht, unnd gesagt er solte gemach thun, darauff diser, wiß nit obs ain priester oder wer er sei, dann es zu abendts umb 9 uhr und schier finster gewest, zu ime gesagt, du bist nit der recht darauff ich gewart, unnd damit den negsten von ime, unnd darvon geloffen,*" ibid., 1 August 1549, Heinrich Khorn.

[7] "*1) Warumb er ainem priester seinen tolchen nachgeworfen,*" "*2) Was in zu solhem neid gegen den geistlichen verursacht hab,*" and "*3) Ob er kainen anschlag wider si gemacht hab,*" ibid., (Fragstück).

[8] "*dann er unschuldig darhinder khomen, und was er wie obgemelt verhanndelt, darzu sei er hochlich unnd großlich verursacht worden,*" ibid., Heinrich Khorn.

the city council took seriously its responsibility to protect the Catholic clergy and seemed to expect trouble. Yet, the testimony of both men fails to reveal any specific animosity towards priests or their faith.

The serious cases of real attacks on Catholic clergy occurred in the years immediately following the introduction of the Interim and the return of the Catholic Church, 1549 and 1550, and then seem to fade away. The first example involves a couple, Georg and Dorothea Schwarz,[9] who shouted insults at a prelate and his lay guests, who were eating in an innkeeper's garden. The prelate's guests were the Schwarz' own neighbors. Abbot Sylvester Gottfried of Oberelchingen had come to Augsburg on some business with the Cathedral Chapter. The Augsburg city council honored this esteemed guest with a gift of good wine, and his host the innkeeper Lienhart Beham had shown him great courtesy.[10] On Saturday evening 13 May 1549, the abbot, his servant, and some guests from the neighborhood (whom he had invited on the innkeeper's recommendation) were enjoying a meal in Beham's garden. According to the abbot's letter to the council, his hosts in Augsburg had made him feel welcome, "with the exception of some people living in the house next-door...including Georg Schwarz' wife."[11]

Ironically, Dorothea Schwarzin instigated the investigation that led to her punishment by registering charges that one of the abbot's guests, Katharina Egglbergerin, had insulted her. Georg and Dorothea Schwarz went to the Discipline Lords to complain that Katharina Egglbergerin had called her (Schwarzin) a "dishonorable, shameful scoundrel...[and said]...she doesn't sit there with honor and piety."[12] When asked to explain the accusation, Egglbergerin testified that as she sat with the Abbot of Oberelchingen and his honorable guests, "she was verbally abused from the Schwarz' house, they made donkeys ears at her and called out, 'look, how they sit a pretty woman next to the monk!'"[13] However, she absolutely refused to admit that she had insulted

---

[9] Although neither Schwarzin nor Egglbergerin are identified by first name in these legal proceedings, the relevant entries in the tax records indicate that they went by the names Dorothea and Katharina, respectively (Steuerbuch 1550).

[10] StadtAA, Reichsstadt, Urg. 17 May 1549 (letter).

[11] Ibid.

[12] "*wie Hannsen Egglpergers hawsfraw sy die Schwärtzin ainen erloser hinckhenden schellmen geschollten, unnd sy sytze nit mit frumkhait und eern aldae,*" ibid., 15 May 1549, Schwarzin.

[13] "*sey sy Egglbergerin auß des Schwartzen hauß ubl geschmecht, Esel oren uber sy gemacht und zum vennster herauß gereden worden, syhe wie setzt man dem munich ain schone frauen an die seytten,*" ibid., Egglbergerin.

Schwarzin at all, and Schwarzin also refused to confess to having insulted her. Since they refused to acknowledge any guilt, both parties, husbands and wives, were ordered to pledge to hold their peace against one another and instructed to bring forth witnesses. The case proceeded when the council received the above-mentioned letter from the abbot of Elchingen, explaining his version of the incident, and Katharina Egglbergerin subsequently called witnesses to testify on her behalf.

Leonhard Abellin, a cooper, who had been eating in Beham's garden with the abbot and the guests, testified that two women in the Schwarz' house had called out, "look how the abbot drinks, look how the monk bleats, and last night there was really something going on, when someone leaned a woman against a tree."[14] Similarly, Leonhard Beham, the innkeeper's son, added that he had heard someone in the Schwarz' house yell, "now the monk drinks, now the monk bleats, and a pretty woman sits at his side."[15] Another of the abbot's guests, Thomas Thalhaimer, corroborated their testimony.

The abbot's servant Martin Weichselbrawn provided the most detailed and comprehensive testimony. According to him, the abbot and his guests were sitting in Beham's garden, when someone in the Schwarz' house yelled, "they would like to see how they can annoy the women, because last night, someone leaned a woman against a tree." Moreover they had shouted, "'look how the monk drinks, look how the monk bleats,' and all together were so disrespectful that—with all due respect—it would have been enough for a brothel." In response to the women's haranguing, Weichselbrawn claimed that the abbot had recited, "a spider in a sack, and a whore in a house do not hide themselves." He testified that when Hans Egglberger also remarked on Dorothea Schwarzin's abusive yelling, she said to him, "he should come up to her and—pardon the expression—look her in the rear end."[16] At this, Weichselbrawn had called Schwarzin a whore. Then Georg Schwarz

---

[14] "*schaw wie drinckht der Abbt, wie plert der munich, unnd gestern gienng es recht zu do man das weib an den paum laniet,*" ibid., 20 May 1549, Lienhart Abellin (witness).

[15] "*yetzt drinckht der munch, yetzt plert der munch, und sytzt ime ain schone fraw an der seyten,*" ibid., Lienhart Beham der Jung (witness).

[16] "*sy wellen gern sehen wie es denen weibern ergern welle, dann nechtu hab man aine an ainen paum gelanit, etc. . . . , schaw wie drinckht der Munich, schaw wie plert der minich unnd in Summa ain solliche schanndt getriben das es (mit gunst zumelden) in ainem gemainen hauß genug were, darauf sein Herr der Prelat gesagt ain spynn in ainem sackh, unnd ain hur in ainem hauß, verbergen sych nit, Die Schwerzin hab auch zum Eggenberger, wie er das herauß schreyen beredt, gesagt, er sol hinauf zu ir geen, unnd ir mit reverentz zemelden, in hindern guggen, do hab er zeug sy die Schwartzin ain hurn geschollten,*" ibid., Martin Weichselbrawn (witness).

wanted to know who had insulted his wife, and the abbot told him he should come on over and he would tell him. When Schwarz had joined them in the garden, the abbot told him about his wife's disrespectful behavior. Schwarz excused himself, claiming that he was ignorant of the entire matter, because he had not been home. He subsequently drank a glass of wine with the abbot, in order to settle things peacefully. Leonhard Abellin also testified that Schwarz had excused the affair by claiming that it was "nothing more than women's business."[17]

Notwithstanding the denunciations of all of these witnesses from the garden, the most damning testimony actually came from Schwarzin's own maid. Veronica Strellmairin swore an oath to tell the truth, a condition required of the other witnesses but specifically emphasized in the record of her testimony, since she was testifying against her employers. She told the following story: her mistress, Dorothea Schwarzin, was sitting by the window when "she said, extra loudly, 'look there's one woman sitting by the monk at table, just short of kissing him on the mouth, but everything else is happening'." The maid, who was also standing by the open window, said, "last night she was fooling around with him. I thought she wanted to get a child from the monk." Then someone in the garden called the maid a "sacramental sow whore" and her mistress said, "now the monk is looking up too." At that her master, Georg Schwarz, had said, "out of the dog, into the monk." According to her, Georg and Dorothea Schwarz had forbidden Strellmairin to report all of this talk, "but for the truth's sake, she didn't want to conceal it."[18]

To settle the libelous accusations, the Discipline Lords required the Schwarz and the Egglbergers to pledge peace towards one another and swear that they knew nothing dishonorable of the other party. In addition, they punished the plaintiffs (Georg and Dorothea Schwarz) who had reported the incident; Georg and Dorothea were both sentenced to spend two days in a tower. Not knowing defeat when it stared them in

---

[17] "*es sey nichts dann weybs deding etc.*" ibid., Lienhart Abellin (witness).

[18] "*ir fraw die Schwerzin am Guggerlin gesessen uberlaut geredt, und gesagt, syhe es sytzt aine bei dem Munch an dem tisch, on das sy den Munch nit gar in das maul khusst, das annder geschicht alles, darauf sy die magt so auch bei offnem venster gestannden gesagt, sy hat necht auch am leben mit im gehabt, ich hab gemaindt sy welle dem Munch ain kindt anmachen, in dem hab ainer in dem garten sy die magt, ain Sacramentische sew hurn geschollten, unnd ir fraw gesagt, yetzt sycht der Munch auch herauff, hab Schwartz gesagt auß dem hundt, in den Munch, Welche Redt Schwartz und sein hausfraw ir zeugin zemelden verbotten, Sy wells aber dannacht umb der warhait willen nit dahinden lassen,*" ibid., Veronica Strellmairin (witness).

the face, the Schwarz contested this punishment and appeared before the council. The council retaliated by doubling the punishment to four days each.[19] Not surprisingly, a few weeks after the case was resolved to the Schwarz' disadvantage, Schwarzin had yet another dispute to settle. This time it involved her maid, Veronica Strellmairin and her parents. Apparently Schwarzin had refused to pay Strellmairin's salary after she had testified against her. The Discipline Book (*Zuchtbuch*) records that Schwarzin was required to pay the maid her earned wages.[20]

What motivated Dorothea Schwarzin to scold the abbot and his guests? She probably did not know the abbot personally. Could it be that she was offended at being excluded from the gathering in Beham's garden, when so many other neighbors had been included? Was she motivated by envy to ridicule those who were invited? Perhaps she was not invited because Beham knew of her anti-clerical sentiments and felt she would be an inappropriate guest for the abbot's party. Or, maybe she and Katharina Egglbergerin were already at odds for other reasons. We know for certain that this case involves more than a question of the two women's honorable reputations. Schwarzin's remarks took an unmistakably anti-clerical form, and her disrespectful behavior towards the abbot was irrefutable, as shown by the abundant testimony above.

The tone of the sentiments expressed by Georg and Dorothea Schwarz and their maid towards the guests gathered in Beham's garden reflects a common theme in medieval and early Reformation era anti-clericalism. Their comments, particularly Dorothea Schwarzin's, illustrate the popularly satirized licentious lifestyle of the clergy. Wine: "look how the monk drinks," Women: "look how a pretty woman sits at his side," and Song: "look how the monk bleats" (depending on what she meant by the term *plert*).[21] The Discipline Lords did not investigate the allegations of a couple fooling around in the garden the night before. Those activities were not part of Schwarzin's original allegations, and were definitely not something the council wanted to know about, especially if they involved the abbot. When Georg and

---

[19] "*Dieweil sich Georg Schwartz unnd sein hausfrau, der verordenten straffherrn aufferlegtten straff zugeben verwidert unnd sich derhalb fur ain Ersamen Rate beruffen, so ist inen dieselb straff wie gebreuchig ist geduppelt worden,*" ibid., RB 1542–49, 21 May 1549.

[20] "*sonnderlichen die Schwarzin zugesagt, die magdt uff Jacobi irs verdiennten lidlons zubezallen,*" ibid., Zuchtbuch der Strafherren, 8 June 1549.

[21] See "pleren" in *Fischer's Lexikon*, vol. I (ABP).

Dorothea Schwarz first went to the authorities they did not accuse Katharina Egglbergerin of adultery—which they could have done if there were anything to prove—but of having injured Schwarzin's honor. Moreover, the events on the evening in question did not constitute an illicit tryst but a public gathering of neighbors.

Why did Dorothea Schwarzin accuse her neighbor Katharina Egglbergerin before the council? Perhaps she truly felt that her honor had been offended by Egglbergerin. Although none of the witnesses mentioned Egglbergerin's having made any statement at all, their testimony certainly does not exclude the possibly that she did say something insulting to Schwarzin. The abbot's letter does not go into any detail about the comments exchanged on either side. He wrote merely that when Schwarzin began to harass them, "I, my servant, and my guests, at first and for a good while remained silent, in the hope that they would give up their insults and jokes...but then my servant and I finally were moved to anger, so that we let ourselves into the quarrel."[22] Nonetheless, it is not unreasonable to think that, in the flurried exchange of insults between the Schwarz and the abbot's guests, Egglbergerin might have joined in the fray in the hopes of shaming Schwarzin into leaving them in peace. But why pick on her, when the men had also made insulting remarks, unless there was a pre-existing argument between the two women?

What still seems inexplicable is how Dorothea Schwarzin thought she could succeed with a charge against a neighbor for disrespectful behavior when her own offensiveness could be proven so easily.[23] Perhaps she truly saw it as a personal matter of honor between her and Katharina Egglbergerin and did not expect the anti-clerical comments to become an issue. In that case, she certainly had misinterpreted the council's position on that subject. Another possibility may be that she was hoping to fend off a similar suit from the Egglbergers or the abbot

---

[22] "*Ich, noch meine diener, auch ernannte meine Gösst, erstlich, unnd ain gute weil, darzu stillgeschwigen, vermainend, sie sollten von solchem verspotten, unnd gelächter lassen, So hatt doch dasselbig nit beschehen wöllen...dardurch sie mich, unnd auch meine diener letzlich zu ettwas zorn, unnd dahin bewögt haben, Das wir uns gegen inen, inn zanck begeben,*" StadtAA, Reichsstadt, Urg. 17 May 1549 (letter).

[23] In a similar case, in seventeenth century Pegau, a man sued his neighbor for having injured his honor by accusing him of property damage and then turned out to be the vandal in question afterall. Eileen Crosby discussed this incident in her paper "Claiming Honor: Litigants, honor, and the legal process in seventeenth- and eighteenth-century Saxony," presented at the Fourth Transatlantic Doctoral Seminar, 22–25 April 1998 in Göttingen, sponsored by the German Historical Institute.

by first discrediting Egglbergerin, as Hans Heinisch's neighbors did with him.[24] If so, her efforts were unnecessary, as well as self-destructive, since the abbot did not write his letter to the council until informed by Hans Egglberger that Schwarzin had sued his wife. It is not surprising to find evidence of resentment towards Catholic clergy, or their supporters, in an overwhelmingly Protestant community. Rather, it makes the friendliness shown to the visiting abbot and his servant by the Behams, Egglbergers and other neighbors even more striking. Clearly it reminds us that not only the wealthy patriciate had harbored Catholic sympathizers during Augsburg's decade of reform.

About a month later a man named Hans Löffler was arrested for verbally abusing several distinguished clerics, namely, three lords from the cathedral chapter. He claimed to have been on his way home from a party and quite drunk. As he passed the priests in the Long Priest Alley, in the Cathedral Quarter, he failed to perform the customary hat removal. When the clerics called him "Lutheran," he retorted, that "he didn't take off his beret for idol-worshippers."[25] They then told him to "kiss their asses." Löffler testified that at this point he got angry and said "he wouldn't kiss the priests of [a false god]."[26]

The council began the interrogations of Löffler with relatively open-ended and unaggressive questions. They wanted to know what he had said, to whom he had said it, where he had said it, and why. They also wondered, in some anxiety, if he was in league with others to bother the clerics and do them some harm. Finally, and somewhat self-consciously, they asked him if he did not think they, the magistrates, would disapprove of his antagonistic behavior and would just let him go unpunished.[27] In other words, what was he thinking?

In this rather fruitless first interrogation, Löffler presented his case as one of harmless squabbling, inebriation, not to mention self-defense, since the priests had insulted him first. After interviewing ten witnesses who lived on the street (half of whom claimed they had heard nothing) and receiving a report from the three prelates involved, the council pursued Löffler more aggressively. The second list of questions begins

---

[24] See Chapter Five.

[25] "*haben sie die pfaffen zu ime gesagt, er were luterisch, darauff er inen geanntwurt, er zuche khain paret gegen kainem gotzendiener ab,*" StadtAA, Reichsstadt, Urg. 18 June 1549, Hans Löffler.

[26] "*hinwider ime die pfaffen haissen, mit Ern zemelden, im hindern leckhen, auf solchs er Löffler inn zorn weiter gegen inen geredt er wolte wie gemelt khainen palmpfaffen leckhen,*" ibid.

[27] StadtAA, Reichsstadt, Urg. 18 June 1549, Hans Löffler (Fragstück).

ominously, "the honorable council has heard his statement and, not neglecting to investigate the matter industriously, has found that things were very different from what he had indicated."[28] With the assistance of witness testimony, the interrogators were able to cite specific offensive statements that Löffler had allegedly made. They used these statements as the basis for the second list of questions, which they then used for the second and third interrogations. The lead question placed significance on the issue of who had spoken first, Löffler or the priests. The list of questions ended with the council's instruction for the interrogators s to have Löffler tortured, if he refused to answer truthfully.

In this second round of interrogations, Löffler initially conceded that he honestly did not know or remember who had started the quarrel, because he had been drunk at the time. This was a reversal of statements he made in his first interrogation, when he claimed unequivocally that the priests had addressed him first for failing to remove his hat. After being threatened by the executioner,[29] Master Veit, Löffler confessed that in fact he had addressed the priests first. Following procedure, the third interrogation began with Löffler confirming this point again without torture. The council's second accusation against Löffler asserted that he yelled at the priests, "the shame of idolators on all you knaves, it's no good with you here, I have to help by striking you dead!"[30] Löffler absolutely refused to admit saying anything of the sort. Even after the being threatened with torture by Master Veit, Löffler emphatically denied having said such a thing. Tougher threatening at the end of the third interrogation, which meant tying his hands together and strapping him up in preparation for the strappado, produced only the admission that he had insulted and cursed the priests but had never threatened to kill them. Instead, he insistently claimed that he had said to the priests, "it would be no good with them until one struck down their idols."[31]

Löffler readily conceded to the allegations that he had slandered the priests, admitting that he had called them, "idol-worshippers and Baal's

---

[28] "*Ain ersamer rate hab sein urgicht gehort, und nit underlassen der sachen mit vleiß nachzu-forschen befynndt die selb vil annderst dann er anzaigt, geschaffen sein,*" ibid., 22 June 1549 (Fragstück).

[29] Threatening the defendant meant showing him or her the instruments of torture which could be used.

[30] "*2) Das dich potzmarter schenndt aller poßwicht, es thuet kain guet weil ir hie seyet, ich mueß euch nachhelffen zu todt schlagen,*" ibid.

[31] "*es werde mit inen khain gut thun, biß man inen ain mal die gotzen, umb den grund schlage,*" ibid., 22 June 1549 (second hearing on that day).

priests" but only in the context of refusing to "kiss their asses."[32] Beyond this, Löffler denied otherwise slandering them, cursing, or blaspheming. Threats of torture and preparations for pulling him up accomplished nothing except to squeeze out the concession that he had wished some sickness on them, such as "St. Valentine's or St. Kirin's [disease]."[33] The council had instructed the interrogators to use torture if necessary, but only on the condition that Löffler's health could bear it. It must have been a relief to Löffler when the scribe noted at the end of the third hearing, "[Löffler] would have been pulled up without weights after he refused to answer the second question [regarding the death threats], but, because of his hernia, which Meister Veit observed, it could not be carried out."[34]

The evidence against Hans Löffler came mainly from the three cathedral lords. Two of them particularly recalled Löffler threatening to harm them, in addition to slandering them. One of their peers also witnessed the incident. Herr Leonhard von Friedberg, vicar of the cathedral, was looking out his window when he heard the other clerics being insulted by Löffler, who then looked up and yelled, "you're another one of those idol-worshippers!" Herr Leonhard told him, "go on home, you know you shouldn't be doing this," and Löffler made his way down the street "cursing and scolding."[35] Two of the clerics who met Löffler on the street that night, Herr Christof and Herr Ott von Bentznaw, took Löffler's threats very seriously, especially after another man joined him. According to them, Löffler had said, "it's no good until we strike all you priests dead!"[36] Herr Christof's servant went to retrieve a weapon for him, and Herr Ott testified that Christof had said

---

[32] "*Es sei war, als ine die pfaffen, wie er das nehner mal anzaigt, leckhen haissen, das er zu inen gesagt, ir gotzendiener unnd palmpfaffen ich leckh khainen etc.,*" ibid., 22 June 1549 (first hearing on that day).

[33] "*So khonne er sich ainmal nit erinnern wie oder mit was woerten er geflucht unnd gescholten hab, annders dann das er gesagt das euch Sant Veltin oder Sant Kirin etc. ankum, etc.,*" ibid., (second hearing on that day). St. Valentine's disease usually refers to epilepsy and St. Kirin's (more commonly St. Quirin) to small pox or some other skin disease.

[34] "*Er were gleichwol mit lerer scheibe nachdem er nit lauter auf obemelte zwen articul anntwurt geben worden auffzogen, hatt aber seines bruhs halben den Maister Veit gesehen, nit seie oder geschehen khonnen,*" ibid.

[35] "*hab wol zu seim hawß herauß gestehen und wie der weber fur sey gangen hab er dry prister hardt geschmecht und zu im hinauff geredt du bist auch der gotzendynner aynner, Da hadt Her Lenhardt in geanttwurdt gan heym du waist wol daß du es nit thon solt, ist er hinab gangen deß gaßlin hinab und geflucht und gescholtten,*" ibid., Herr Leonhard von Friedberg (plaintiff).

[36] "*Ey es thudt kain gudt wir schlagen dan uch pfaffen all zw todt,*" ibid., Ott von Bentznaw (plaintiff).

to Löffler, "if I had a weapon, you wouldn't strike me dead!"[37] Herr Christof testified that he had taken a sword from his servant and then exchanged words with Löffler, saying, "knave, do you want to kill me too?" To which Löffler had merely retorted, "I'm not a knave," and then left them.[38] So who was the unidentified man who had approached Löffler and waited silently? Herr Christof commented at the end of his testimony: "he was worried about the other man, but since then [Christof] had learned that this man had also had a quarrel with [Löffler] and didn't want to walk in front of him."

Claus Bendler, a lay witness, identified Löffler only as "a man with a red beard," but heard him say to the priest looking out the window (Herr Leonhard von Friedberg), "the time will come when we'll see if God is God or if Baal is God."[39] In other words, Löffler was expressing the Protestant opinion that Catholic priests were idol-worshippers and warning that the time would come when the true God would triumph over the idols, Protestants over Catholics. Bendler also mentioned that, "the priest had nothing nice to say to [Löffler] either, saying 'may God's [wounds] shame you, you are a disgrace to your craft.'"[40] Then, according to Bendler, another man—presumably the same one Herr Christof saw—came up to Löffler and tried to lead him away and make him be quiet, but "[Löffler] swore at him and at Bendler too and cursed at them both harshly, he was very drunk."[41] Löffler's hostility seems to have been directed rather indiscriminately.

Anna Schweglerin witnessed the events first-hand and provided further details about Löffler's offensive behavior. She testified that Löffler had said, "Nothing's good since the devil brought you idol-worshippers back in here... you knave, you disgraceful priest, kiss my ass, I have no pants on!" Schweglerin also stated that she and that unnamed man on

---

[37] "hadt Her Cristoff gesagt locker so ich ain wer hadt du wurdest mich nit zu todt schlagen," ibid.

[38] "hadt Herr Cristoff sein were genomen von dem buben, hadt zw dem gsagt beschwicht willt mich auch schlagen da hadt der gsagt ich pin kain boßwicht und ist also von im gangen," ibid., Herr Christoff (plaintiff).

[39] "ainer in ainem Rotten bart..., da hab der im bart gesagt (den er sonst nit kent, ist aber in seines nachpaurn hauß ain pfaff oben im laden glegen) es wirt ain mal darzu komen ob got got sei, oder bal got," ibid., 18 June 1549, Claus Bendler (witness).

[40] "als er den pfaffen erzirnet hat im der pfaff auch nit vil guter wort geben und gesagt Ey daß dich botz etc. schend du bist deines handtwercks ain schelm," ibid.

[41] "hab in ain ander weck gefuert und in stillzuschweigen gepetten, er aber hab im nur bese wort geben dessgleichen ime Bendler auch und inen beden ubel geflucht, gleich wol er sei voll weins gewesen," ibid.

the street scolded Löffler and told him to be quiet, but he just swore at them both.[42]

The punishment issued by the council reads as follows:

> Hans Löffler...disrespectfully addressed noble clerics and other people without cause, insulted them verbally, called them idol-worshippers, Baal's priests, and knaves, cursed terribly, and said—among other things—it would be no good until one knocked the heads off the priest's idols. Because such speech leads to rebellion, opposition, and discord, the honorable council could have proceeded against him with a much harsher sentence, but in consideration of the intercessions from the same clergy and other influential persons, it is declared that [Löffler] be whipped out of town, to be an example to avoid similar disrespectful, malicious, rebellious slander.[43]

Thus, Hans Löffler was banished from Augsburg on 25 June 1549. One year later and again the year after that the council rejected his petitions for their permission to re-enter the city. A change in the city's political fortunes would finally bring Löffler a reprieve. On 23 April 1552, after nearly three years in exile and, more significantly, about three weeks after Duke Moritz's Protestant troops occupied Augsburg and Herbrot returned to office, Löffler was pardoned and permitted to re-enter the city, but with the warning that he not repeat his offensive behavior.

The day of Löffler's sentencing back on 25 June 1549 was an unfortunate one for his friends, particularly Wilhelm Lyndenmair,[44] who was arrested for protesting Löffler's punishment. Although Lyndenmair's

---

[42] *"ey es ist kain gluck seider der deuffel die getzen diener herein gefuert hat,... ey du schelm, du schelmischer pfaff du leckst mich, ich hab kain hosen an, si zeugin aber und ainer so in weck gefuert haben in gestraft er soll doch schweigen aber inen nur bese wort geben und ubel geflucht,"* ibid., Anna Schweglerin (witness).

[43] *"Gegenwurtiger Hanns Löffler von Augspurg so auff dem prannger steet, hat etliche geistliche adels unnd annder personen unverursacht freuenlich angewendt, mit worten geschmecht gotzendiener palmpfaffen unnd schelmen gescholten, ubel geflucht auch under anderm gesagt, es thue kain gut, man schlag dann den pfaffen die gotzen umb die kopf, Dieweil dann solche reden zu auffrur unwill unnd unainigkait dienen, hett ain ersamer rat wol ursach mit ernnstlicher straff gegen ime zuverfaren, aber auff der geistlichen selbs unnd annder ansehenlichen furbitt ist erkannt das er mit Ruten soll ausgehauen werden, menigclich zu ainem Exempel, sich vor dergleichen freuenlichem mutwillen, und auffrurischen schmachreden zuverhuetten wissen,"* ibid., 25 June 1549, Hans Löffler (Urteil).

[44] Wilhelm Lyndenmair appeared in a number of hearings over a period of five years. His name varies, including in 1549 as Wilhelm Weisser from Todtenweiss, Willibald or Wilpold Weisser from Todtenweiss; in 1552 as Wilhalm Leupold weisser; and in 1554 as Wilhalm Lindenmair weisser, and Wilhelm or Wilbold Lyndenmair galgenweisser. I've chosen the form by which he went in his last hearing in 1554. The terms *"weisser"* and *"galgenweisser"* were probably nicknames referring to his origin from the village of Todtenweiss.

criticism of the council's judgment would seem to fall in the category
of critical speeches, it appears here with the attacks on clergy because
of Lyndenmair's connection to Löffler and because of the anti-clerical tone of his later speeches. As we have seen, it is difficult, if not
impossible, to separate religious and political issues.[45] Lyndenmair's
interrogation reveals that he was Löffler's drinking companion and
was moved to pity him for being beaten and exiled. While Löffler was
being whipped, Lyndenmair announced to the crowd "there is innocent
blood on the scaffold, and the council has dealt with him unjustly, if
only everyone would do something and plead for him, so that Löffler
might be freed."[46] Furthermore, he said, "if we had proper lords, the
poor man would be protected and sheltered; they often throw stones
at him, and no one wants to stop it."[47]

In response to the interrogators, Lyndenmair denied being in league
with Löffler or knowing of any plot to attack the clergy or authorities in Augsburg. He also denied wanting to cause an uprising to free
Löffler with force. He readily admitted that he did not like the clergy,
but with good cause, he said. Some time in the past he had worked
as a musician, playing the trumpet marine.[48] One day three priest's
servants had come to him and insisted he play for them. He had told
them "he couldn't do it, because he wouldn't violate my lords' ban, so
they punched him in the face. That's why he hates the priests, but he
never did anything to them."[49] Without a doubt, Lyndenmair gave the
council grounds to suspect him of being an anti-clerical trouble-maker.
Between his outspokenness at Löffler's sentencing and the hostility he
admitted to in his interrogation, Lyndenmair earned himself a swift
punishment.

---

[45] See, for example, the case of Hans Streler discussed earlier in this chapter.

[46] "*Er hab gesagt, es stee das unschuldig plut auffm prannger, unnd ain E. Rat thue ime unrecht,
wann man gleich ains thete unnd jederman fur ine bethe, damit er Loffler ledig wurde*," StadtAA,
Reichsstadt, Urg. 26 June 1549, Wilhalm von Todtenweiss.

[47] "*Er hab nit annders gesagt, dann wann man recht herren hett, so wurde der arm mann
beschutzt, unnd beschirmbt, dann man ine offt mit den Stainen werffe, unnd wölle ime niemanndts
darvor sein*," ibid.

[48] The "*trummensheit*" or *Trumscheit*, known in English as a trumpet marine, is a
single-stringed instrument that sounds like a trumpet.

[49] "*Als er auff ain zeit, mit dem trummensheit gangen, seien ime 3 pfaffenknecht khomen, und zu
ime gesagt, er solt inen ains hofirn, do hab er inen geantwurt, es were ime nit glegen, dann er meiner
heren gepott, nit verachten wolt etc., do haben sie ine ins maul geschlagen, derhalben er inen den pfaffen
feindt gewest, hab aber doch khainem nicht thon*," ibid. A number of decrees from the 1530s
and 1540s banned the playing of musical instruments on public streets or at night.
See the discussion of Barbara Hertnitin's case in Chapter Four.

Two days later, on 27 June 1549, Wilhelm Lyndenmair was banished with the threat of corporal punishment if he returned to Augsburg. Despite this warning, Lyndenmair illegally entered Augsburg some time in the following months. Once again he was arrested for insulting the authorities and punished on 27 December 1549. The Punishment Book explains that Lyndenmair had illegally entered the city after being previously threatened with physical punishment and, in addition, had said, "all sorts of insulting things about the authorities." Consequently, he was "disciplined in irons" and then banished once again with the warning that, "if he came back in without permission, the council would hold him in a tower for life."[50] Lifetime imprisonment was an almost unheard-of procedure at this time, and using it as a threat against Lyndenmair shows how exasperating the council found him.

Yet that was not the end of Lyndenmair's encounters with Augsburg's city council. On 23 March 1552, about a week before Duke Moritz's Protestant forces arrived (1 April 1552), Lyndenmair once again faced interrogation, this time for speaking in front of the Weavers' Guild Hall. Among other things, he was accused of saying, "the only reason this war is coming is because [they] sent the pious preachers out and put the present traitors in their place."[51] He was referring to the conditions of the Interim, which forced many of Augsburg's preachers to leave the city and led the council to replace them with more conservative Protestants. In August 1551 Augsburg's council finally required the ministers to follow the Interim or leave.[52] Many of the replacements were related to the magistrates by kinship or some other tie. In his testimony, Lyndenmair amended this statement, claiming that he had actually said, "we have good preachers, but no one follows them, things are just the same as they were before."[53] When the interrogators asked him if he knew who had expelled the preachers, Lyndenmair answered that he had heard that the emperor wanted them to be driven out. Perhaps

---

[50] "*Wilpold Weisser... hat sich mit allerlay schimpfflichen reden wider die oberkait vernemen lassen, Darumb er... inn den eisen gezuchtigt, unnd... werde er on erlaubnus wider herein geen, so wolle ine ain E. Rate sein lebenlanng inn ainem thurn vennkhlich enthalten,*" ibid., SB 27 December 1549.

[51] "*Item er hab under anderm gesagt, diser krieg khom allain aus dem, das man di frommen predi-canten hinaus geschafft und di jetzigen lauren an ir statt herein genommen hab,*" ibid., 23 March 1552, Wilhelm Leopold (Fragstück).

[52] Katarina Sieh-Bürens, *Oligarchie, Konfession und Politik im 16. Jahrhundert: Zur sozialen Verflechtung der Augsburger Bürgermeister und Stadtpfleger 1518–1618,* (Munich: Verlag Ernst Vogel, 1986) 177.

[53] "*er hab also nit geredt, sonder gesagt, man hab gut prediger, aber es thue niemand darnach, sei glich nach wie voran,*" ibid., Wilhelm Leopold.

the council was trying to figure out if Lyndenmair held the emperor or the council responsible. Just how high did his treason go?

Not only had Lyndenmair complained about the preachers, but he had also criticized the city's treatment of the poor, particularly in the sense of their disadvantages in buying food. For example, he said that, "there is plenty of grain growing, and there's good weather, but the prices have been driven up so high that no one gives anyone else a chance...the innkeepers make only small soups for the poor day workers."[54] Furthermore, "when a poor man is shopping in the grain warehouse, if a richer man is there he can pay more, and the poor man has to wait behind him."[55] When asked what had caused him to say such things at the Weavers' Hall, Lyndenmair responded, "someone asks him and leaves him no peace, the people make him talk."[56] The interrogators also asked him why he had not taken his previous punishment as a warning and accused him of wanting to revenge himself on the authorities by making the common people hate them. Lyndenmair denied this and explained that he had been careful since being punished before, "but the bad boys plague him and provoke him, that he has to talk, they ask him if he's heard anything new and if he's a traitor."[57]

The minutes of the council's record books state that Wilhelm Lyndenmair had spoken offensively against the "whole city" (gemeine Stadt) and, in consideration of "the dangerous times" he was to be held in prison.[58] No length of time was named for the duration of this imprisonment, and no subsequent record indicates the date of his release. There is reason, however, to believe that he was eventually banished after being released from prison. A subsequent hearing in 1554 indicates that he

---

[54] "er hab gesagt, es wachs khorn gnug, und sei gut wetter, aber der wucher vil, das ainer dem andern nichts zu gute laß khomen, ... Item di wirt machen khlaine supplen, den armen tagwerckhern," ibid.

[55] "Wann ain armer man in der schrand khauffen wol, so sei ain reicher da, geb mer drumb so mieß der ander hinder sich steen," ibid. The "Schrand" or grain warehouse, where grain was sold in Augsburg, stood in front of St. Moritz's church and directly across the street from the Weavers' Guild House where Wilhem Lyndenmair was arrested.

[56] "Man frag ine, und laß im khain ruhe und mahen ine di leit reden," StadtAA, Reichsstadt, Urg. 23 March 1552, Wilhelm Leopold.

[57] "er hab ja hievor sein straff empfangen, und sich jetzo gehuett, aber di bosen buben plagen ine also, und raitzen ine an, das er ettwo reden mueß, fragen ine imer waß er neuß hor ob er ain verether sei, etc." ibid.

[58] "Wilhelm Leupold weisser hat sich vorm Weberhauß, inn gegenwurt etlicher personer vill poser strafflicher reden wider gemaine Stat vernemen lassen, Darumb er inn verhafft genomen unnd erkannt wordenn, das er inn betrachtung diser gefarlicher leuffd, inn den eisen soll vennklich enthalten werdenn," ibid., RB 1550–55, 24 March 1552.

had re-entered the city after a banishment, which must have resulted from the incident in March of 1552. A few months after that incident, Lyndenmair tried his luck with Mayor Herbrot's new government. On 16 July 1552, Lyndenmair petitioned the council for assistance to buy himself a new cloak, a petition which the council rejected due to his previous offensive speeches against the city. Lyndenmair had made himself a reputation as a troublemaker and, therefore, did not count among the deserving poor, even with the new regime.

In his next hearing, two years later on 13 August 1554, Wilhelm Lyndenmair explained that, like Löffler, he had received permission to re-enter the city in the summer of 1552, while Duke Moritz of Saxony was in residence. With the help of a friend, he had successfully petitioned Mayor Rudolf for permission to return to Augsburg. At that time, the change in political influence, in favor of the anti-imperial party, had worked to Lyndenmair's advantage. By 1554, however, the emperor had regained the upper hand in Augsburg, and Lyndenmair once again ran into trouble with the authorities for insulting the Catholic clergy. According to the list of questions, Lyndenmair had talked "evilly and insultingly" about the clergy and called them "scoundrels and knaves." Lyndenmair confessed readily to this and admitted that "unfortunately" he had also said, "things wouldn't be right until one killed the monks and priests and all their followers."[59] He claimed to have heard from his old friend Löffler, as well as others, that things would soon change, because the Catholic clergy would soon be chased out of the city again.

With a little encouragement, Lyndenmair further admitted to calling Mayors Ilsung and Rehlinger, "monks' and priests' servants," even claiming that "they were not his authorities, rather they were priests' servants, he couldn't stand to look at them…"[60] As in his 1552 hearing, Lyndenmair explained that his behavior resulted from being "very vexed and plagued," though not drunk. In particular, he was offended by insults to Schertlin von Burtenbach, Augsburg's famous general, who led Protestant forces in 1546's unsuccessful War of the Schmalkaldic

---

[59] "3) Er hab den geistlichen allerhalb ubel und schmechlich nachgeredt, sy schelmen und poßwicht gescholten… 4) Item er hab zwm offtermal gemelt es thue khain gueth, bis man munchen und pfaffen zu tod schlag und alle die inen anhangen," ibid., Urg. 13 August 1554, Wilhalm Lindenmair (Fragstück).

[60] "7) Er hab den Hern Burgermaister Ilsung offentlich fur ain munchs und pfaffen knecht ausgerueft… 8) Deßgleichen auch vom Hn. Burgermaister Rechlinger vermeldet mit dem anhang, sy weren sein obrikh[ait] nit, sunder pfaffen knecht, er wolle sy auch nit ansehen…" ibid.

League. Lyndenmair explained that his anti-clerical comments, "were provoked by the priests' students, because they made fun of him and said that his lord Schertlin [von Burtenbach] was going to be hanged."[61] Once more the council undertook to punish Lyndenmair, hoping to silence him once and for all. On 14 August 1554, Lyndenmair was "disciplined in irons" and afterwards "laid in a hut belonging to the Hospital," presumably to recuperate.[62] A few months later, on 9 October 1554, the council released Lyndenmair from his imprisonment on a petition from none other than Schertlin von Burtenbach himself, with the earnest admonishment "that [Lyndenmair] be the master of his mouth from now on."[63]

Wilhelm Lyndenmair presents a fascinating case for a number of reasons. For one, the council had a great deal of difficulty in silencing him, as seen when the interrogators asked him after his second arrest, "why didn't you take the last punishment as a warning?"[64] The council was unable to get rid of this nuisance, and Lyndenmair even had the nerve to ask them to help him buy a new cloak. Secondly, despite his repeated run-ins with the city government, Lyndenmair does not seem to have presented any real threat or danger, otherwise the council would have had grounds to deal with him more severely, through permanent exile, public whipping, or branding. Instead, the council recognized in him not a plotter or a rebel, but a man who was not "the master of his mouth." Although Lyndenmair had repeatedly insulted the Catholic clergy in Augsburg—which he readily admitted—the council treated him as a case for discipline and rehabilitation. The example of Lyndenmair's persistence shows both an individual's ability to defy the authorities' attempts to mold his behavior and the authorities' patience with his eccentricity. Finally, the history of Lyndenmair's encounters with the city government through a very tumultuous period reflects the city's changing fortunes. Events at the level of imperial politics could affect

---

[61] "10) Darumb das er sehr gefatzt unnd geplagt worden," and "2)... darzu durch die pfaffen schuler verursacht worden, dann dieselben umberdar sein gespott, unnd gesagt man werde seinen Hern den Schertlin henckhen," ibid., Wilhalm Lindenmair. "Schertlin" was Sebastian Schertlin von Burtenbach, Augsburg's military commander who led troops for the Protestant forces in the Schmalkaldic War.

[62] Ibid., SB 14 August 1554.

[63] "Wilbold Lyndenmair sonnst galgenweisser genannt soll inn ansehung des herrn Schertlins furbit der vennkhnus wider erlassen unnd ime mit ernnst eingebunden werdenn hinfüro seines mauls maister zusein," Ibid., RB 1550–55, 9 October 1554.

[64] Ibid., Urg. 23 March 1552, Wilhelm Lyndenmair (Fragstück).

the fate of one relatively insignificant person. Lyndenmair occasionally benefited and frequently suffered from the regime changes that Augsburg witnessed in the late 1540s and early 1550s. He, like the council, often found himself at odds with the community around him.

The summer of 1550 saw numerous cases which illustrate a variety of religious tensions in Augsburg, including anti-Catholic, anti-Protestant, and general anti-clerical behavior. In July of 1550 Leonhard Bader, who also went by the name Teufel (devil), got involved in an argument with Provost Hans Probst and Pastor Michael Hausmann from Oberhausen, a village lying near the northwest corner of Augsburg. The three men were in the *Schwarzbad*, a bathhouse which stood along the river on the western side of the city. Teufel was a fountain or well-maker and a decided Protestant. He presented the following testimony of his encounter with the men from Oberhausen.

> First, he had said in the common bath, that he had to take in soldiers as well, and if they wanted to give him two soldiers and a whore, he'd rather just have four soldiers. Then the pastor and provost of Oberhausen asked him, 'who likes the whores?' to which Leonhard responded, 'no one likes the whores more than soldiers and priests. After this the provost came over and sat by Leonhard on the bench, and the pastor, sitting across from him, slapped both hands on Leonhard's knees and said, 'you are the Devil and will remain the Devil, you belong to the devil with body and soul for eternity, I know it.' Leonhard answered him, 'I'm no idol-worshipper, no adulterer, no whoremonger, no thief, no robber, because none of these will enter the kingdom of God.' The pastor asked [Leonhard] if he meant him, to which Leonhard responded, 'if you're one of them, then you know it.' Then the provost shoved him in the side with his elbow three times and asked him if his lord [the bishop of Augsburg] was also one of those?' Leonhard answered, 'he didn't know anything about him, except that he had recently put in a well for him at the palace and had dealt honorably with him...and that he had known him when [Teufel] was a young boy.' During this talk the pastor had grievously insulted, slandered, and damned the Lutherans. In his final word to the two men, Leonhard said, '*Verbum domini manet in eternum*, and before that passes away, heaven and earth will pass away,' and walked out without another word.[65]

---

[65] "*1) Erstlich, er hab deßmals inn gemain im bad gesagt, er mueste auch lanndtsknecht haben, unnd wann man ime zwen landtsknecht unnd ain huren einlegen wolt, so wolte er lieber vier landtsknecht dafur haben, Darauff unnder den zwayen der der ain der Pfarrer und der ander der Vogt von Oberhausen sein soll. Er aber derselben khainen gekhonnt, zu ime gesagt, und gefragt wer die hurn mache, auf sollichs er ime hinwider geanntwurt, niemandts macht die hurn mehr dann die landtsknecht unnd pfaffen etc., nach disem hab sich der Vogt zu ime Lenhart auf die laßbanckh gesetzt, unnd der Pfar-*

The motto *"Verbum domini manet in eternum"*[66] adorned banners carried by soldiers of the Schmalkaldic League in 1546.[67]

According to Teufel, the interaction started out conversationally but took a wrong turn when he imprudently claimed that priests liked whores, to which the provost and pastor not surprisingly took offense. Did he not recognize that they were clerics? Did he not think they would mind? Or did he set out to irritate them? While portraying his remarks as harmless, he implied that the provost's and pastor's reactions were far more offensive and threatening. His casual remarks led to bullying and physical violence from them.

Provost Hans Probst portrayed his encounter with Teufel very differently.

> As he and his pastor were sitting in the Schwarzbad, the well-builder Teufel, said many derogatory things about priests and spoke of prophecies against them, among other things saying they were doing villainy. Despite [their] respectful requests, Teufel refused to stop. When the pastor reminded him of the decree (the Interim) and that he should not speak in violation of it, Teufel said, 'it's all villainy, and the devil will lead all the priests away.' At this point the Provost said to Teufel, 'according to what you say, my lord [bishop] of Augsburg must also be a villain and likewise his Imperial Majesty who is on his side.' Since Teufel would not stop, the Provost felt obliged to do his duty and report Teufel to the authorities. Teufel just cursed the Provost's warning and told him to go ahead and report him.[68]

---

rer so vor im uber gesessen mit baider herden auf seine knie geschlagen, unnd zu ime Lenhart gesagt, du bist der Teufl, unnd bleibst der teufl, unnd bist deß teufls mit leib unnd seel ewigclich das wais ych, Hierauf er Lenhart geantwurt nit also verdamt niemandt, und weiter geredt, bin ich doch khain gotzendiener khain Eebrecher, khain hurer, khain dieb, und khain rauber, dann diser khainer inn das Reich Gots kheme, auf diß der Pfarrer gefragt ob er ine mein, darauf er gesagt, seye ers so wiß ers wol, Nachdem allem hat ine der Vogt inn die seiten mit dem elenbogen 3 mal gestossen, unnd gefragt ob sein gn'stn herr auch ain sollicher sei, Er Lenhart geantwurt Er wisse nichts von ime, dann er seiner f. gn. neulich ainen Brunnen auf der pfaltz … geschöpft, und hab ine erlich unnd wol gehalten, hab ine auch als er ain junger knab gewest, gekhant, dise antwurt hab er ime Vogt zum drittenmal auf sein anhalten geben. … Inn disen reden, hab der Pfarrer die luterischen zum höchsten geschendt, geschmeht und verdambt, hab aber gleich wol nit sonders acht darauf gehabt, Aber er Lenhart sei noch obgemelter verloffnen handlung auffgestanden, sein wasser genomen, unnd zu ime Pfarrer gesagt, Hera bruederlin, es steet unns noch ain wörtlin, nemlich Verbum domini manet in eternum, unnd ehe dasselb zergen, wurt ehe himel unnd erterich zergeen, unnd sei damit zur thur hinaus ganngen, unnd khain wort mehr weder zu dem Vogt noch dem Pfarrer gesagt," ibid., Urg. 7 July 1550, Lenhart Bader genant Teufl.

[66] Trans: the word of God will last forever.

[67] Roth, *Augsburgs Reformationsgeschichte*, vol. 3, 384.

[68] *"Hans Probst Vogt von Oberhausen sagt als er und sein pfarer gestern im schwartzenbad gesessen, hab N. Teufel prunnen schepfer vil schmechlicher reden von priestern getriben von propheceyen wider sy geredt, und under anndern gesagt, es sey schelmenwerch warmit sy umbgeen, hab auch uber*

In the provost's version, Teufel ignored their polite requests to stop, continuing to harass him and his clerical colleague even after they warned him that his insults slighted the bishop, the emperor, and the Interim.

Three bathhouse employees, Hans Widenman, Valentin Poxlar, and Hans Stromer, also witnessed Teufel's encounter with the pastor and provost. Widenman testified that Teufel had insulted the Catholic clergy and called them knaves. According to him, Teufel had also said that the priests did nothing but villainy and all of their followers were also villains.[69] Widenman, like Valentin Poxlar, also heard Teufel declare that certain persons would not come into heaven. Widenman heard him say usurers, adulterers, and pre-emptive buyers, while Poxlar heard blasphemers, whoremongers, drunks, robbers, and misers.[70] Hans Stromer heard the provost warn Teufel, "I've heard you suggest that my lords also do villains' work, I advise you—meaning Teufel—to be quiet, you've said enough about that."[71] All three witnesses testified that they did not hear much of the conversation, because they had to take care of their work. The evidence regarding Teufel's statements suggests that he resented the Catholic clergy, for rather traditional grounds of immorality, but also disapproved of the Catholic faith and "all who... believe in the Mass."

Based on the testimony of the provost and the bathhouse employees, the council was able to pursue a second interrogation of Leonhard Bader, alias Teufel. In the second hearing, the interrogators were instructed to threaten Teufel with "hard questioning" or torture. The list of questions for the second hearing began, "[we] know and have reliable information that he grievously defamed the clergy, therefore he

---

bettlichs ansuechen nit nachlaßen wollen und als im der pfarer derhalb zugesprochen er soll des berueffs inngedenkh sein und solher reden demselben zw wider mueßig steen hab er wider gesagt, es sey ja alles schelmen werch und der teufel werd di pfaffen alle hin furen, er Vogt hab auch gesagt, sein reden nach mueßt mein gn'stn herrn von Augspurg auch ain schelm sein, deßgleichen Kay. Mt. die ob inen hallt, und dhweil er ir nit nachlaßen woll, mueß ers sein pflichten nach von im klagen, darauf ine Teufel trutzlich und schimpflich geantwurt, er soll und mags wol klagen," StadtAA, Reichsstadt, Urg. 7 July 1550, Hans Probst (witness).

[69] "die Pfaffen thuen sonst nichts dann das sie nur schelmerei treiben, es werde sich auch ir schelmerei nit lang mehr verbergen khonnen, sonder bald an tag khommen, welcher auch meß hab unnd damit umbgange die seien schelmen, etc." ibid., Hanns Widenman (witness).

[70] Ibid., Hanns Widenman and Valentin Poxlar (witnesses).

[71] "ich hör wil meine herrn geen auch mit schelmennwerckh umb Ich rat dirs ime teufl mainend, schweig still dann es ist gnug von der sach gerett," ibid., Hanns Stromer (witness).

should tell the truth and not give cause to greater seriousness."[72] Despite all of the evidence against him, Teufel denied the charges, including that he had called the priests villains or that "all those who read the Mass or believe in the Mass are all villains."[73] He also denied that the pastor or provost of Oberhausen had ever pointed out to him that his insults could be interpreted to refer to the bishop of Augsburg and the emperor. Teufel was never tortured, in spite of his refusal to "tell the truth." The council's instructions to the interrogators limited them to threatening the defendant with torture but not actually utilizing it for a confession. Teufel was sentenced to spend eight days in a tower and earnestly warned not to speak like that again.[74]

Like Wilhelm Lyndenmair, Teufel continued to present trouble for the city councilors, until eventually they ran out of patience with him. Four years later, in August 1554, Teufel was finally banished for making threatening statements and then insulting the court that interrogated him. In the months following his banishment, the council turned down repeated petitions to secure Teufel's return, until the council lords at last instructed his friends to stop bothering them.[75] Unlike Lyndenmair, Teufel posed a more significant danger to the council because of his ability to express his hostility more articulately, nor did he ever attempt to justify his actions as expressions of anger or irritation. Moreover, by turning his animosity against the council and its court, as he did in the latter case, his offenses inclined toward treason rather than just anti-clericalism or religious dissent.

Another case from this same summer exemplifies the anti-institutional aspect of attacks on clergy or church property in the Reformation. In this incident, from 8 August 1550, a group of Spaniards (members of the imperial Habsburg forces) vandalized the Protestant preaching house at St. Ulrich.[76] Before the reformation many churches had had separate buildings for preaching to the laity. Because they were often owned by the city rather than the church, during the early years of reform they were some of the earliest sites of evangelical preaching. When the Interim of 1548 returned Catholic services to the city,

---

[72] *"Man wiß und hab in gueter erfarung das er den geistlichen ubel geredt hab darumb soll er di warhait sagen und zu merern ernst nit ursachen geben,"* ibid., 9 July 1550, Lenhart Bader Teufel (Fragstück).

[73] *"Item wer meß les und mit der meß umbgang sei alles schelmerei,"* ibid.

[74] See ibid., SB 14 June 1550.

[75] Ibid., RB, 9 October 1554.

[76] Ibid. Urg. 18 August 1550, Peter beim Brunnen and Caspar Eckhart.

many of the former preaching houses were designated as places were
Protestant services could be held. This change in venue was seen as a
demotion for the Protestants and a source of irritation to the Catholic
clergy. In 1550 Catholic vandals attacked a haven for Protestant worship, and may have planned to vandalize the house of the minister
Jacob Dachser as well. The list of questions used for the interrogation
indicates that pews were ripped out and a painted hanging was torn
down from the wall. The property damage may have been intended as
intimidation or to prevent Protestant services from taking place. The two
men interrogated in the case were officeholders of the Catholic church
at St. Ulrich, the Sacristan, Peter beim Brunnen, and the Schoolmaster,
Caspar Eckhart. The men did not participate in the actual vandalism, but were suspected of playing an instrumental role in giving the
Spaniards encouragement and access to damage the preaching house.
The council was in no position to prosecute the Spanish soldiers, but
they used the occasion to investigate troublemakers among their own
citizens. Both men claimed innocence in the matter. Because the council could not find enough evidence against them, the two men were
released after a day in custody, on the condition that they reappear if
new evidence came to light.[77] Unlike verbal offenses directed at Catholic
clerics in Augsburg, this attack focused on Protestant worship, not the
clergy as such.

   One of the most interesting and unusual cases appeared in quick
succession after the incidents at the bathhouse and St. Ulrich. In September of 1550 the culprit was a woman, Catherina Frenckin. Frenckin
ridiculed a procession of clerics and lay people, including a number of
Spaniards, who were taking the Eucharist from the Cathedral of Our
Lady to a sick man, Simprecht Hofman. In this unique case, Frenckin
expressed anti-Catholic sentiments not just to the clergy but also to the
lay participants in the ceremony. In most other cases, religious-based
hostility was directed at members of the clergy rather than lay persons.
As the procession passed the house of weaver Sebastian Onsorg, his
wife, Catherina Frenckin, leaned out her window and said, laughing,
"oh, look, how they have to carry a torch in front of the fools!" The
sacristan, Augustin Schroter, who was carrying the torch, shouted back

---

[77] Ibid., SB 19 August 1550.

to her, "you old whore, what business is it of yours?"[78] In his testimony
Shroter asserted that if he had not been directed ahead of time not
to revenge himself, he would have thrown the torch in her face, so
that she could see her lies. Anna Weißin corroborated both Frenckin's
alleged speech and Schroter's response and added that if she had not
considered God and the honorable authorities, she would have broken
the window herself. Stefan Walkircher, a *Stuhlbruder* of Our Lady, also
heard Frenckin's verbal attack. He and Anna Weißin both noted in
their testimony that several Spaniards were with them in the procession, which raised the incident to the level of imperial interest.[79] The
testimony of a man identified only as Klainentaler, who lived by the
slaughterhouse, agreed with the other witnesses. He added that Frenckin
had also ridiculed them before and after her comment about carrying
torches in front of fools. Furthermore, the Spaniards walking with them
had wanted to know what the woman had said, so he told them.

A letter from the cathedral dean, Philip von Rechberg, to Mayor
Anthony Welser substantiated the witnesses' testimony. Although not
present at the procession, Rechberg had looked into the matter and
was able to report what he had heard from Schroter, the sacristan,
and several other observers. The leader of the procession, the assistant
(*Helfer*), Hans Finsternach, had heard Frenckin say something but had
not paid attention, because he was praying, and he did not know who
she was. However, a number of women, who were attending a baptism
in the Cathedral after the procession, reported that they had also heard
Frenckin, as did a translator, probably one of the Spaniards. Although
any of these witnesses could have justified reporting Frenckin to the
authorities, it appears that Rechberg wrote this letter in response to an
inquiry from the council. As he concluded his report, Rechberg wrote,
"I did not want to withhold this, according to your wishes, because I
want to show you good will."[80]

---

[78] "*er hab... ain prinende fakhel vortragen... und als er fur Bastian Unsorgen haws khommen
hett sein hausfraw so man Katherina Frenkhin nennet, zwm fenster heraus gesehen daruber gelacht
und gesagt sich wol tragt man den naren die fakhel vor, darauf er geantwurt du allte hur was geet es
dich an, und da ime nit hievor befolhen worden, sich selbs nit zu rechen, wollt er ir wol das liecht
inns angesicht gestoßen haben damit sy ir leugen khenen,*" ibid., 11 September 1550, Catherina
Frenckin, Augustin Schroter (witness).

[79] See testimony of Anna Weißin and Steffan Walkircher, ibid.

[80] "*solchs hab ich awff Ewer beger nit wollen verhaltten dan uch fruntlichen willen zu bewisen
pin ich willig etc.*" ibid., Philip von Rechberg (letter).

In Catherina Frenckin's first interrogation, before witnesses testified about the incident, she explained the affair so innocently as to be almost comical. She claimed that when she had heard the sacristan ringing a bell, she naturally thought a mute person was coming, so she wanted to show him some charity. When Frenckin looked out her window and saw the procession with the priests, she turned to her husband and said, "look, they're burning a light, although you can see enough by day."[81] She claimed that she spoke without thinking and did not mean anything bad. Frenckin also denied other alleged instances of her making fun of women who carried rosaries by calling them priests' wives or concubines.[82] Given the overpowering testimony of multiple witnesses against Frenckin, the council decided to interrogate her once again, placing special emphasis on her exact statements. An entry in the council minutes, on 13 September 1550, notes that Catherina Frenckin should be questioned and threatened with torture.[83]

A few days later, the council directed that Dr. Has (one of the council's legal advisors) be shown Frenckin's interrogation and advised that she is "weak and fragile in body."[84] The council wanted to make sure that Frenckin was healthy enough to endure the application of torture. Although a second list of questions was prepared, there is no extant copy of a second hearing. It seems plausible that after consulting Dr. Has the council decided it could not proceed against Frenckin with torture, and, therefore, figured that a second interrogation, pursued without force, would be useless. The statement of her sentencing in the Punishment Book confirms this with an unusual expression. Most verdicts state unequivocally that the relevant person committed such and such a crime, while Frenckin's crimes had to be described accurately in the verdict as alleged, "according to report and testimony of the sacristan of Our Lady and several other people."[85] While other criminals were sentenced after being brought to confess their offenses, Frenckin

---

[81] "*such sy haben ain liecht anzunt, unnd gesehen in gnug beim tag,*" ibid., 10 September 1550, Catherina Frenckin.

[82] "*man trage auch gut wissenn das sy die frawen verspotte und verachte, so pater noster tragen, und zeiche sy seien pfaffen weiber,*" ibid., (Fragstück).

[83] Ibid., RB 1550–55, 13 September 1550.

[84] "*Catherina Frennkin halb ist erkannt das doctor Hasen ir urgicht unnd das sie schwachs unnd gebrechlichs leibs sey, soll anzaigt werden,*" ibid., RB 1550–55, 16 September 1550.

[85] "Catherina Frennkin soll…, nach ansag unnd bekundschafftung des mesners zu Unser Frauen unnd etlicher annder personen, gesagt haben…" ibid., SB, 23 September 1550.

had not confessed—since the council had not been able to complete its interrogation without the use of force. It should be noted that the lack of a confession did not prevent the council from punishing her.

Catherina Frenckin's case, especially her punishment, is unusual for another reason. The record clearly states that the Holy Roman emperor himself had commanded Frenckin's punishment. She was to be escorted out of the city by the correction officials and then banished "for all times" and never allowed back in with or without a petition.[86] The presence of Spaniards in the procession, very likely members of some imperial official's retinue, would have drawn the emperor's attention to the case. Sources show that the council obediently carried out the dictated punishment. When Frenckin's husband Sebastian Onsorg petitioned on her behalf the following June of 1551, the council rejected his plea, with the explanation that the emperor had ordered that she be banished permanently. However, if Onsorg could secure a pardon from the emperor, the council would acknowledge it.[87] In February of 1552 Onsorg's petition was turned down once more. The council minutes (*Ratsbuch*) note that Onsorg should be informed that it was not within the council's power to pardon his wife, but if he could succeed with the emperor, the council would allow it. No succeeding entries indicate that this ever happened.

Catherina Frenckin's case illustrates a different kind of hostility towards the Catholic Church, which differs from typical anti-clericalism. She directed her antagonism towards Catholics and their ceremonies and practices—such as wearing rosaries or carrying torches in daytime processions—rather than aiming at the clergy. The other incidents of attacks on clergy (verbal or physical), described above, usually took aim at clerics—priests, monks, or higher prelates. While some, as in the cases involving the abbot of Oberelchingen or the pastor of Oberhausen, attacked the lifestyle of the clergy, others, like Hans Löffler, attacked the Cathedral Lords for spreading false or idolatrous beliefs. In all of these cases, the defendants targeted the clergy as representatives of the Catholic Church and as members of an odious class. Frenckin's case, therefore, shows a rare occurrence of a citizen ridiculing her neighbors, rather than just the clergy, for participating in what she considered

---

[86] "*Darumb die Römischen Kay. Mt. unnser allergenedigster herr bevolhen hat, das sie durch den zuchtinger aus der Statt soll beglaittet unnd derselben zu ewigen zeiten verwisen sein, also das sie weder mit noch on furbitt nit mehr darein gelassen werdenn soll,*" ibid.

[87] Ibid., RB 1550–55, 30 June 1551.

superstitious practices. As seen from the other cases, citizens who disliked the Catholic religion usually did not express hostility toward fellow citizens but rather toward officials of the church. It is also interesting to note that while the council clearly took seriously its responsibility to protect the Catholic clergy in Augsburg, the clergy had been advised to act with restraint and not retaliate, although they seem not to have hesitated in bringing up legal charges. Catholic authorities apparently anticipated some hostility, especially in response to a public procession, and attempted to cooperate with the council by trying to diffuse the situation.

RELIGIOUS DEVIANCE

The term "religious deviance," which is used to describe the following group of cases, reflects the view of contemporary authorities regarding people whose religion deviated from the legally prescribed norms. After 1547 Augsburg's government officially permitted Catholic worship or the Augsburg Confession as defined by the Interim.[88] This group of cases includes a variety of offenders or suspected offenders, ranging from Anabaptists to followers of Arius.

The case of Thomas von Löven stands out for several reasons. For one, he was well-connected to a number of prestigious Prostestant clergy, including Philip Melanchthon. Secondly, he was a well-educated foreigner. Thirdly, and most importantly, his is the earliest case in Augsburg's interrogation records in which the council asked a person to declare his or her religious affiliation and used the term "confession" to do so. Even interrogations of Anabapists in the 1520s and 1530s did not ask what the person's religion was or even if the person was an Anabaptist or [Wieder-] Täufer but rather if the person had been baptized.

According to his story, Thomas von Löven left the city of Louvain, Belgium, around 1541. He appears in the matriculation records of the University of Wittenberg in 1541, which notes that he had fled from religious persecution in the Netherlands at the hands of Habsburg

---

[88] The Augsburg Confession was a very moderate expression of Protestantism, initially drafted by Philip Melancthon in an attempt to appease the emperor in 1530. It included communion in both forms and marriage of priests, but not much more. Hence, it was rejected by Zwinglians, not to mention many Lutherans.

authorities. He seems not to have finished his course of studies with a degree, since he was still calling himself a student, rather than master, when arrested in Augsburg in 1550. Perhaps as an exile he did not have the funds to pursue his education to completion. Since the early 1540s von Löven had been in and out of Augsburg, where he had met and on occasion stayed with the Zwinglian preacher Bonifacius Wolfart, who died in 1543. In his interrogation, von Löven claimed to have recently arrived from Wittenberg, where he had left Philip Melanchthon. Among his friends in Augsburg he counted an estimable crowd. Besides Wolfart, there were the schoolmaster from St. Georg (with whom he was currently staying), the Lutheran preacher Johann Flynner, the schoolmaster of St. Anna, Sixtus Birk, the preacher at the Spital, and the wealthy Catholic financier and book-collector, Hans Jakob Fugger. In the previous year, von Löven and Birk had together to register Hebrew books for Fugger's library, giving them Latin names and inscribing titles on their covers.

Von Löven seems to have earned his way by undertaking various opportunities for short-term employment, such as the project in Fugger's library. During the Imperial Diet in Augsburg in 1547–48, he had tutored a Spanish noble, Bernhardinus de Granada, who gave him a book of psalms in Hebrew in exchange. At the time of his arrest, von Löven's other books included Latin and German psalters, a small Bible, Hippocrates' *Medicine*, a book of Gospels in Czech, and Aristotle's *Problemata* in Spanish. The Latin and German psalters, as well as the Bible were gifts he had received in Wittenberg, probably from other patrons or clients whom he had served. His reading materials included Christian and pagan texts, religious, philosophical, and medical subjects, and a range of at least five languages, showing the impressive results of a humanist education.

On 23 June 1550 von Löven, the itinerant scholar, was arrested in Augsburg on suspicion of heresy. Questions six and seven from the interrogatory get at the heart of the council's interest in Löven. "6) Did he not speak to his host conversationally about religious matters and in what way? 7) What is his confession or belief?"[89] Von Löven's answers to questions six and seven are very interesting because of how he identifies

---

[89] "*6) Ob er nit ettwo von glaubens sachen mit inen geselliger weis geredt hab und uff was weis... 7) Was sein confeßion oder glaub sei*," StadtAA, Reichsstadt, Urg. 23 June 1550, Thomas von Löven (Fragstuck).

his faith. To question six he replied, "he only spoke about matters of faith in the way that they think in Wittenberg, which confession he followed entirely." Then to question seven, in response to the direct inquiry about his confession, he said, "I believe, regarding matters of faith, in the way it's done in Wittenberg, here [i.e. Augsburg], and Nuremberg and in no other way."[90] The term "confession" was already in use among some theologians and scholars, but it appears in the court records of Augsburg for the first time in 1550, and von Löven seemed reluctant to use it. Von Löven's answers seem strikingly similar to those of the Kretzweschers' daughter, Elizabeth Schenk, who seventeen years earlier said she preferred the services at Holy Cross and the Franciscan churches.[91] Both of them defined their religious preferences by naming the locations where worship took place in the manner they approved. Although von Löven alluded to a Wittenberg confession, a somewhat identifiable entity, his definition of his religious beliefs was more vague. He had no label with which to identify his faith. Rather than calling himself Lutheran, Philippist, or evangelical, he referred instead to places, cities whose religious position was similar to his own, although none of them was identical. Augsburg and Wittenberg had been at odds over theological issues for years before the Interim. Although the term "confession" may have been in use by 1550, it did not yet appear to be a customary way for people to identify their religious affiliation.

In addition to asking him explicitly what his confession was, the council also asked von Löven, in separate questions, if he were an Anabaptist and, then, if he were an Arian. To both questions he responded adamantly in the negative. Not only was he not a follower of Anabaptism, but "he didn't even like to hear it talked about. May God protect him from Anabaptism ... [von Löven] thought even less of the teaching of Arius, because he is a great enemy of God for denying the eternal life of Christ."[92] Apparently it was easier for him to articulate what he did not believe than what he did.

---

[90] "6) Er hab auff khain ander weiß, mit jemandts der glaubens sachen halben nie geredt, dann wie man es zu Wittemberg dem Confession er gentzlich anhengig sei, halte etc. ... 7) Wie man es zu Wyttemberg, hie, und Nürmberg der Religion, unnd deß glaubens sachen halben halte, also glaube ers unnd anderst nit," ibid., Thomas von Löven.

[91] See Chapter One.

[92] "8) Er sei der widertaufferischen sect mit nichten anhenngig, dann er auch davon nit möge reden hören, Es solle ine auch gott vor dem widertauff verhueten, ... 9) Er halte noch vil weniger von deß Arry leer, dann derselb der groß veindt gottis sei, dhweil er die ewigkhait Christi nit halt etc." ibid.

Aside from general questions about von Löven's business in Augsburg, his contacts, his residence, and so on, the council also asked what he had preached and taught, where, and for how long. This line of questioning demonstrates the council's efforts to discover not only the followers of illegal sects but also the roots of such movements by regulating who preached and what they preached. Von Löven's unofficial preaching to the poor in the Holy Ghost Hospital had initially slipped past the council's notice. He explained to them that he had only preached to poor people in Wittenberg and in Augsburg, starting in Bonifacius Wolfart's time, especially to those in the Hospital. He also added, humbly, that "he had learned far more from others, than he had taught anyone."[93] The activities of itinerant preachers contributed to the vigor of popular religious life on the periphery of official establishments, just as they did before the Reformation.

For every inquiry, in a relatively long list of twenty-three questions, von Löven had an answer guaranteed to impress the council with his piety, learning, humility, and reputable friends. In all fairness, the council soon realized that it was on the wrong trail. The Punishment Book entry acknowledges that it was a case of mistaken identity, justifying the investigation because, "in face, height, and weight he looked just like a known follower of the damaging and misleading teaching of Arius…but after examination and careful investigation, he was shown to be innocent." He was released on an old bond.[94]

Von Löven was not the only person to be arrested as a suspected Arian in this period. A few years earlier, Claudius Allodius, from Geneva, and Georg Nuber had been arrested for being Arians. In particular the council worried about their denial of the trinity. The council resolved the issue by having several ministers attempt to secure a recantation by explaining Scripture to them. When the Genevan Claudius Allodius recanted, he was released and then escorted out of town.[95] Despite his

---

[93] "Er hab nie sonders gepredigt dann alain hie unnd zu Wytemberg armen leuten, hab es auch seider Bonifacius zeiten her geuebt, er hab aber vil mehr von andern gelernt, dann das er jemandts andern gelert hab," ibid.

[94] "Thomas von Louen, ist an gstalt lennge unnd grosse der person, ainem der der schedlichen verfurischen leer Arry angehanngen, gannz gleich unnd anlich gewest,…Dieweil er aber nach gepflegner erkundigung unnd examination fur den unrechten unnd unschuldigen befunden, ist er der vennkhnus aff ain alte urphed erlassen worden," ibid., SB, 28 June 1550.

[95] Ibid., RB 1543–49, 17–28 January 1547, Claudius Allodius (a.k.a. Wassermenlin) and Georg Nuber.

recantation, the council apparently did not want to take any chances, and, as always, foreigners were easily dismissed.

Even less so than von Löven, Anthoni Schnedl does not fit easily into any single religious category. The spur-maker was arrested in February of 1552. Although probably not a follower of the Catholic church, Schnedl differed from most Protestants as well, at least on the issue of baptism. In that respect he set himself apart from the prevailing Christian opinion regarding the baptism of infants. Schnedel came to the authorities' attention for declining to have his newborn child baptized promptly after birth. This failure consequently drew suspicion on him as a possible Anabaptist. Since the city's reformation in 1537, The council had issued more than one decree requiring midwives to make sure each child received an appropriate baptism by clergy and to report parents who refused.

Schnedl's delinquency in baptizing his child had led to a specific order from Mayor Leonhard Christof Rehlinger to have the child baptized immediately, but he refused. On Saturday, 19 February 1552, eleven days after the birth of his child, Schnedl was arrested. In addition to withholding his child from baptism, he had also spoken disrespectfully to the city guards when they came to arrest him. Regrettably, it is not clear how the mayor learned of the matter. Possibly one of the midwives reported him, as the law required, or it might have been a neighbor or pastor.

Although the council initiated legal measures against Schnedl to ensure that his child received a proper baptism, he actually claimed that he had not withheld his child or refused to have it baptized. On the contrary, he explained that while he did in fact believe in baptism, he simply did not think that godparents were necessary, because, he claimed "Christ hadn't commanded anything about godparents."[96] He told the interrogators, "he was not opposed to baptizing his child, he just wanted to leave out the human additions."[97] He explained further, "the godparents make a promise in baptism that they cannot keep, because they don't know how the child will be later."[98] When asked whether or not he was an Anabaptist and what he thought about Anabaptism,

---

[96] "2) Er hab sein khyndt nit vorgehalten zu teuffen oder gewegert, das er aber gevatterschafft darzu bitten sollen, das achts er nit von notten sein, dann Christus nichts von der gevatterschafft bevolhen," ibid., 19 February 1552, Anthoni Schnedl.

[97] "4)... so sei er nie dar wider gewest, sein khind zutauffen, Allain die menschen satzungen achte er darbei zu underlassen sein," ibid.

[98] "5)... dann je die gevattern ain ding globen ws den Tauff das sie nit halten khonnen, dann sy nit wissen, wie das khind geradten werd," ibid.

Schnedl responded succinctly that he did not know anything about it and had nothing to do with it, thereby answering the interrogators' two questions with one answer. For good measure, he added that plenty of people who could confirm his rejection of Anabaptism.

The interrogators also asked Schnedl about his disrespectfulness towards the city guards. According to them, he had allegedly said, "if his child is baptized by them, and it's damaged from it, he would recover himself for it with the authorities."[99] Schnedl's explanation of these remarks differed little from this report. Schnedl testified that he had said to the city guard, "because he was so insistent... 'take the child, baptize it, but make sure you don't drown it for me, otherwise I'll have nothing to say about it, that would have been a droll speech.'"[100]

Schnedl's testimony apparently convinced the council that he was not an Anabaptist or a similar kind of threat. He objected not to infant baptism but to the form of the rite of baptism. Evangelical reformers frequently opposed what they saw as "human additions" or man-made laws in Christian rituals. Schnedl's opposition may have stemmed from theological issues, as his comments about wanting the baptism performed without "human additions" suggests, but that may been a cover for personal reasons. Perhaps he did not get along with the people who customarily would have been asked to be godparents, or perhapps he felt uncomfortable turning to people he did not know well. It is also possible that in a very human sort of reaction, the more Schnedl was pushed by others, the more he resisted, making a bigger issue out of it than it really was. In the end, the council did not know what to make of this man—eccentric, cantankerous, or insubordinate. The day after his hearing he was released from prison on a petition, "because sometimes he is not in his right senses."[101] The council's final treatment of the defendant, as someone who did not have all his wits about him, calls to mind the case of Katharina Kunigin, who was arrested in 1541 for not having had one of her children baptized in infancy.[102] The council dismissed her, like Schnedl, as being not in her

---

[99] "wan im sein khind getaufft werd, und ainicher schad daran zuestee, das er sich deßelben bei der obrikhait gedenkhen zw erholen," ibid. (Fragstück).

[100] "er hab zum Statkhnecht Kholen, weil er so embsig angehalten das khind tauffen zelassen,... Also gesagt, nembts hin, taufffs, seht aber ertreckht mirs nit gar, ich wird sunst kain red darzu haben, das sey ain schwankh red gewest," ibid, Anthoni Schnedl.

[101] "inn ansehung das er bisweiln nit wol bey synnen ist, widerumb auff furbitt daraus gelassen wordenn," ibid., SB, 20 February 1552.

[102] See the discussion of Katharina Kunigin's case in Chapter Four.

right senses. Perhaps this was the only way the council could explain people who differed from the more popular Christian faiths and yet did not belong to a particular sect. Schnedl and Katharina Kunigin both interpreted their faith independently, while not seeing themselves as belonging to a particular confession other than those endorsed by the city.

No discussion of religious deviance in the 1540s and 1550s would be complete without considering the Anabaptists. Despite three decades of repeated persecution, the Anabaptist movement managed to survive in Augsburg, partially aided by new members. Some Anabaptists, like Pilgram Marbeck, were even tolerated by the city council so long as they did not spread their beliefs. Although many more than we know about probably managed to live in obscurity, a few ran into trouble with the city council. Two notable examples, Georg Probst (Maler) and Georg Seifrid, faced repeated arrests over several decades. The mere fact that they survived so many encounters with Augsburg's government and continued to live in the city says something about the limits of the judicial system's efficacy or about the council's toleration. The 1550s saw a few people—all men—prosecuted for Anabaptism for the first time in Augsburg. Despite the impression of continuity with the 1520s, something important had changed, at least for the city council, and this change explains why the defendants in the 1550s were all men, a distinct contrast to earlier decades, when women usually made up half of the Anabaptists arrested on any given occasion. The council records regarding Anabaptists in the 1550s deal almost exclusively with the social rather than the religious aspects of their behavior. Specifically, the council's chief concern was that the men did not want to swear an oath to help protect the city from enemies. Their refusal to swear the oath apparently drew the council's attention to them, not an attempt to seek out Anabaptists. Each of them was given the option to stay in the city, if he agreed to recant. Preachers met with them, and a few did indeed recant. Bernhart Unsynn, brother-in-law of the Protestant minister Johann Ehinger, struggled with the council over this issue for quite a while but eventually agreed to recant. Yet—in what must have been a heartrending moment—when the council read aloud the official statement in which he was supposed to acknowledge his errors, he refused.[103] This period saw continued efforts to come to terms with

---

[103] Ibid., RB 1550–55, 9 August–10 December 1554.

and assimilate known Anabaptists but no organized attempts to root them out as a group.

MISCELLANEOUS

The next case brings us full circle. Leonhard Widenman vividly exemplifies the spirit of the 1520s as it resurfaced in Augsburg two decades later, after the introduction of the Interim. One of the city's poorer residents, Widenman drew the council's attention because of his self-styled claim to fame. Widenman, who tried to scrape together an income by begging from door-to-door, claimed to be one of seven men who had petitioned for the evangelical preacher Johann Schilling in 1524.[104] The popular Schilling had been forced into exile by the council in 1524, and hundreds of supporters had rallied against the council, in the so-called Schilling Uprising. During the uprising, the populace gathered on the City Hall square and demanded that the council reinstate Schilling as preacher at the Franciscan Church. A quarter of a century later in 1549 Widenman declared that he was responsible for "keeping the Gospel in the city," in other words saving the cause of reform in Augsburg. Shortly after the introduction of the Interim, that boast was sure to win sympathy amongst oppressed Protestants, or so Widenman thought. Unfortunately for him, to the council they sounded like fighting words. The council feared that Widenman's purpose might be to encourage those he met, by going door-to-door, to rise up against the government. The councilors even considered the possibility that Widenman had purposely left the public welfare system, in order to carry out his house-to-house campaign to rally support for a "mutiny and rebellion like the one for the Franciscan monk years ago."[105] Widenman himself had inadvertently encouraged this impression by protesting his arrest, with the alleged statement, "Christ had to suffer in innocence, and because this council is no good, the same may happen to me."[106] According to Widenman, what he actually said

---

[104] See the discussion of the Schilling Uprising in Chapter Two.

[105] "*9) Ob er sich nit eben darumb aus dem almusen gethan, das er verhofft wan er allso von haus zu haus petteln gehe, er mog dardurch ain meutterei und aufrur anrichten, in maßen er vor jarn des predigers halb, zum Parfueßen auch gethan hab,*" ibid., Urg. 24 April 1549, Leonhart Widenman (Fragstück).

[106] "*7)... Christy hab umb unschuld leiden mueß, und dhweil dise obrikhait nit gueth sey, mog im auch allso geschehen,*" ibid.

was merely, "If the good lords knew of his poverty, they wouldn't let [him] be taken away."[107]

Widenman's references to the long ago Schilling Uprising are very interesting and apparently unique. It is the only case after 1524 in which someone claimed to have supported Schilling and petitioned for him, and then used his role in one of the most notorious events in Augsburg's history as a claim to fame. After all, the uprising had been a debacle for the government, and a terrifying moment for many of the council members, at least one of whom was injured. Although few of those men were probably still members of the council, even the newer members were unlikely to forget it. Though the council had eventually succeeded in pacifying the irate crowd back in 1524, it had come at a price. While maintaining its exile of Schilling, the council had been forced to agree to hire a new reform-minded preacher to replace him.

The authenticity of Widenman's claim cannot be substantiated. Extant interrogation records from the 1524 uprising do not include Leonhard Widenman, nor do any of the arrested men mention him as one of the leaders. According to a report from the council in 1524, however, he does appear among a list of people who gathered in front of the City Hall during the Schilling Uprising.[108] So we can place Widenman there, but he certainly does not appear to have played the crucial role in the uprising or its resolution that he alleged. Regardless of whether Widenman's claim is valid, what is interesting is the usefulness he expected it to have for acquiring alms from Augsburg's residents, on the one hand, and the impact it actually had on Augsburg's magistrates by raising suspicions of a plot, on the other. Recalling one of the most traumatic and shocking events the city had seen in recent memory, Widenman had touched a raw nerve with the uneasy Interim council.

Despite the council's concern about the rebellious nature of Widenman's claim, he cannot simply be labeled a "critical speech" maker. Among his many faults, he was accused of insulting the Alms Officials (*Bettelknechte*), begging illegally, meeting with Anabaptists, allowing his wife to fool around with their tenants (which apparently had led to her spending some time in a tower), and drinking all his income. Although

---

[107] "7)...wissten di frumen herrn mein armut sy liessen mich nit daher bringen, so wiß er nichts args von der oberkhait, und trow inen alles guets zue," ibid., Leonhard Widenman.
[108] Ibid., Urg. 6 August 1524 (report).

he was originally arrested for begging illegally, the council investigated a wide variety of issues. In Widenman's first and second hearings, on 24 and 26 April 1549, the interrogators asked him if he had preached to the soldiers who stayed in his home. In the first interrogation Widenman testified that he had not preached, but his wife had washed shirts for them. The second time he explained more fully that he had not preached and "could not read a single letter of the alphabet." In his third hearing on 29 April, they asked him if he was an Anabaptist, which he absolutely denied. He had never been rebaptized and had nothing to do with the sect. Why the council suspected Widenman of being an Anabaptist is unclear. It is true that quite a number of Widenmans were arrested for Anabaptism in Augsburg in 1528, but none by the name of Leonhard. Widenman was a fairly common name in Augsburg, and Leonhard may have been related to one or more of those arrested then. Maybe the council confused him with one of them or perhaps they jumped to the conclusion that religious deviance might be behind his unusual behavior.

In any case, one has the impression from the broad range of the interrogators' questions, in three different interrogations, that the council did not know what to do with Widenman or how to interpret his behavior. Was he a political threat, a religious deviant, an immoral householder, or a welfare case? Perhaps all of the above; the council decided to resolve the dilemma by banishing him from the city. Twice in the following months Widenman entered the city illegally in order to petition for legal permission to return. Each time he was arrested, and the councilors began to wonder why he did not take them more seriously. He pleaded for help, because he was "a poor, sick, miserable man in body." After the third arrest, they finally put him in the Hospital where he would be under house arrest but cared for, which was all he had really wanted. Widenman's case presents an interesting combination of issues intertwined in one person. It illustrates the point that these cases are rarely simple or straightforward. The timing of Widenman's nostalgic claim, that he had supported Schilling and saved the Gospel in Augsburg, reveals something about the period. Widenman expected his fellow citizens—who saw the cause of Protestantism threatened once again, this time by Charles V's intervention—to sympathize with him and perhaps show gratitude in the form of alms. The council, however, saw his behavior not only as inappropriate (for boasting about participation in an insurrection) but dangerous, if he encouraged people to recall the events of 1524 when residents had protested the religious policies of the regime.

The timing of Widenman's reference to Johann Schilling and the council's reaction to it show the disparity between the views of Augsburg's populace and its council in this period. The council was very sensitive to the potential for rebellion as a consequence of enforcing unpopular religious terms. The Interim not only returned Catholicism to the city but altered the nature of Protestant worship in ways that threatened the popular mode of religious expression in Augsburg, which had been primarily Zwinglian.[109] Not unlike the days of the the Schilling Uprising, in 1548 and again in 1551 a number of Augsburg's ministers had been forced into exile for refusing to accept the conditions of the Interim. Several cases, therefore, show that the dissatisfaction with the Interim, and resulting tensions, stemmed not just from the reintroduction of Catholicism into a Protestant community (thus, religious coexistence) but from resentment about the restrictions placed on how Protestants were allowed to worship.

A final case presents the only recorded occasion in the period from 1548 to 1555 of neighbors fighting with each other over religious differences and using confessional epithets as insults. In August 1552, during the last days of the Protestant occupation of Augsburg, a young man named Hans Scheber, an apothecary's journeyman, filed an official complaint with the mayors against two barber surgeons, father and son, both named Matheus Sonntag (also known as Sundau). Although there are no extant interrogation records for this case, the report from Scheber, the testimonies of twelve witnesses, and a petition from Matheus Sonntag the Younger still exist. Seven numbers marked by a scribe in the text of Scheber's report correspond to the seven points on which the witnesses were questioned and make up for the lack of a list of questions. Not surprisingly, religious hostility was not the sole cause of the altercation between the parties. Honor, politics, and even ill-health played a role in instigating the main incident between Scheber and the Sonntags and led to the official complaint, which followed a long history of antagonism.

According to Scheber's report, which was largely substantiated by the witnesses whom he called, the older Sonntag had often called him a Lutheran knave or heretic. Moreover, Sonntag had said that "all those

---

[109] Philip Broadhead, "One Heart and One Soul: The Changing Nature of Public Worship in Augsburg, 1521–1548," (*Ecclesiastical History Society Papers*, 1997–1998) 118.

who go to the Lutheran sermons, including the preachers, are false and dishonorable people."[110] In this way Sonntag not only insulted Scheber but all of the Protestant population and preachers of the city. Scheber reported that Sonntag had also threatened to file complaints against him and other Lutheran "knaves and scoundrels" and "to set the Spaniards at their throats," as soon as the emperor returned to the city.[111] So Sonntag had threatened Scheber with legal as well as physical danger. Futhermore, Sonntag had warned Scheber that "within fourteen days an upset would come to the city and there would be a change in the guilds, so the preachers ought to run away on their own," instead of waiting to be banished.[112] Scheber then admitted that all of Sonntag's slander against the Gospel and the preachers and his threats had forced Scheber to return the insults. Sonntag had retaliated by promising to file a complaint as soon as a new pro-imperial government came into power, to which Scheber said that "if he sues me, he's obviously a knave and scoundrel himself."[113] Lastly, Scheber asserted that Sonntag had shamed him in front of his master, Matheus Schöllenberg, by saying that "[Scheber] did not serve his master faithfully but instead rejected and drove away his customers." In response, Scheber had said that Sonntag "lies brazenly, like a dishonorable man."[114] While Scheber and Sonntag were exchanging insults, Sonntag's son joined them and confronted Scheber. "You Lutheran traitor, what business do you have with my father? You double heretic, there's no Lutheran heretic like you in the entire city, and you're a liar like your Duke Moritz [of Saxony]."[115] Like father like son, the younger Sonntag also called Scheber

---

[110] "1) Erstlich daß der altten mich zum offtermols, ein Luterischen schelmen, ketzer hatt offentlich gescholtten,..., 2) ursach er sagt offentlich, daß alle die so in die Lüterische predig gen, auch die predicanten seien meineidige und erlose leutt," ibid., 13 August 1552, Matheus Sonntag (a.k.a. Sundau), Hans Scheber (plaintiff).

[111] "3) Auch welle er, so baldtt der kaiser in die statt wieder kome, mich mitt sambt anderen Lutherischen schelme und beßwichtten verklagen und mirr und andern Spanier iber den halß schicken die unß wol sollen zu vesten, etc." ibid.

[112] "4)...man soll noch 14 dag wartten so werde noch jomer werden in der statt, und ein grosst verenderung in den zünfftten, 5) so sollen auch die predicanten von inen selbß hiewecg lauffen," ibid.

[113] "Auff solchß hab ich mich gegen im eingelossen und im erzeltt seine bese stuck, hatt er von stundt an 6) gesagtt er welle mich wol finden, und mich verklagen, so ein andere oberkaitt ist,..., hab ich geantworttet, so er mich nichtt verklagtt sei er ein offentlicher selbß schelm und beßwicht, er sei auch eben der den er mich nembtt, so lang er solchß auff mich bringe," ibid.

[114] "weitter in bei sein meinß hern, 7) sagtt er ich diene meine hern nichtt treulich sonder ich abweise und vertreibe im alle seine kinden, darauff ich geantworttet, er liege mich an wie ein unerlich man, etc." ibid.

[115] "1) du Lüterischer laur waß hastu mitt meinen vatter zu thun, du doppelter ketzer, kein solcher Lüterischer ketzer ist in der gantzen stat nichtt, und du bist meineidig wie dein Hertzog Moritzen," ibid.

a Lutheran knave and claimed that he served his master unfaithfully and drove away all his customers. He said many other things which Scheber had been "too angry to remember."[116]

In his report, Scheber made it clear that his reason for filing an official complaint was to defend his honor. Not only had the two men slandered his religion ("*Schmehung deß hailigen Ewangeli*"), but they had also called him a knave and had accused him of unfaithful service, a damaging reputation for a journeyman to have. At the beginning of his report, Scheber pointed out the significance of Sonntag's having slandered him publicly.

> The old one…abused me openly, in the street, (otherwise we had conversed with each other about all sorts of things discreetly and privately in the past), but because he impugned my honor so openly, as mentioned, we would have come to blows, if I had not respected his age.[117]

Later, after describing the Sonntags' combined offenses, Scheber declared that "if they give me my honor again openly (as is fair), then I will be well satisfied."[118] In concluding his report, Scheber requested from the mayors that "you might help me, a poor journeyman, so that I might acquire and have my honor again, so that no one can or may attack me with such slander."[119] It is difficult to say what aspect of the Sonntags ' insults offended Scheber the most. Was it the religious, the personal, or the professional slight? Scheber's main concern, so far as seeking justice went, seems to have focused on the insult to his professional honor. More importantly, Scheber did not distinguish among different kinds of honor, and it would be inappropriate to separate them, since they seem to have been so intricatedly entwined. As we have often seen, whenever religious differences appeared in conflicts between neighbors other factors played a role too.[120]

---

[116] Ibid.

[117] "*1]…daß der altten mich…hatt offentlich gescholtten, uff der Gassen, (wyr haben wol sunst mitt ein ander in der stille und heimlich vormoln mer mitt einander von allerhant sachen conversiertt) aber die weil er mich so offentlich (wie gemelt) an meine Eeren antastet hatt wo ich seins alters nicht hette verschonett, Daß wir weren zu schlagen kommen,*" ibid. The parentheses are Scheber's.

[118] "*wan sie mirr mein Eer offentlich (wie billich) wider geben, so bin ich schon wol zu friden,*" ibid. The parentheses are again Scheber's.

[119] "*Ich bitte der halben…, sie welle mirr armen gesellen behelfflich sein, daß ich mein Eer mege wider haben und erlangen do mitt mier niemant solche schmoch wortt auffrupffen kan oder moge,*" ibid.

[120] See, for example, the case of George Zeindelweber and Heinrich Meckenloher in Chapter Two.

Witnesses' testimonies add another dimension to the scene described by Scheber. In general the witnesses corroborate Scheber's story, which is to be expected, since Scheber called them himself. Few of the witnesses had observed the entire incident, but altogether their testimonies covered each of the points Scheber raised. One significant point which emerges is that the hostility and verbal abuse between Scheber and the Sonntags was reciprocal. Hans Gfider, a purse-maker, testified that "the younger Sonntag said, 'why do you call my father a traitor, you're a traitor yourself and a knave and no better,' then [Scheber] called him [the son] names too."[121] Scheber's master, Matheus Schöllenberg, a wealthy Augsburger and the first witness, testified to the exchange of insults, stating that "they called each other Lutheran and Papist knaves."[122] According to Schöllenberg, the incident had begun when Matheus Sonntag the Elder, had come to him to complain about Scheber. Sonntag told Schöllenberg that his journeyman had called him "a priest's servant and a traitor."[123] At this point Scheber came out of the apothecary's shop and began the quarrel described above. In other words, the antagonism between the parties predated the reported incident, and Scheber was certainly no innocent victim. Another witness, Andreas Kuttenkoffer, testified that when he heard the men quarreling he had asked Schöllenberg what they were fighting about. Schöllenberg told him that Sonntag had complained about Schöllenberg's servant, upon which Schöllenberg had advised Sonntag to let one of the mayors make peace between them. Then Kuttenkoffer heard the young Sonntag say to Scheber, "don't slander my father!" and then the two of them called each other knaves.[124]

By the time Charles V returned victoriously to Augsburg a week later (19 August 1552) the Sonntags had already been ordered into exile. Matheus Sonntag the Younger petitioned the emperor for assistance and explained his own version of the incident. The most interesting

---

[121] "*warumb schilts mein vatter ain laurn, du bist selbs ain laur und schelm und nit besser, hinwiderumb appoteckher ine auch gesschollten,*" ibid., Hans Gfider (witness).

[122] "*das sy ainannder Lutterisch unnd Babstisch schelmen geshollten,*" ibid., Matheuß Schellenperger (witness).

[123] "*vor unnd ehe sych die sach zugetragen hab Maister Matheiß ime zeugen clagßweise angezaigt, wie sein gesell der Schöberlin, ine ain pfaffenkhnecht unnd ain verretter geschollten mit bit ime darvor zusein, in dem sein gesell der Schoberlin uß der appoteckhen kommen mit dem alten Sundau zu zannckhen angefanngen,*" ibid.

[124] "*in dem der Jung Sundau zum Schöberlin gesagt er solle sein vatter ungeschmecht lassen, allso ainannder schelmen gescholten,*" ibid., Enndriß Khuttenkoffer (witness).

aspect of Sonntag's petition is his description of the mitigating circumstances under which the altercation occurred. Most significantly,
he explained that his father had suffered a sort of stroke thirty years
earlier and since then was a sick and crippled man who was easily
angered, especially when the "old religion" was disrespected. He also
added that the apothecary's journeyman knew it well and often grievously irritated his father for the fun of it and with vicious words would
bring him to the point that he would be laid up sick for two or three
days. Although Sonntag had often asked Scheber to leave his father
alone regarding his faith and the old Catholic religion and not to play
him for a fool, Scheber would not let it go.[125] On 11 August, Scheber
had insulted his father, called him a heretic and a priest's servant, and
badgered him for so long that the old Sonntag was finally driven out
of anger—and for no other reason than that, insisted the son—"to
say some things against the new religion and its followers." At first,
claimed Sonntag the Younger, Scheber found this amusing, but then
the younger Sonntag, who had grown tired of seeing his father goaded,
grew angry and said some things against the new religion himself.
Consequently, Scheber maliciously brought both Sonntags, father and
son, up on charges. Sonntag the Younger explained that if they had
not yielded, they would have been put in prision. He insisted that he
had innocently become involved in the matter and that neither he nor
his father would ever have said such things if they had not been provoked by Scheber's harassment of his father. On the back of Sonntag's
supplication to the emperor, a note instructed the council to consider
Sonntag's request and directed them to permit him to re-enter the city,
if the situation was as Sonntag described.[126] The father and son, thus,
returned to the city shortly after their exile.[127]

Curiously, Sonntag's petition assures the Catholic emperor that he
meant no disrespect to the "new religion." His comment reflects his

---

[125] "*mein lieber vatter, Matheus Sundaw vor dreyssig jaren mit dem gwalt gottes berurt, unnd
er seyderher ain krancker prechenhafftiger mann gewesen, unnd ganntz leichtlich, besonnder aber wa
die alte Religion wurdt verachtet, zu zorn zubewegen, das dann ain apotegker knecht zu Augspurg,
bey dem Herrn Schellenberger an ime wol gewißt, und ine deßhalben offtermals seins gefallens zum
hefftigisten erzurnet, unnd dahin mit spötlichen wortten gepracht, das er ettwann zwen oder drey tag
darnach kranck gelegen, Unnd wiewol gedachter apotegker knecht ettlich mal freuntlich gepetten worden,
das er meinen vatter seines glaubens unnd alter Catholischen Religion halb, wöllte unbekemert lassen,
unnd nit also fur ain Narren umbziehen, so hat ers doch nit wöllen underlassen,*" ibid., 23 August
1552, Matheus Sundaw (petition).
[126] Ibid.
[127] Ibid., RB 1550–55, 29 August 1552.

society's sensitivity to religious feelings and the desire to avoid conflicts. Perhaps he suspected that even the Catholic emperor would not appreciate a trouble maker. In addition, the terms "old religion" and "new religion" went back a generation, and Sonntag's use of them in 1552 reflects the as yet rudimentary distinction between religious beliefs. The appearance of the word Lutheran (*luterisch*) in the Sonntag's dispute with Scheber cannot be assumed to refer to a particular confession, since the term was so commonly used for any type of reformer, especially by followers of the old religion.

These cases illustrate what a crucial role the upheavals in regime could play in determining the fate of defendants arrested by the council. It must have frustrated Augsburgers to know that the changing circumstances resulted primarily from external forces which were beyond their control. The varying fortunes of the city government in the early 1550s were largely determined by military might supported by financial backing from wealthy Augsburgers, rather than any kind of popular consensus.[128] Soon, the Peace of Augsburg in 1555 would permanently regulate the constitution of the city to ensure that such changes and reversals would no longer upset the status quo. In the late 1540s and early 1550s, Augsburg's population, including the authorities, feared or anticipated that military intervention would lead to one faith's gaining sole control of the religious institutions in Augsburg. Yet, through most of the Reformation era the city had contained a religiously diverse population. In 1555 the Peace of Augsburg merely recognized *de jure* what the city already experienced *de facto*: the coexistence of more than one faith.

---

[128] Augsburg's wealthy merchants sometimes provided financial support to opposing sides in the imperial conflicts in the late 1540s and early 1550s. Sieh-Bürens, *Oligarchie*, 163–187.

CONCLUSION

The representatives of the city of Augsburg... stated that their lord governors, mayors, and councils... allowed both religions to exist next to one another.[1]

King Ferdinand to his brother, Emperor Charles V, 1555

When the Imperial Diet drafted the Peace of Augsburg in 1555, it signaled the end of war and the acceptance, however reluctant or provisionally of religious diversity in the Holy Roman Empire. The treaty introduced the innovative principle, later known as *cuius regio, eius religio*, which allowed each state's ruler or government to choose the religion of its territory and expel dissenters. As part of the peace settlement, Article Twenty-Seven required the sixty-five free imperial cities to tolerate religious minorities.[2] For example, even if the town's population was essentially evangelical, it still had to tolerate Catholic residents. For the vast majority of imperial cities, who were overwhelmingly Protestant or Catholic, this article did not have a great impact. Eight of the cities, however, were acknowledged as bi-confessional, because of the substantial size of the minority faith (Catholicism in all cases). Of those eight cities, an even smaller group of four, including Augsburg, shared the government between the two faiths, allowing Lutherans and Catholics to worship openly, maintain their own churches, and hold offices.[3] Since 1549, Hans Jakob Fugger, sometime mayor of Augsburg, had been interceding energetically with the emperor for the coexistence of the religious communities in the city.[4] During the imperial diet in 1555 the magistrates communicated their wishes to King Ferdinand, maintaining that the Augsburgers "did not feel burdened by the coexistence of two religions... and wanted to tolerate and manage both

---

[1] *"Darauf aber der stat Augsburg verordnete alsbald vermeldet, das ire hern statpfleger, bürgermeister und räte in dieser stat Augsburg auch baide religionen neben einander halten liessen,"* August von Druffel, *Briefe und Akten zur Geschichte des 16. Jahrhunderts* (Munich 1882) 717, #667.
[2] R. Po-chia Hsia, *Social Discipline in the Reformation: Central Europe 1550–1750* (New York: Routledge, 1989), 73–88.
[3] Warmbrunn, *Zwei Konfessionen in einer Stadt*, 11–14.
[4] Sieh-Bürens, *Oligarchie*, 183.

in the future."[5] This was a remarkable statement for the time, hardly one to be predicted and yet not as surprising as it first appears given Augsburg's history.

The city's business interests are often credited with determining its religious destiny. In other words, as an internationally active trading center, Augsburg's merchants saw no sense in antagonizing valued partners in Catholic regions, such as Italy, Spain, Austria, and neighboring Bavaria. More importantly, in the 1520s and 1530s Augsburg's magistrates lacked consensus in religious matters among themselves and, therefore, dragged their collective feet, while many other cities where Protestantism had popular support were introducing the Reformation officially. In 1537, a change in leadership moved the newly elected mayors to ban the Catholic Mass and clergy and introduce a new Protestant church ordinance—one should add that this occurred despite ongoing business connections with Catholic states and not without repercussions. After a ten-year exile, Catholic worship returned in 1548 at the command of Emperor Charles V, who restored the clergy, removed guild leaders from government and replaced them with loyal Catholic and Protestant patricians during the Interim, while permitting only Catholic and moderate Lutheran worship (based on the Augsburg Confession) to continue. The year 1552 saw two more fluctuations in Augsburg's confessional allegiance as the result of warfare between Lutheran Duke Moritz of Saxony and the Catholic emperor. Moritz' forces took over the city in the spring, and a new regime once again outlawed Catholicism, only to be overturned in the summer, as an imperial army regained control of the city. The succeeding years, up to 1555, saw growing resentment of the emperor's Catholic occupying force and its interference in Augsburg's religious and political affairs.

On the surface, a chronology of Augsburg's official religious arrangements reveals little to suggest that Augsburgers would recognize themselves in the magistrates' declaration that the city wished to tolerate two religions. It is true the city council endorsed moderation even during the height of Protestant success in Augsburg, perhaps to appease important Catholic residents, perhaps to avoid conflict, but surely not because it valued religious toleration in and of itself, or did it? Most studies contend that neither tolerance as an intellectually formulated principle nor even toleration as a policy were widely held or considered

---

[5] Zorn, *Augsburg*, 227.

preferable to religious unity in the early modern period.[6] On the other hand, hidden from the record of official religious policy, the stories of ordinary Augsburgers, culled from interrogation transcripts demonstrate the practice of toleration among citizens and magistrates despite the undeniable potential for conflict. The cases studied in this book assess the impact of a changing religious world on individuals in an urban community by highlighting the experiences of ordinary people, who witnessed the innovations and upheaval firsthand, at the very beginning of the reform movement. By listening to the voices of residents in Augsburg in the first half of the sixteenth century, the anonymous mass of believers becomes individuals, and the existence of an often puzzling tangle of motives, influences, and passions, which complicated their relationships to religious belief and practices, comes to light. Appreciating the variety of factors that played a role in developing a person's religious convictions and shaping his or her encounters with others gives us a much better understanding of the diverse ways that people reacted to the discord of the early Reformation and contributed to a community that became bi-confessional.

For many people differing religious beliefs seem to have been a surmountable obstacle in relationships among friends or relatives. In the Germair house, an Anabaptist mother, Sabina Hieberin, and her evangelical daughter, Elisabeth Schenk, readily supported one another's divergent religious beliefs. Although rival interpretations of the true Gospel may have created a battleground for theologians, they did not necessarily have the same impact on individuals' lives. In fact, theology rarely appears as the most important indication of one's identity. Many people in Augsburg showed openness to religious curiosity and experimentation, and this openness characterized their interactions with others. Furthermore, the willingness of a landlord like Michael Germair to wink at his tenants' suspect spiritual activities, despite his adherence to the old faith, facilitated the carrying on of day-to-day life in the early Reformation. Consequently, our understanding of the early Reformation's impact on sixteenth century society should include a more restrained and nuanced view of the divisiveness of theological disputes.

---

[6] Hans R. Guggisberg, "Wandel der Argumente Argumente für religiöse Toleranz und Glaubensfreiheit im 16. und 17. Jahrhundert," in *Reformation und Gegenreformation*, ed. Heinrich Lutz (Munich: Oldenbourg, 1979), 455–481.

Not all was so rosy. Georg Zeindelweber and Heinrich Meckenloher, neighbors and fellow employees in the city's military establishment, entered into a verbal duel one evening amidst a gathering of neighbors. When Meckenloher brought Zeindelweber before the council on charges of blasphemy, the encounter came to light and fortunately has been preserved. Their dispute opens a window onto interactions between Augsburg's citizens in the late 1520s, revealing the experience of religious debate in casual social gatherings and the potential for very different views on religious belief and behavior to emerge. This case is one of the most significant examples of a religious conflict between the city's residents in the 1520s and yet nothing remotely like confessional differences between the two men can be recognized. Both showed interest in Protestant reforms. Purportedly a case of blasphemy against the mother of God, Zeindelweber's criticism of authorities who oppress religious dissidents also troubled the Council. Sympathetic to those who suffer "for a small misbelief," Zeindelweber disliked Meckenloher's boasts that he would fight Jews who insulted Mary, while Meckenloher resented Zeindelweber's attack on his honor as a man and fighter. The two men not only disagreed on religious beliefs but also on how people with unorthodox beliefs should be treated and how one could best prove his manliness. In this excellent example, a simple case of blasphemy disguises a much more complicated incident, and a supposed religious conflict reveals many other layers of meaning. As in so many cases, the religious elements are intricately entangled with other factors that contributed to conflicts between individuals.

The extensive investigation into Anabaptists in the late 1520s and early 1530s provides some of the most interesting insights into the formation of religious identity in this period and suggests the possibility of finding similar characteristics among the other Christian groups. The Anabaptists's testimonies demonstrate a whole spectrum of ways in which people became involved with the movement. People like Dorothea Duchschererin could attend meetings on a friend's invitation but choose not to be re-baptized. Some were baptized under questionable circumstances and seemed to regret their decision later, such as Hans Gabler who was baptized while drunk and later recanted. Others, like Agnes Vogel, turned to the preaching of Anabaptist ministers out of frustration after finding the other preachers too contradictory. A number of Anabaptists, such as Ursula Germairin, developed such a deep faith that they resisted oppression under any circumstances. Many Anabaptists joined with family members, others in spite of them. Some recanted after a brush with the law, others aided the movement in any way they could regardless of official sanctions. Coming to their religious convictions and participating in a variety of ways, they also exhibited various degrees of commitment and passion about their faith.

Signs of a similar phenomenon can be observed among Catholics and Protestants in Augsburg. For instance, when the city council prohibited Catholic ceremonies in 1537, Barbara Hertnitin switched from attending Catholic Mass to Protestant sermons rather readily it seems. After all, as she stated in her own words, "she likes the evangelical sermons just as much, and she listens to them as gladly as to the others." Yet just a few years earlier, she and her husband had fired a servant for not attending Catholic Mass. Despite her willingness to attend evangelical services, it seems Hertnitin did not fully internalize the Protestant message and its rejection of Catholicism. She continued to participate in and support Catholic rites outside of town, such as weddings and church festivals, because she placed greater value on social customs and obligations than on religious orthodoxy. Hertnitin's religious practices were shaped by a mixture of influences, including political authorities and social responsibilities, and by an openness to spiritual guidance from conflicting sources. She seems to have seen no obstacles in crossing whatever tentative boundaries existed between the Protestant and Catholic faiths in the late 1530s.

During Augsburg's brief experiment with religious uniformity from 1537 to 1547, variations of Christianity continued to survive beyond just the old Catholicism. Many Anabaptists and Schwenkfeldians—most of whom never appeared before the Council—managed to live peacefully in Augsburg, even organizing their own printing presses to publish their writings. In addition to them, people like Katharina Kunigin and Anthoni Schnedl defy any attempt to categorize them. They cannot be adequately described as independents, because Kunigin belonged to the evangelical community and relied on its ministers to carry out God's message. Yet she clearly developed her own unique beliefs in certain particulars and, even under arrest, never doubted her right to maintain them. She readily shared with the interrogators her vision of her relationship with Christ, and the Council cast no aspersions on her claim to have special insights into God's will.

In the 1550s Protestants like Lenhart Teufel and Catherina Frenckin vocalized their religious position passionately and without hesitation; more precisely put, they vocalized their opposition to Catholicism. When confronted in a bathhouse by the pastor and provost of Oberhausen,

Teufel unhesitatingly revealed his dislike of all Catholic clergy and their supporters. Likewise, Catherina Frenckin imprudently mocked Catholics in a procession to a sick man's house and apparently had ridiculed others before. During the Interim in Augsburg, both Teufel and Frenckin put themselves in jeopardy by criticizing the newly rein-troduced religion. The council punished them not in order to suppress the defendants' religious beliefs but to keep the peace. Protecting a minority faith helped to make possible the formation of Augsburg as a bi-confessional city, even if it was not their first preference. They were making the best of a situation that had been forced on them by circumstances beyond their control.

Two significant points emerge from this study of Augsburg's populace in the first half of the sixteenth century. First, religious groups were amorphous and indistinct, with individual preachers agreeing on some issues and diverging on others, some reformers wanting to stay loyal to Rome and some priests wanting to reform. As in the Middle Ages, a particular church or preacher might develop a following but distinct confessions of faith were not considered. Therefore, identifying oneself or others with a particular label was not only problematic but not even an issue. Even Anabaptists were not nearly as exclusive as has usually been thought. As repeatedly demonstrated, Augsburgers usually did not identify their faith by name or describe themselves as belonging to a particular group, though this does not mean that they were unaware of differences in religious beliefs or practices. Instead they tended to express preferences for attending sermons held at a particular church or by a particular preacher. This non-confessional form of religious identity reflected the religious culture and may have played a role in maintaining the relatively peaceful relations among townspeople in the early years of the Reformation.

Second, while tensions and conflicts certainly did exist—between citizens and magistrates or between neighbors—they seem to have been the exception rather than the rule and usually involved more issues than just religious differences. Even where religious distinctions could be seen clearly, in the case of some Anabaptists, numerous incidents show that people maintained relationships with one another despite differences. These two observations regarding the ambiguous nature of religious identity and the relatively peaceful communal relations contrast sharply with an older view of the Reformation as a time when bitter confessional feuds triggered riots and wars and a blazing battle of words among theologians. The anachronistic desire to fix confessional

labels to individual Christians in the early reformation does not fit at all with the evidence from the period.

This study of the pre-confessional period complements the growing body of scholarship that demonstrates people's ability to overcome religious boundaries later on in the confessional age, such as Judith Pollmann's study of the Dutch Republic. Evidence from Augsburg shows that, while some people had strong beliefs or opinions about religion and recognized differences among themselves, so many more things seem to have held them together: an appreciation of their shared Christian piety (hence the need to fight blasphemy), a sense that they were all "children of the city," their economic interdependence, social and familial bonds, and shared values, like honor, friendship, peace, modesty or good neighborliness. That should not lead to the illusion that Augsburg was a sort of oasis of religious freedom; it certainly was not for the Anabaptists. Also, at the mid-point of the sixteenth century we begin to see the stakes change in Augsburg, apparently as a consequence of the city's defeat in the Schmalkaldic War. As observers of and occasional participants in imperial affairs, Augsburgers began to associate certain religious beliefs with political parties, recognizing, for example, that the fate of Catholicism in Augsburg depended on the emperor's influence on the city council. Thus, Catholics tended to support the emperor and the council that did his bidding, while Protestants opposed him and the new magistracy. Less and less could religious differences be overlooked as "a small matter of misbelief," as Zeindelweber put it, but were recognized more and more as signs of adherence to a traitorous cause. It appears as a form of confessionalization from below, as ordinary people began to view the religious identities of themselves—and their neighbors differently, though in the 1550s still without great subtlety.

By exploring the lives of common people in Augsburg, rather than theologians or magistrates, this project distinguishes—but does not separate—them from the experiences and interests of authority figures. As a result, we see that faith was lived on a broad spectrum of degrees of involvement and commitment, motivated by a range of interests, concerns and experiences. Before the distinctness of religious groups materialized in the mid-sixteenth century and thereafter, Augsburgers did not have to identify themselves with one particular faith. They had a freedom to experiment and sample different religious views that is largely lost with confessionalization, though perhaps not to the extent we sometimes think. In addition, we see that the common person could develop his or her own religious position relatively independently from friends and family and from spiritual and secular leaders. This observation by no means discounts the influence of one's social, political, or even economic circumstances, rather it reveals the complexity of motivations and interests that formed people's experiences and decisions and our inability to predict them. In order to understand the Reformation's impact on a sixteenth-century community, we need to look first at how people experienced the Reformation and developed their convictions. Only by examining how people regarded their own beliefs, can we begin to understand how they felt about others. Evidence suggests that people did not experience differences to the degree that they would later and could often overlook disagreements in belief or practice. This study of individuals in an urban community in the first half of the sixteenth century suggests that most people did not make religious agreement a criterion for peaceful relations with their neighbors, even if they might have preferred it.

A new understanding of the development of religious identity in early Reformation Augsburg informs our perception of relations among people of diverse religious beliefs. Most histories of the Reformation used to take the existence of conflicts between religious groups for granted. The documentation of theologians' disputes and magisterial policy-making presents ample evidence of dissent and of contemporary concern for violence and danger resulting from competing religious factions.[7] The more recent focus of historians, such as Olivier Christin and Benjamin Kaplan, on common people's experiences has revised that view and unearthed more and more evidence of toleration even if contemporaries did not consider it ideal. The exploration of Augsburg's legal records adds another dimension to our understanding of religious identities and conflicts by showing how minor a role one's religious faith seemed to play in everyday encounters with others. Almost all documented incidents of religious conflict took place between authority figures (either secular or spiritual) and citizens and not among citizens themselves. Indeed, many cases reveal people demonstrating

---

[7] Jacob Sturm of Strasbourg, for example, contended that nothing was more divisive than discord over religion. Jacob Sturm to Georg and Bernhard Besserer [of Ulm], Strasbourg, 15 December 1534, in *Politische Correspondenz der Stadt Strassburg im Zeitalter der Reformation*, ed. Hans Virck, et al. 5 vols. (Strasbourg: Trübner, 1882–98; Heidelberg: Carl Winter, 1928–33), 2:237, no. 259. See Thomas A. Brady, Jr., *Protestant Politics: Jacob Sturm (1489–1553) and the German Reformation*. Atlantic Highlands, NJ: Humanities Press, 1995.

sympathy for one another in spite of different religious beliefs, even illegal ones.

In Augsburg uniformity imposed from above created a thin veneer of consensus, which was not internalized for decades or perhaps much longer. In the first half of the sixteenth century, people in Augsburg did not express their religious commitments as being something (a Catholic, Zwinglian, or an Anabaptist) but as doing something (going to Holy Cross, listening to Michael Keller). If they defined their religious life at all, they did so by where they went and what they did, not by their creed or confession. Likewise their interactions with others seemed more often determined by whether they shared common social values, or piety, rather than creeds. Not surprisingly, Augsburg does not show signs of confessionalization understood as the use of religious disciplining as a political tool to develop a modern state, a process usually believed to have occurred much later, particularly after confessions became better defined, nor confessionalism as the development of sharply defined confessional identities. What one does see happening in the late 1540s and early 1550s, however, is an example of the politicization of religion, when a particular political agenda becomes associated with a certain religious group. Robert Scribner refers to this process as "stigmatization," which he says "became more intense…when a particular group could be associated in a casual manner with a specific threat or problem.[8] This happens clearly in Augsburg when the Catholic emperor demolishes the city's guild-based political system in 1548. As a result, the forcible return of the old Catholic faith becomes associated with the loss of traditional political rights for the citizens. Support for the old Catholic faith implies a betrayal of the city, while support for Protestantism suggests disloyalty to the emperor and the city's new government. Thus, the confluence of religious groups and political agendas inspires the visible increase in agitation among Augsburg's citizens after 1548.

This unforeseen, though not unprecedented or even very surprising, development rather than any systematic attempt to instill religious belief or enforce conformity seems to be responsible for the growing divide which characterizes social relations in the middle of the sixteenth century and beyond in Augsburg, and it seems to begin with the Interim of 1548. First, Charles V demolished the centuries-old representation of

---

[8] Scribner, "Preconditions of Tolerance and Intolerance," in *Tolerance and Intolerance*, 41.

the guilds in Augsburg's city government, replacing them with patricians and overturning the city's reformation by bringing back the Catholic clergy and expelling obdurate Protestant ministers. Then, Protestants rallied briefly, when Duke Moritz of Saxony's defeat of imperial forces enabled Jakob Herbrot to reinstate the old guild-led government and ban Catholicism again. Within months Catholic Masses were being said in the cathedral once more, after the emperor's victorious return. The back-and-forth changes to the religious establishment as the result of military victories by different forces aggravated the situation and further entrenched the notion that there was no security for anyone's church without political dominance. There can be no doubt that over time secular and spiritual institutions that attempted to inculcate orthodox belief and practices and to claim exclusivity to truth contributed to the creation of more confessionally aware or sensitive societies. Yet the awareness of difference does not seem to have been enough to motivate hostility among ordinary lay people. Rather, the association of a particular religious faction with political influence or economic power, rather than theological discrepancies, disrupted the sense of interdependency between groups and led to tension between individuals. Doctrinal or liturgical disputes could inspire conflict between theologians, but they do not move lay people to aggression unless other interests are also at stake. We see this repeatedly in Augsburg in cases that appear before 1548 as well. Even after 1548, we see that most residents intended and expected to be able to coexist peacefully with one another.

The suppression of guild power in the city at the hands of the Catholic emperor and the continuation of warfare between competing Catholic and Protestant forces in the empire added a new political dimension to the religious differences between citizens in Augsburg. While these events tended to exacerbate religious tensions, paradoxically they also coincide with Augsburg's commitment to maintain a confessionally mixed community. While Augsburgers became more aware of religious differences after 1548, their desire to keep the community intact overcame the common preference for religious unanimity. One could say unity triumphed over uniformity, despite contemporary assumptions about the necessity of having only one religion to achieve domestic peace. In the intimate relations of families, friends, and neighbors, the people of Augsburg in the first half of the sixteenth century generally found that to be true.

BIBLIOGRAPHY

ABBREVIATIONS

BMB   Baumeisterbuch
Lit.   Literaliensammlung
RB   Ratsbuch
SB   Strafbuch
StB   Steuerbuch
StAA   Staatsarchiv Augsburg
StadtAA Stadtarchiv Augsburg
StBA   Staats- und Stadtbibliothek Augsburg
Urg.   Urgichtensammlung

UNPUBLISHED SOURCES

Stadtarchiv Augsburg
Anschläge und Dekrete 1524–1552
Bauamt
    Baumeisterbücher 1496–1539
Geheime Ratsprotokolle (Protokolle der Dreizehner) 1–7
Literalien
    1527–1555
    "Schwenkfeldiana"
    "Widertäufer und Religionsakten"
Ratsprotokolle (Ratsbücher) 24–28
Schätze 16
    1, 28, 35, 39, 44, 54, 67, 114, 116, 130, 133
Steueramt
    Steuerbücher 1524–1555
Strafamt
    Strafbücher 1517–1562
    Urgichten 1508–1555

Staats- und Stadtbibliothek Augsburg
4° Aug. 1021, Ordnungen, 2. Abt., 5 Bd., No. 3

PUBLISHED SOURCES AND LITERATURE

Andor, Eszter and István György Tóth, eds. *Frontiers of Faith: Religious Exchange and the Constitution of Religious Identities 1400–1750.* Vol. 1, *Cultural Exchange in Europe, 1400–1750.* Edited by Robert Muchembled. Budapest: CEU and European Science Foundation, 2001.
Blickle, Peter. *Communal Reformation: the Quest for Salvation in Sixteenth-Century Germany.* Translated by Thomas Dunlap. Atlantic Highlands, NJ: Humanities Press, 1992.
———. *The Revolution of 1525.* Translated by Thomas A. Brady, Jr., and H. C. Erik Midelfort. Baltimore: The Johns Hopkins University Press, 1981.

———. H.-C. Rublack, and R. Schulze. *Religion, Politics, and Social Protest: three studies on early modern Germany*. Boston: German Historical Institute (Allen & Unwin), 1984.

Böhm, Christoph. *Die Reichsstadt Augsburg und Kaiser Maximilian I: Untersuchungen zum Beziehungsgeflect zwischen Reichsstadt und Herrscher an der Wende zur Neuzeit*. Sigmaringen: Jan Thorbecke, 1998.

Bosl, Karl. *Bosl's Bayerische Biographie: 8000 Persönlichkeiten aus 15 Jahrhunderten*. Regensburg: Pustet, 1983.

Brady, Thomas A. *Protestant Politics: Jacob Sturm (1489–1553) and the German Reformation*. Atlantic Highlands, NJ: Humanities Press, 1995.

———. *Ruling Class, Regime, and Reformation at Strasbourg, 1520–1555*. Leiden: E. J. Brill, 1978.

———. "Confessionalization—The Career of a Concept." In *Confessionalization in Europe, 1555–1700: Essays in Honor and Memory of Bodo Nischan*, edited by John M. Headley, Hans J. Hillerbrand, and Anthony J. Papalas. Burlington, VT: Ashgate, 2004.

Broadhead, Philip. "Guildsmen, Religious Reform and the Search for the Common Good: The Role of the Guilds in the Early Reformation in Augsburg." *The Historical Journal* 39, No. 3 (1996): 577–597.

———. "One Heart and One Soul: The Changing Nature of Public Worship in Augsburg, 1521–1548," *Ecclesiastical History Society Papers* (1997–1998): 116–127.

Brunner, Heinrich. *Deutsche Rechtsgeschichte*. Leipzig: Duncker, and Humblot, 1906–1928.

Chrisman, Miriam Usher. *Conflicting Visions of Reform: German Lay Propaganda Pamphlets, 1519–1530*. Atlantic Highlands, NJ: Humanities Press, 1996.

———. *Strasbourg and the Reform; a Study in the Process of Change*. New Haven: Yale University Press, 1967.

Clasen, Claus-Peter. *Anabaptism: a Social History, 1525–1618: Switzerland, Austria, Moravia, South and Central Germany*. Ithaca: Cornell University Press, 1972.

———. *The Anabaptists in South and Central Germany, Switzerland, and Austria: their names, occupations, places of residence, and dates of conversion, 1525–1618*. Scottdale, PA: Mennonite Quarterly, 1978.

Dixon, C. Scott. *The Reformation in Germany*. Oxford: Blackwell Publishers, 2002.

———. "Urban Order and Religious Coexistence in the German Imperial City: Augsburg and Donauwörth, 1548–1608," *Central European History* 40, (2007): 1–33.

Ehrenpreis, Stefan and Ute Lotz-Heumann. *Reformation und Konfessionelles Zeitalter*. Wissenschaftliches Buchgesellschaft, 2002.

Fassl, Peter. *Konfessionspolitik, Wirtschaft und Politik: von Reichstadt zur Industriestadt, Augsburg 1750–1850*. Sigmaringen: J. Thorbecke. 1988.

Fischer, Hermann, ed. *Fischer's Schwäbisches Wörterbuch*. Tübingen, 1908.

Forster, Marc. *Catholic Revival in the Age of the Baroque: Religious Identity in Southwest Germany, 1550–1750*. Cambridge: Cambridge University Press, 2001.

———. *The Counter-Reformation in the Villages: Religion and Reform in the Bishopric of Speyer, 1560–1720*. Ithaca: Cornell University Press, 1992.

———. "With or Without Confessionalization: Varieties of Early Modern German Catholicism." *Journal of Early Modern History* 1, no. 4 (1997): 315–343.

François, Etienne. *Die unsichtbare Grenze: Protestanten und Katholiken in Augsburg, 1648–1806*. Sigmaringen: J. Thorbecke, 1991.

Ginzburg, Carlo. *The Cheese and the Worms: The Cosmos of a Sixteenth-Century Miller*. Baltimore: Johns Hopkins University Press, 1980.

Gray, Emily Fisher. *Good Neighbors: Architecture and Confession in Augsburg's Lutheran Church of Holy Cross, 1525–1661*. Diss. University of Pennsylvania, 2004.

Grell, Ole Peter and Bob Scribner, eds. *Tolerance and Intolerance in the European Reformation*. New York: Cambridge University Press, 1996.

Greyerz, Kaspar von. *Religion und Kultur: Europa 1500–1800*. Vandenhoeck and Ruprecht, 2000.

———. "Sanctity, Deviance and the People of Late Medieval and Early Modern Europe. A Review Article." *Comparative Studies in Society and History* 27, No. 2 (April, 1985): 280–290.

———, Hans Medick, und Patrice Veit, eds. *Von der dargestellten Person zum erinnerten Ich: Europäische Selbstzeugnisse als historische Quellen (1500–1850)*. Cologne: Böhlau Verlag, 2001.

———. Manfred Jakubowski-Tiessen, Thomas Kaufmann, und Hartmut Lehmann, eds., *Interkonfessionalität—Transkonfessionalität—binnenkonfessionelle Pluralität: neue Forschungen zur Konfessionalisierungsthese*. Gütersloh: Gütersloher Verlag, 2003.

Grünsteudel, Günther, Günter Hägele, and Rudolf Frankenberger, eds. *Augsburger Stadtlexikon*. Augsburg: Perlach Verlag, 1998.

Guderian, Hans. *Die Täufer in Augsburg: Ihre Geschichte und ihr Erbe*. Pfaffenhofen: Ludwig Verlag, 1984.

Haemmerle, A. *St. Ulrichs-Bruderschaft Augsburg: Mitgliederverzeichnis 1466–1521*. Munich: (privately printed), 1949.

Hoffmann, Carl A. "Strukturen und Quellen des Augsburger reichsstädtischen Strafgerichtswesens in der ersten Hälfte des 16. Jahrhunderts." *Zeitschrift des Historischen Vereins für Schwaben* 88 (1995): 57–108.

Hsia, R. Po-chia. *Social Discipline in the Reformation: Central Europe 1550–1750*. New York: Routledge, 1989.

———. *Society and Religion in Münster, 1535–1618*. New Haven: Yale University Press, 1984.

———, ed. *A Companion to the Reformation World*. Malden, MA: Blackwell Publishing, 2004.

———, ed. *The German People and the Reformation*. Ithaca: Cornell University Press, 1988.

——— and Henk van Nierop, eds., *Calvinism and Religious Toleration in the Dutch Golden Age*. Cambridge: Cambridge University Press, 2002.

Jesse, Horst. *Die Geschichte der Evangelischen Kirche in Augsburg*. Pfaffenhofen: Ludwig Verlag, 1983.

Karant-Nunn, Susan. *Zwickau in Transition, 1500–1547: the Reformation as an Agent of Change*. Columbus: Ohio State University Press, 1987.

Kießling, Rolf. *Bürgerliche Gesellschaft und Kirche in Augsburg im Spätmittelalter*. Augsburg: Verlag H. Mühlberger, 1971.

Kiraly, Bela K., ed. *Tolerance and Movments of Religious Dissent in Eastern Europe*, Eastern European Quarterly. New York: Columbia University Press, 1975.

Kraus, Jürgen. *Das Militärwesen der Reichsstadt Augsburg 1548–1806*. Augsburg: Verlag H. Mühlberger, 1980.

Kselman, Thomas, ed. *Belief in History: Innovative Approaches to European and American Religion*. Notre Dame: University of Notre Dame Press, 1991.

Künast, Hans-Jorg. *'Getruckt zu Augspurg:' Buchdruck und Buchhandel in Augsburg zwischen 1468 und 1555*. Tübingen: Max Niemeyer Verlag, 1997.

Kunze, Michael. *The Highroad to the Stake: A Tale of Witchcraft*. Chicago: University of Chicago Press, 1987.

Ladurie, Emmanuel LaRois. *Montaillu: The Promised Land of Error*. New York: G. Braziller, 1978.

Lieu, Judith M. *Christian Identity in the Jewish and Graeco-Roman World*. Oxford: Oxford University Press, 2004.

Luria, Keith P. *Sacred Boundaries: Religious Coexistence and Conflict in Early-Modern France*. Washington, D.C.: The Catholic University of America Press, 2005.

Lutz, Heinrich, ed. *Reformation und Gegenreformation*. Munich: Oldenbourg, 1979.

Moeller, Bernd. *Imperial Cities and the Reformation, Three Essays*. Translated by H. C. Erik Midelfort and Mark U. Edwards, Jr. Philadelphia: Fortress Press, 1972.

Nischan, Bodo. "Ritual and Protestant Identity in Late Reformation Germany." In *Protestant History and Identity in Sixteenth Century Europe*, edited by Bruce Gordon. Vol. 2. Aldershot, UK: Scolar Press, 1996.

Oberman, Heiko A. and Peter A. Dykema, eds. *Anticlericalism in Late Medieval and Early Modern Europe*. New York: E. J. Brill, 1993.

Ocker, Christopher, and Michael Printy, Peter Starenko, and Peter Wallace, eds. *Politics and Reformations: Communities, Politics, Nations, and Empires. Essays in Honor of Thomas A. Brady, Jr.* Boston: Brill, 2007.

Packull, Werner O. *Mysticism and the Early South German-Austrian Anabaptist Movement 1525–31*. Scottdale, PA: Herald Press, 1977.

—— and Geoffrey L. Dipple, eds. *Radical Reformation Studies: Essays Presented to James M. Stayer*. Ashgate: Brookfield, USA, 1999.

Peters, Edward M. *Torture*. Philadelphia: University of Pennsylvania Press, 1996.

Pettegree, Andrew. *Reformation and the Culture of Persuasion*. Cambridge: Cambridge University Press, 2005.

Racaut, Luc and Alec Ryrie, eds. *Moderate Voices in the European Reformation*. Ashgate: Burlington VT, 2005.

Reinhard, Wolfgang. "Zwang zur Konfessionalisierung? Prolegomena zu einer Theorie des konfessionellen Zeitalters." *Zeitschrift für Historische Forschung* 10 (1983): 257–277.

——, ed. *Konfession und Konfessionalisierung in Europa*. München, 1981.

—— and Heinz Schilling, eds. *Die Katholische Konfessionalisierung: Wissenschaftliches Symposion der Gesellschaft zur Herausgabe des Corpus Catholicorum und des Vereins für Reformationsgeschichte*. Gütersloh: Gütersloher Verlagshaus, 1995.

Rogge, Jörg. *Für den gemeinen Nutzen: Politsches Handeln und Politikverständnis von Rat und Bürgerschaft in Augsburg im Spätmittelalter*. Tübingen: Max Niemeyer Verlag, 1996.

Roper, Lyndal. "Going to Church and Street: Weddings in Reformation Augsburg." *Past & Present* 106 (1985): 62–101.

——. *The Holy Household: Women and Morals in Reformation Augsburg*. Oxford: Clarendon Press, 1989.

Roth, Friedrich. *Augsburgs Reformationsgeschichte*. 4 vols. Munich: T. Ackermann, 1901–11.

Schiersner, Dietmar. *Politik, Konfession und Kommunikation: Studien zur katholischen Konfessionalisierung der Markgrafschaft Burgau 1550–1650*. Berlin: Akademie Verlag, 2005.

Schilling, Heinz. *Konfessionskonflikt und Staatsbildung: eine Fallstudie über das Verhältnis von religiösem und sozialem Wandel in der Frühneuzeit am Beispiel der Graftschaft Lippe*. Gütersloh: Gütersloher Verlagshaus Mohn, 1981.

——. *Religion, Political Culture, and the Emergence of Early Modern Society: essays in German and Dutch History*. New York: E. J. Brill, 1992.

Schorer, Reinhold. *Die Strafgerichtsbarkeit der Reichsstadt Augsburg 1156–1548*. Cologne: Böhlau Verlag, 2001.

Schulze, Winfried ed. *Ego-Dokumente: Annäherung an den Menschen in der Geschichte*. Berlin: Akademie Verlag, 1996.

Schwab, Paul Josiah. *The Attitude of Wolfgang Musculus Toward Religious Tolerance*. Scottdale, Pa.: Mennonite Press, 1933.

Scribner, Robert. *For the Sake of Simple Folk: Popular Propaganda for the German Reformation*. New York: Cambridge University Press, 1981.

——. *Popular Culture and Popular Movements in Reformation Germany*. London: Hambledon Press, 1988.

——. *Religion and Culture in Germany (1400–1800)*. Edited by Lyndal Roper. Leiden: Brill 2001.

——, ed. *Germany: A New Social and Economic History*. Vol. 1, *1450–1630*. London: Arnold Publication, 1996.

—— and C. Scott Dixon. *The German Reformation*, 2nd ed. New York: Palgrave Macmillan, 2003.

Seebass, Gottfried. *Die Reformation und ihre Aussenseiter: Gesammelte Aufsätze und Vorträge.* Edited by Irene Dingel. Göttingen: Vandenhoeck & Ruprecht, 1997.

Sender, Clemens. *Die chronik von Clemens Sender von den ältesten zeiten der stadt bis zum jahre 1536.* In *Die Chroniken der deutschen Städte vom 14. bis ins 16. Jahrhundert.* Vol. 5. Edited by Friedrich Roth. Leipzig: S. Hirzel, 1894.

Sieh-Bürens, Katarina. *Oligarchie, Konfession und Politik im 16. Jahrhundert: Zur sozialen Verflechtung der Augsburger Bürgermeister und Stadtpfleger 1518–1618.* Munich: Verlag Ernst Vogel, 1986.

Snyder, C. Arnold and Linda A. Huebert Hecht, eds. *Profiles of Anabaptist Women: Sixteenth-Century Reforming Pioneers.* Waterloo, Ontario, CA: Wilfrid Laurier University Press, 1996.

Strauss, Gerald. *Nuremberg in the Sixteenth Century.* New York: Wiley, 1966.

Stuart, Kathy. *Defiled Trades and Social Outcasts: Honor and Ritual Pollution in Early Modern Germany.* Cambridge: Cambridge University Press, 1999.

Tlusty, B. Ann. *Bacchus and Civic Order: The Culture of Drink in Early Modern Germany.* Charlottesville: University Press of Virginia, 2001.

Uhland, Friedwart. *Täufertum und Obrigkeit in Augsburg im 16. Jahrhundert.* Diss. University of Tübingen, 1972.

Volkland, Frauke. *Konfession und Selbstverständnis: Reformierte Rituale in der gemischtkonfessionellen Kleinstadt Bischofszell im 17. Jahrhundert.* Göttingen: Vandenhoeck & Ruprecht, 2005.

Wandel, Lee Palmer. *The Eucharist in the Reformation: Incarnation and Liturgy.* Cambridge: Cambridge University Press, 2006.

———. *Voracious Idols and Violent Hands: Iconoclasm in Reformation Zurich, Strasbourg, and Basel.* New York: Cambridge University Press, 1995.

Warmbrunn, Paul. *Zwei Konfessionen in einer Stadt: das Zusammenleben von Katholiken und Protestanten in den paritätischen Reichsstädten Augsburg, Biberach, Ravensburg und Dinkelsbühl von 1548 bis 1648.* Wiesbaden: F. Steiner, 1983.

Weyrauch, Erdmann. *Konfessionelle Krise und soziale Stabilität: das Interim im Strassburg (1548–1562).* Stuttgart: Klett-Cotta, 1978.

Zeeden, Ernst Walter. *Konfessionsbildung. Studien zur Reformation, Gegenreformation, und Katholischen Reformation.* Stuttgart: Klett-Cotta, 1985.

Zorn, Wolfgang. *Geschichte einer europäischen Stadt.* Augsburg: Wißner, 1994.

INDEX

Studies in Central European Histories

Edited by Thomas A. Brady, Jr. and Roger Chickering

19. Patrouch, J.F. *Negotiated Settlement*. The Counter-Reformation in Upper Austria under the Habsburgs. ISBN 0 391 04099 5

20. Haude, S. *In the Shadow of "Savage Wolves"*. Anabaptist Münster and the German Reformation during the 1530s. ISBN 0 391 04100 2

21. Caldwell, P.C. & Scheuerman, W.E. *From Liberal Democracy to Fascism*. Legal and Political Thought in the Weimar Republic. ISBN 0 391 04098 7

22. Brenner, A.D. *Emil J. Gumbel*. Weimar German Pacifist and Professor. ISBN 0 391 04101 0

23. Bell, D.P. *Sacred Communities*. Jewish and Christian Identities in Fifteenth-Century Germany. ISBN 0 391 04102 9

24. Myers Feinstein, M. *State Symbols*. The Quest for Legitimacy in the Federal Republic of Germany and the German Democratic Republic, 1949-1959. ISBN 0 391 04103 7

25. Hobson, R. *Imperialism at Sea*. Naval Strategic Thought, the Ideology of Sea Power, and the Tirpitz Plan, 1875-1914. ISBN 0 391 04105 3

26. Edwards, K.A. *Families and Frontiers*. Re-creating Communities and Boundaries in the Early Modern Burgundies. ISBN 0 391 04106 1

27. Lavery, J. *Germany's Northern Challenge*. The Holy Roman Empire and the Scandinavian Struggle for the Baltic 1563-1576. ISBN 0 391 04156 8

28. Healy, R. *Jesuit Specter in Imperial Germany*. ISBN 0 391 04194 0

29. Geehr, R.S. *Aesthetics of Horror*. The Life and Thought of Richard von Kralik. ISBN 0 391 04201 7

30. Safley, T.M. (ed.). *Reformation of Charity*. The Secular and the Religious in Early Modern Poor Relief. ISBN 0 391 04211 4

31. Lindemann, M. (ed.). *Ways of Knowing*. Ten Interdisciplinary Essays. ISBN 0 391 04184 3

32. Ulbrich, C. *Shulamit and Margarete*. Power, Gender, and Religion in a Rural Society in Eighteenth-Century Europe. Transl. by T. Dunlap. ISBN 0 391 04145 2

33. Funck, M. & Chickering, R. (eds.). *Endangered Cities*. Military Power and Urban Societies in the Era of the World Wars. ISBN 0 391 04196 7

34. Beachy, R. *The Soul of Commerce*. Credit, Property, and Politics in Leipzig, 1750-1840. ISBN 0 391 04142 8

35. Mayes, D. *Communal Christianity*. The Life and Loss of a Peasant Vision in Early Modern Germany. ISBN 0 391 04225 4

36. Aaslestad, K. *Place and Politics*. Local Identity, Civic Culture, and German Nationalism in North Germany during the Revolutionary Era. ISBN 0 391 04228 9

37. Burnett, S.G. & Bell, D.P. (eds.). *Jews, Judaism, and the Reformation in Sixteenth-Century Germany*. ISBN 90 04 14947 3

38. Safley, T.M. *Children of the Laboring Poor*. Expectation and Experience among the Orphans of Early Modern Augsburg. ISBN 0 391 04224 6

39. Hartston, B.P. *Sensationalizing the Jewish Question*. Anti-Semitic Trials and the Press in the Early German Empire. ISBN 90 04 14654 7

40. Janik, E. *Recomposing German Music*. Politics and Musical Tradition in Cold War Berlin. ISBN 90 04 14661 X

41. Canoy, J.R. *The Discreet Charm of the Police State*. The *Landpolizei* and the Transformation of Bavaria, 1945-1965. ISBN 978 90 04 15708 8

42. Head, R.C. & Christensen, D. (eds.). *Orthodoxies and Heterodoxies in Early Modern German Culture*. Order and Creativity 1550-1750. ISBN 978 90 04 16276 1

43. Steinhoff, A.J. *The Gods of the City*. Protestantism and Religious Culture in Strasbourg, 1870-1914. ISBN 978 90 04 16405 5

44. Johnson, M.W. *Training Socialist Citizens*. Sports and the State in East Germany. ISBN 978 90 04 16957 9

45. Hanson, M.Z. *Religious Identity in an Early Reformation Community*. Augsburg, 1517 to 1555. ISBN 978 90 04 16673 8

46. Friedrich, K. & Pendzich, B.M. (eds.). *Citizenship and Identity in a Multinational Commonwealth*. Poland-Lithuania in Context, 1550-1772. ISBN 978 90 04 16983 8

47. Coy, J.P. *Strangers and Misfits*. Banishment, Social Control, and Authority in Early Modern Germany. ISBN 978 90 04 16174 0